Law and Philosophy Library

Volume 130

The Law and Philosophy Library, which has been in existence since 1985, aims to publish cutting edge works in the philosophy of law, and has a special history of publishing books that focus on legal reasoning and argumentation, including those that may involve somewhat formal methodologies. The series has published numerous important books on law and logic, law and artificial intelligence, law and language, and law and rhetoric. While continuing to stress these areas, the series has more recently expanded to include books on the intersection between law and the Continental philosophical tradition, consistent with the traditional openness of the series to books in the Continental jurisprudential tradition. The series is proud of the geographic diversity of its authors, and many have come from Latin America, Spain, Italy, the Netherlands, Germany, and Eastern Europe, as well, more obviously for an English-language series, from the United Kingdom, the United States, Australia, and Canada.

More information about this series at http://www.springer.com/series/6210

Nicoletta Bersier Ladavac • Christoph Bezemek •
Frederick Schauer
Editors

The Normative Force of the Factual

Legal Philosophy Between Is and Ought

Springer

Editors
Nicoletta Bersier Ladavac
Thémis Institute
Genève, Switzerland

Christoph Bezemek
Institute of Public Law and Political Science
University of Graz
Graz, Austria

Frederick Schauer
School of Law
University of Virgina
Virgina, VA, USA

ISSN 1572-4395 ISSN 2215-0315 (electronic)
Law and Philosophy Library
ISBN 978-3-030-18928-0 ISBN 978-3-030-18929-7 (eBook)
https://doi.org/10.1007/978-3-030-18929-7

Cover design: eStudio Calamar, Berlin/Figueres

This Springer imprint is published by the registered company Springer Nature Switzerland AG.
The registered company address is: Gewerbestrasse 11, 6330 Cham, Switzerland

Preface

The idea for this volume originated in the aftermath of a panel organized by the editors at the XXVIII World Congress of the International Association for the Philosophy of Law and Social Philosophy (IVR) in the summer of 2017. Although the title of the panel was based on Georg Jellinek's notion of a "Normative Force to the Factual," the panelists came up with a broad range of ideas revolving around the topic so defined. Thus, the papers presented in Lisbon addressed not only Jellinek's theory of how facts may merge into norms but also the dichotomy of "is" and "ought" according to Kelsenian theory, the connection between law and force, the question of how discourse shapes our understanding of the normative sphere, and the fundamental problems of the concept of "normativity."

The diversity of these accounts reassured us that it would be useful to pursue further the topic of the interrelation of facts and norms and to ask still more friends and colleagues to join the conversation. We were pleased that so many of them accepted our invitation and we are even more pleased to present the result of our common efforts in this volume.

We would like to thank the editors of Springer's "Law and Philosophy Library" for including the volume in the series and Anitha Chellamuthu of Springer International for diligently looking after the volume. Anja Krasser and Laura Christandl kindly assisted in correcting the proofs. We are grateful for their support.

Finally, we would like to thank the contributors to this volume for sharing their knowledge and wisdom and thereby significantly enhancing our understanding of many of the aspects that are to be considered when it comes to the ties of facts and norms. We hope that our readers will benefit from their insights just as much as we did.

Geneva, Switzerland
Graz, Austria
Charlottesville, VA, USA
February 2019

Nicoletta Bersier Ladavac
Christoph Bezemek
Frederick Schauer

Contents

Introduction

Nicoletta Bersier Ladavac, Christoph Bezemek, and Frederick Schauer

Law's 'normativity', its capacity to impose obligations, is among the great mysteries of jurisprudence; or so the bulk of the literature dedicated to the topic strongly suggests. As mysteries typically do, the mystery of law's 'normativity' (if there is indeed such a thing) derives from various sources. One of them (and one of major importance) is the question as to the interrelation of facts and norms.

This interrelation has become complicated as well as contested, at the very least since David Hume introduced the "Is-Ought-Problem" to moral philosophy 1739 in his paradigm-shifting "Treatise on Human Nature". There Hume denied that prescriptive statements could be deduced from descriptive statements. More than 150 years later G.E. Moore described what is nowadays commonly referred to as the 'naturalistic fallacy'. In his "Principia Ethica", published in 1903, Moore emphasized the difference between 'natural' and 'moral properties'. From a jurisprudential perspective the separation of 'is' and 'ought' remains a central tenet of positivist theory in general and of Hans Kelsen's "Pure Theory of Law", first published in 1934, in particular. To this day the relationship between 'is' and 'ought' persists as one of the major topics in any field of practical reasoning and, thus, for legal theory and legal philosophy.

Against this background, this volume intends to revisit the question of normativity and the interrelation of facts and norms from various perspectives and based on

N. Bersier Ladavac (✉)
Thémis, Centre de Philosophie du droit, de Sociologie du droit et de Théorie du droit, Geneva, Switzerland
e-mail: nberserier@iprolink.ch

C. Bezemek
University of Graz, Graz, Austria
e-mail: christoph.bezemek@uni-graz.at

F. Schauer
University of Virginia, School of Law, Charlottesville, VA, USA
e-mail: fschauer@law.virginia.edu

N. Bersier Ladavac et al. (eds.), *The Normative Force of the Factual*, Law and Philosophy Library 130, https://doi.org/10.1007/978-3-030-18929-7_1

various theoretical approaches. The volume's title pays tribute to a concept introduced by the great constitutional theorist Georg Jellinek in his "Allgemeine Staatslehre", originally published in 1900. Analyzing what he designated the "Normative Force of the Factual", Jellinek raises questions such as: How does non-law become law in the first place? Which phenomena lie at the roots of this transformation? How is its result upheld? And how does it elapse?

To answer these questions, Jellinek dissects the human tendency to infer rules from recurring events, to perceive a certain practice not only as a fact but as a norm; a norm which not only allows to distinguish regularity from irregularity, but at the same time, to treat deviance as transgression.

Jellinek, arguably one of the greatest legal scholars of his time, remains understudied in Anglo-American academia. This volume, while dedicated to normativity and the interrelation of facts and norms in general and not to Jellinek's work in particular, seeks to take a step to lessen that gap, as the notion of a "Normative Force of the Factual" still allows for new insights into the interrelation of law and fact, into the emergence of normativity, and into the efficacy and the defeasibility of (legal) norms. This inquiry leads us back to early legal history, connecting anthropology with legal theory, and demonstrating the interdependence of law and the social sciences. In short, exploring the normativity of law invites us to transcend disciplinary boundaries.

At the same time, Jellinek himself would have cautioned us against accepting this invitation lightheartedly: Although he encouraged the analysis of the phenomena of law and state from various disciplinary perspectives, his approach remains opposed to excess methodological 'syncretism'. The various disciplines that help us to understand legal normativity are synergistically vauable, but they persist as separate perspectives. To adequately understand the notion of a "Normative Force of the Factual", thus, presupposes to understand Jellinek's scientific approach to the concept of the state.

In the first chapter of this volume, Oliver Lepsius' contribution fosters a Jellinek type of understanding, thereby also providing an introduction to those chapters that are arranged around Jellinek's position and its obvious tension to the separation of 'is' and 'ought' in positivist thought. It is this tension that the second chapter, written by Nicoletta Bersier, explores, in focusing on the problem of normativity according to Hans Kelsen's position and in raising the question as to the interplay of natural and positive law. Following that, in the third chapter, Matthias Klatt discusses two elements of Jellinek's thought: the "Normative Force of the Factual" and the "Two-Sided-Theory of the State"; assessing them in the light of Kelsen's position as described in the previous chapter and the nature of legal argumentation. In the fourth chapter, Christoph Bezemek sets out to reconcile Jellinek's and Kelsen's approach by emphasizing the dichotomous interrelation of fact and norm in light of a close analysis of the "Normative Force of the Factual". The fifth chapter, written by Andreas Th. Müller, brings in another core concept of Jellinek's work, the "three-elements-doctrine of the state", to the test of international law doctrine, raising the question of the relation of a fact-based approach to the formation of the state to issues of legitimacy.

Following on many of the positions discussed in these first five chapters, (while still going beyond them), a second group of contributions places the interrelation of facts and norms on a broader foundation. In the chapter "How the Facts Enter Into the Law", Clemes Jabloner asks the question of how the facts enter into the law, distinguishing 'facts of reality'—things as they are—and the 'state of facts' as established by a court when rendering a judgment. Michael Potacs, in the chapter "The Fact of Norms", introduces a difference between the 'normative' and the 'factual' existence of norms as a difference between a norm's validity and its meaning. And Alexander Somek, in the chapter "Ex facto jus oritur", explains how the concept of the 'legal relation' helps to understand the origins of the norm based on the facticity of practical reasoning by others.

A third group of contributions concludes this volume by focusing on (select aspects of) the problem of 'normativity'.

Jorge Nunez, in the chapter "The Many Forces in Law: Rational, Physical and Psychological Coercion", examines how Kelsen understands different variants of coercion (rational, physical and psychological) and why the Hartian tradition misunderstands the Kelsenian approach. The chapter "Legal Facts and Reasons for Action: Between Deflationary and Robust Conceptions of Legal Normativity", written by Noam Gur—takes the problem of normativity seriously, addressing the question whether the fact that the law requires an action can constitute a reason for its performance. Frederick Schauer's final chapter offers a contrasting approach, arguing that 'normativity' may not pose a distinct puzzle at all, but rather a non-puzzling instantiation of an array of different traditional perspectives, none of which proves to be particularly puzzling in its own right.

The different angles this volume offers on the problem (if there is indeed such a thing) of normativity and on 'is' and 'ought' are intended to serve three (even if hardly separate) purposes: to reintroduce Georg Jellinek's important theoretical concepts to the contemporary jurisprudential debate in Anglo-American academica; to clarify the interrelation of fact and norm in positivist thought; and to (somewhat) demystify the phenomenon of 'normativity'. Of course: accomplishing any of these goals would be no small achievement.

Georg Jellinek's Theory of the Two Sides of the State ("Zwei-Seiten-Lehre des Staates")

Oliver Lepsius

Abstract This chapter focusses on Georg Jellinek's specific approach to the concept of State: the Two-Sides-Theory which differentiates between a social and a juridical conception of the State. It analyses claim, content, methodology and context of this theory and shows that, from an interdisciplinary, epistemological and normative standpoint, the concept of State as expounded by Jellinek has retained its scientific attraction to the present day.

The concept of State has intensely intrigued legal studies, humanities, economics and social science, particularly in Germany.[1] The debates around the State almost inevitably pose methodological questions. Sometimes, they even turn out to be expressions of fundamentally diverging methodological convictions. "The State" is therefore a popular subject of general epistemological considerations, and Georg Jellinek, being one of the leading German legal theorists around the turn from the nineteenth to the twentieth century,[2] set new scholarly standards. Which discipline is competent for exploring its nature? From a juridical point of view, one may ask in particular whether the legal concept of the State is conceivable without taking into consideration sociological, historical, philosophical or political aspects. How can one overcome these interdisciplinary epistemological difficulties?

The expression "state" may denote a given situation as well as an ideal. It may refer to a state of affairs or to a normative standard—to an "Is" or an "Ought". No matter from which disciplinary perspective one approaches "the State", one has to acknowledge that it comprises both factual and normative components. How can one grasp a dimension that oscillates between the "Is" and the "Ought"? As a rule, the concept of State is linked to expectations regarding the political ordering. Yet how can one canvass these expectations without resorting to value judgements while

[1] See, e.g. Kelsen (1925), pp. 3–5; Thoma (1926), Matz (1974), Draht (1987), Boldt et al. (1990), and Vollrath (1998).

[2] On the biography of Georg Jellinek, see Kempter (1998). For brief accounts see Sinzheimer (1953), p. 61; Sattler (1993), and Kersten (2015).

O. Lepsius (✉)
University of Münster, Münster, Germany
e-mail: oliver.lepsius@uni-muenster.de

N. Bersier Ladavac et al. (eds.), *The Normative Force of the Factual*, Law and Philosophy Library 130, https://doi.org/10.1007/978-3-030-18929-7_2

retaining a critical distance to ideology? A theory of State that claims to be "general"—as does Jellinek's *Allgemeine Staatslehre*—has to face the following issues: the relation of the academic disciplines to one another (interdisciplinary issues), the relation between the object and the method of investigation (epistemological issues), the relation of value-free science and political ideas (issue of theory and practice). With his theory of the two-sided State, Jellinek responded to all of these issues, offering a novel conception of the concept of State. It is not least due to these aspects that the theory has retained its importance up to the present day.

1 The Claim of the Two-Sides-Theory

1.1 Definition and Theoretical Basis

"The theory of the State has to explore the different sides of the state's nature. In accordance with the two perspectives, from which the state can be considered, the theory has two focuses. On the one hand the State is a social entity; on the other hand, it is a legal institution. Hence the theory of State has to be divided into the social theory of the State and the legal theory of the State."[3] In Jellinek's own words, this is the quintessence of the 'Two-Sides-Theory'. Jellinek claims that the State has a twofold nature being both a social entity, hence a matter of fact, and a legal institution, that is, a system of normative powers. The 'Two-Sides-Theory' considers the State as a single object of recognition with two different manifestations which have to be distinguished epistemologically and methodologically. It is this differentiation of methodological approaches that constitutes the Theory of the two-sided State. Jellinek (1900), pp. 19–20 sets out to investigate the same object, the state, using different methods which he refers to as "causal" approach and "normative" approach ("Kausalwissenschaft und Normwissenschaft"). The normative approach allows determining the legal side of the State, while the causal approach accounts for its factual side. Jellinek provides the juridical theory of State—the *Staatsrechtslehre*—with a specific normative epistemology while leaving everything else, that is, "the State" in its historical, philosophical and sociological dimensions to an unspecified "causal science". In his own words, "[t]his results in an important methodical difference between the social *Staatslehre* and the juridical *Staatsrechtslehre*. The former concerns the objective, historical and, as has been said not quite correctly, 'natural' being of the state, while the latter deals with the legal norms which are supposed to be materialized in this real being."[4] This methodological dualism reflects the

[3] Jellinek (1914), pp. 10–11: "Die Staatslehre hat den Staat nach allen Seiten seines Wesens zu erforschen. Sie hat zwei Hauptgebiete, entsprechend den zwei Gesichtspunkten, unter denen der Staat betrachtet werden kann. Der Staat ist einmal ein gesellschaftliches Gebilde, sodann eine rechtliche Institution. Dementsprechend zerfällt die Staatslehre in die soziale Staatslehre und in die Staatsrechtslehre."

[4] Jellinek (1900), p. 20: "Daraus ergibt sich ein wichtiger methodologischer Unterschied zwischen sozialer Staatslehre und Staatsrechtslehre. Die erstere hat das gegenständliche, historische, wie

Two-Sides-Theory: It explains what the theory is about and, at once, presents itself as the logical consequence of the latter.

Jellinek sets out the Two-Sides-Theory in the first pages of his "General Theory of the State" (*Allgemeine Staatslehre*). The fundamental differentiation governs the entire work.[5] Jellinek divides his "General Theory" into the parts: "Introductory Analysis", "General Social Theory of State" and "General Legal Theory of State". The first part mainly provides a methodological justification for differentiating the two sides of the State, both of which are subsequently illustrated in the second and third part. Further methodological justifications are provided at the beginning and the end of the second part.

1.2 The Program of the Two-Sides-Theory

Starting his analysis, Jellinek makes clear that the State is a multifarious phenomenon that can be considered from many different points of view. By fundamentally dividing his work into a "General Social Theory of the State" and a "General Legal Theory of the State" Jellinek puts this diversity into an order. He admits that the law is vital for the State as the State could not be conceived without it. However, he maintains (1900, 11) that the theory of the State should not be identified with the juridical theory of the State. Jurisprudence only forms a part of the overall area of investigation. It must be supplemented by the social theory of the State which considers its object as a social entity and which should be contrasted to the legal theory of the State. This differentiation and contrast is due to the diverging methodological approaches that prevail in both areas. Hence, confounding legal phenomena with that which antecedes the law is not permissible in the scientific representation of the issue."[6] According to Jellinek, only the combination of both aspects, the legal and the social theory of the State, can account for the epistemic goals of a general theory of the State: to scientifically depict the State as a uniform object.

Thus, Jellinek (1900), p. 12 opposes the line of thought according to which only a non-legal (sociological, historical, political) explanation of the state is appropriate[7] as well as the opposite opinion that maintains that "only the jurist was competent for resolving all the issues linked to the phenomenon of the State, with his own means of investigation." Jellinek distinguishes legal epistemology from all other kinds of epistemology. He argues that law is a genuinely different object of investigation. Law as the epitome of norms does not belong to the realm of the "Is", but is part of that what should be—the "Ought". Legal concepts do not aid in recognizing

auch wohl nicht ganz zutreffend gesagt wurde, natürliche Sein des Staates, die letztere hingegen die in jenem realen Sein zum Ausdruck kommen sollende Rechtsnormen zum Inhalt.".

[5] Jellinek (1900), pp. 9–12; see besides that in particular 50–52, 136–140, 174–183.

[6] Jellinek (1900), pp. 11–12; regarding the clarity of methods see 25–30, 50–51.

[7] Jellinek (1900), pp. 12, and 162: a completed recognition of the state was impossible without the knowledge of its legal nature.

the reality, but are consulted for its evaluation. "By legal norms one cannot recognize reality. It is not up to jurisprudence to determine the "Is" of the state as such, but to arrange the given phenomena under fixed categories for certain purposes and to evaluate them in accordance with the abstract legal norms. Hence, jurisprudence is a science of norms (*Normwissenschaft*). It resembles logics which do not teach us what things are, but how they are to be conceived in order achieve consistent knowledge." (1900, 138) Legal recognition of an object fundamentally differs from the recognition of matters of fact. Its subject is "the recognition of legal norms originating from the State which are intended to govern the State's institutions and functions and the relationship between its factual elements and its legal standards. The juridical investigation of the State has to complement the social-scientific approach but should on no account be confounded with it. Its methodology is exclusively juridical." Jellinek proceeds (1900), pp. 138–139: "The misjudgment and obliteration of the difference that is illustrated here, has up to the present day been the cause of one of the most fatal misconceptions. The legal nature of the State and its institutions is continuously being confounded with its social reality. Indeed, it has not been realized at all that there are different ways of exploring the nature of the State."

1.3 The Juridical Starting Point of the Two-Sides-Theory

The Two-Sides-Theory is the corollary of a specific conception of juridical methodology. Since juridical methods are devised solely for the recognition of legal phenomena, complementary perspectives are necessary in order to grasp the State's nature. Lawyers are not able to recognize the State's nature by employing their methods. They are only competent for organizing and evaluating aspects of the State in light of normative criteria. According to Jellinek, the State "per se" (*an sich*) cannot be identified that way. The restriction and the "scientification" of juridical methodology calls for the expansion of the object of recognition in order to be able to describe a uniform phenomenon such as the "State". The Juridical theory of the State examines the norms of "State law" (*Staatsrecht*). The social theory of the State examines the State as a "social entity". This includes considering the law "in its capacity as a social function" (1900, 51), as an "actual factor in the life of the people" (1900, 21). By contrast, the juridical concept of the State does not aim at apprehending the "real nature" of the State, but at rendering it legally conceivable, that is, devising a conception under which all legal features of the State can be comprehended without any contradiction (1900, 163).

Therefore, the State has two sides: one legal and one social. Only their combination can describe the State as a uniform object. Differentiating the way of dealing with the state into a juridical and a sociological approach is not the result of two a priori manifestations of the state, but a methodological corollary. Juridical methodology is as unsuitable for grasping the social side of the State as is sociological methodology for understanding its legal nature. The different methodological approaches call for distinguishing the State into its two sides (1900, 27), but they do not divide up the State as such. On the contrary, it has to be retained as a uniform object.

Jellinek had already outlined a large part of his methodological foundations before writing the "The General Theory of State". Eight years earlier, he insisted in his book "The System of Subjective Public Rights" ("Das System der subjektiven öffentlichen Rechte") that it was impossible to find a preexisting epistemological object, and that these objects rather had to be scientifically established by employing the methodology of the respective disciplines (1892, 15–20). As a consequence, by employing juridical methodology, one cannot contemplate an "Is", but only an "Ought" (1892, 16–17). One can understand the "General Theory of State" as a monumental implementation of the program already outlined before, and the theory of the two-sided State as its state-theoretical manifestation. In the "System of Subjective Public Rights", Jellinek had examined the methodologically appropriate recognition of an object by adducing a purely normative phenomenon as an instance. In the "General Theory of State", he applied his methodology to another object of investigation, one that cannot be clearly categorized as either "factual" or "normative": the State.

1.4 *The Uniformity of the State as a Juridical Problem*

According to Jellinek (1900), pp. 140–158, the nature of the State cannot be determined without presuppositions. In his eyes, it is neither an objective fact nor a moral organism. Jellinek opposes conceptual realism, misguided objectivity and naturalistic conceptions of state. He aims at rationalizing and "scientificating" epistemology by an approach free of value judgements and critical of ideology. Facticity and normativity are supposed to check on one another. Legal norms select the normatively relevant from the "factual mass" while facticity limits legal validity. Therefore, Jellinek (1900), pp. 172–175 controverts both realism and idealism insofar as they pretend to be objective. Nevertheless, he thinks fit to call his theory a "general theory" of State since only by employing juridical methodology can one grasp the State's uniformity and therefore its "generality". Every other individualistic or collectivistic, naturalistic or intellectual approach, in Jellinek's opinion, merely pretends to be realistic and empirical while still unable to explain the uniformity of the State. Hence, sociological, historical or philosophical examinations of the state are of limited value for him. At best, they may be of use for explaining aspects of the State which, in turn, depend largely on subjective presuppositions.

For Jellinek, the State's uniformity cannot be conceived as an objective intellectual or empirical entity, but only as an imagined entity. Thus, he poses the question: How we think of the State as a uniform entity? Jellinek (1900), p. 165 does not devise a theory for grasping the state in its real nature, but for discovering the concept of the State under which all legal features of the state can be conceived without any contradictions. As a general phenomenon, independent of specific historical and social emanations, the "State" can indeed be conceived as a legal creation (1900, 183). Thus, Jellineks "General Theory" is primarily a juridical theory of the State.

2 The Content of the Two-Sides-Theory

2.1 The Social Conception of the State

Jellinek defines the social conception of the concept of State as follows: "The State is an association of sedentary people vested with original authority."[8] How does Jellinek arrive at this definition? According to him, neither the "Is" nor the "Ought" can be recognized autonomously. As a factual entity the State is subject to normative influences as much as it reconnected to facticity, being a creation of law. These reciprocal influences are coupled by psychological phenomena, namely the recognition of the belief that what exists ought to exist. The social conception of the State is, thus, the result of subjective attributions. It is neither naturalistic nor objective, but subjective and psychological. It results from a function of the mind (1900, 174). This psychological function that focusses on the human being shapes the social conception of the State.[9] Jellinek does not examine the social conception of the State as such, but rather he poses the question the other way round: How does a social entity come into existence by human recognition?

To be sure, the State, being a social entity, cannot be created by an individual mental operation. Its creation requires corresponding states of mind of all those who accept the State as a conceived order. Hence, the State as a social entity owes its existence to "the concurrence of mind of a majority of people".[10] Jellinek illustrates this by referring to the example of tradition. Although tradition may be powerful in infusing all social affairs, it does not derive its (objective or naturalistic) power from

---

[8] Jellinek (1900), pp. 180–181: "Der Staat ist die mit ursprünglicher Herrschermacht ausgerüstete Verbandseinheit seßhafter Menschen."

[9] Jellinek (1900), p. 174: "Social relations between humans in certain activities appear to be the sum/amount of the final objective elements of the state. More precisely they are, because the term amount/sum already implies a form of subjective synthesis, a juxtaposition and succession of certain activities that become clear in the relations between people. Therefore, it is in no way a substance but exclusively a form of function. The substance that underlies this form of function are the people. But this form of function is exclusively of psychological nature, an even if it also causes physical effects, these are always psychologically conveyed." In the original: "Als letzte objektive Elemente des Staates ergeben sich eine Summe bestimmter in Tätigkeiten sich äußernder sozialer Beziehungen zwischen Menschen oder, noch genauer gesprochen, da der Begriff der Summe bereits eine Form subjektiver Synthese bedeutet, ein Neben- und Nacheinander bestimmter, in Beziehungen von Menschen zu Menschen sich äußernder Tätigkeiten. Er ist somit nach keiner Richtung hin Substanz, sondern ausschließlich Funktion. Die dieser Funktion zugrundeliegende Substanz sind und bleiben Menschen. [Abs.] Diese Funktion ist aber ausschließlich psychischer Art, und wenn sie auch physische Wirkungen hervorruft, so sind diese doch stets psychisch vermittelt."

[10] Jellinek (1900), p. 176: "in den Willensverhältnissen einer Mehrheit von Menschen".

"the outside", but rather from "inner creation".[11] History has a bearing on the social theory of the State. It cannot be conceived objectively or naturalistically, but is to be learned by each generation anew. This way, Jellinek tries to explain why certain historical events trigger intellectual effects while others fall into oblivion. Forgotten events are not included in the collective "concurrence of mind". Therefore, basically every factor may influence the social theory of the State—political ideas as well as social circumstances. Of course, empirical conditions may become relevant too, but not by virtue of them being empirical—thus not due to being objective or naturalistic—, but by virtue of acknowledgement. We can think of numerous concurrences of mind, which are able to constitute different associations. In the context of State theory, Jellinek is of course, interested in the concurrences of mind that are related to authority. To be sure, Jellinek does not limit the State to the exertion of authority, but he understands authority as being constitutive of the State. For it is only the State that is able to unconditionally enforce its will against opposing intentions, and that, in doing so, exerts authority.[12] On this assumption, Jellinek may justifiably assert that the State is "an association of sedentary people vested with original authority".

In the course of his analysis, Jellinek applies these conceptual considerations to a couple of basic problems. In particular, he discusses the justification of the State, (1900, 184–229) the State's purpose, questions of emergence and demise of statehood and the historical prototypes of the State (1900, 287–331). This selection of topics shows that what really matters to him is the juridical recognition of the State. For this purpose, the social conception is merely instrumental.

2.2 *The Juridical Conception of the State*

The juridical conception of the State terminologically differs only slightly from its social counterpart. Jellinek gives the following definition: "Thus, as a legal concept the State is the corporate body of a sedentary people, vested with original authority" or "territorial entity vested with original authority."[13] The social and the juridical

[11] Jellinek (1900), p. 176: "Dark, subconsciously operating forces do not shape the continuity of all human affairs in a mystical way. The entire knowledge and skills of the past have to be recreated by an inner experience of every new race, by learning and experience. These processes predominantly belong to the sphere of consciousness." In the original: "Nicht dunkle, unbewußt wirkende Kräfte gestalten in mystischer Weise die Kontinuität aller menschlichen Verhältnisse. Vielmehr muß das ganze Wissen und Können der Vergangenheit durch inneres Erleben eines jeden neuen Geschlechts, durch Lernen und Erfahrung von neuem erzeugt werden, und diese Prozesse fallen überwiegend in die Sphäre des Bewußtseins."

[12] Jellinek (1900), p. 180: "Diese Macht unbedingter Durchsetzung des eigenen Willens gegen andere Willen hat nur der Staat."

[13] Jellinek (1900), p. 183: "Als Rechtsbegriff ist der Staat demnach die mit ursprünglicher Herrschermacht ausgerüstete Körperschaft eines seßhaften Volkes", bzw.: "die mit ursprünglicher Herrschermacht ausgestattete Gebietskörperschaft."

conception differ only in their references to legal categories—"territorial entity" (*Gebietskörperschaft*) instead of "corporate body" (*Verbandseinheit*), "a people" (*Volk*) instead of "people" (*Menschen*).

In order to illustrate the juridical concept of the State, Jellinek presents a sequence of attributional concepts of law. The general attributional concept "territorial entity" is divided into several elements which consistently are legal concepts and need not be derived from the tension between normativity and facticity, as in the case of the sociological-attributional concepts. Legal concepts are normative and can be applied with far less epistemological presuppositions.

Jellinek (1900), pp. 394–434 commences, introducing the following three elements that constitute the legal status of the State: people, territory, and authority (Staatsvolk, Staatsgebiet, Staatsgewalt). He examines important features like sovereignty, indivisibility of the State's authority and the ability of self-organization and self-governance. Jellinek describes the legal side of the State regarding its organization. The chapters on "constitution", "government bodies", "representation" and "representational bodies" are followed by chapters on the division of powers, decentralization and self-governance. Subsequently, a long section deals with the different types of government, primarily monarchy and republic from a historic and systematic point of view. A chapter on "associations of States" concludes the "General Theory of State". In this last substantial chapter, Jellinek deals with confederations and other legal forms of associations. What follows under the heading "The Guarantees of Public Law" is not more than a couple of pages on how the validity of law may be ensured by social, political and legal safeguards. These safeguards are not particularly elaborated. Hence Jellinek's *opus magnum* does not conclude with a summary or a synthesis of the two conceptions of the State.

Neither the general social theory nor the general juridical theory of the State addresses contemporary issues. The fact that they underlie many chapters of his book as *leitmotif* is due to Jellinek's methodological impetus aimed at overcoming State positivism and recognizing the importance of political ideas for constitutional law. Jellinek does not present suggestions for the solution of specific contemporary problems as this would contradict the theoretical standard of the book that claims to be a "general" theory of State. It would of course have enhanced the vividness of his considerations, had Jellinek illustrated his theory by practical applications.

2.3 The Systematic Relationship Between the Social and the Juridical Side of the State

It becomes clear that Jellinek's general theory of the State clings to a distinctive juridical point of view. Employing legal attributional categories, the "General Theory of the State" is an implementation of his epistemological program of explaining the State by legal concepts. In doing so, Jellinek has established many long lasting insights and concepts (i.e. the "Three-Elements-Doctrine" and his reflections on the associations of states). However, the individual chapters of the "General Theory of the State" do not contribute innovative arguments, but elaborate the program outlined before.

It is remarkable that, according to Jellinek, only the juridical approach can establish the epistemological object—the State—despite its differentiation into the two sides. Social aspects only interest him as a complementary perspective. Therefore, Jellinek's "social conception of the State" is not an empirical conception. It remains a theoretical construct because only the law provides the interconnecting element of Jellinek's theory. Actually, Jellinek opens the law of the State to non-legal topics. This opening remains however under "legal control" (concurring Möllers 2000a, pp. 33–34). The elements of law are constitutive of the State, and this also applies to its social theory whose facts only become relevant within a legal setting.[14] In the final analysis, Jellinek reduces the "State" as the epistemological object more severely to the legally relevant parts than it is generally perceived. Being a uniform object, the "State" is not deduced from the epistemological object but inductively recognized by the process of epistemology.

3 The Two-Sides-Theory as an Expression of Three Problems of Juridical Methodology

Why does Jellinek, being a jurist, strive to devise a general theory of the State? Should his methodological starting point not have made him aware of the impossibility of this endeavor? One would expect Jellinek to be satisfied with the observation of the state from a juridical point of view. According to his own standards, as a jurist, he was not able to go further in recognizing the State's nature. Why then include a "social theory of the state" in his general theory? Would it not rather be the task of a sociologist, historian or political theorist to establish a social theory of the state? Including the social theory into the overall framework only complements a primarily legal epistemological object—the State in its legal side.

Jellinek is convinced that recurring to the "Is" is indispensable in legal epistemology. That is why he finds himself compelled to complement his juridical State theory by the social dimension. The Two-Sides-Theory is the answer to this methodological claim. It does not primarily express a special feature of the state, but rather appears as the methodological corollary of legal epistemology which, at one point, necessarily refers to the "Is". The "State" stands just *pars pro toto* for a general epistemological problem which is not rooted in the concept of the State, but in the concept of law.[15]

---

[14] Dissenting Friedrich (1997), pp. 288–289, who classifies the general theory of the state as "sociological".

[15] Jellinek (1900), p. 162: "[…] law always has to come from real facts beacause it, however it may be, has the purpose to be applied to real facts." Legal terms never enabled the recognition of the real being, "but always nothing but norms, that are determined to be implemented by human acts."

3.1 The Concept of Law as the Epistemological "Trigger" of the Two-Sides-Theory

In the "General Theory of the State", Jellinek deals with the concept of law in the last chapter of the social theory, hence, just before discussing the juridical theory of the State (1900, 332 ss.). This position already demonstrates that the concept of law connects both sides of his theory, and that this connection is crucial for its understanding. Like the Two-Sides-Theory, Jellinek's concept of law expresses a specific interrelation of normativity and facticity. (See also Kersten 2000, pp. 352–375; Lembcke 2016).

Jellinek deduces legal norms from intentional human acts, that is, from normative statements. Legal norms, however, cannot be conceived purely as normative statements as they owe their existence, validity and content to "causes" from outside the normative sphere. In addition, factual preconditions may have an influence on the content of norms. According to Jellinek, these preconditions are primarily human psychology, historical developments and social circumstances. They underlie, enable and limit legal norms. Legal objects of recognition are both motivated and caused by these factual circumstances. Without including them in his theory, it would be impossible for Jellinek to adequately apprehend the normative level. The factual circumstances generate the conditions for the existence of legal norms. Facticity and normativity remain separated, but they are not unconnected. They affect each other. An epistemology that confined itself to the normative side of the law, would, in Jellinek's eyes, not even be sufficient from the juridical perspective. It would not be able to appropriately grasp legal norms as it neglects the "background influences" of facticity. Hence, facticity and normativity are separated on the one hand and connected on the other hand.[16] At a certain point, legal validity must be traced back to the "Is" as it cannot be explained by normative statements any further without something essential missing.

The validity of law is a typical and fundamental issue of jurisprudence. According to Jellinek, validity is based on the fact that the "psychological effectiveness" of the law is ensured. In his words, law is effective "if the motivating power of its norms is enhanced by socio-psychological powers in such a way that these norms are able to prevail over opposing individual motives as reasons for action."[17]

The connection of the law to the "Is" particularly manifests itself in Jellinek's dictum of the "normative force of the factual". (Jellinek 1900, pp. 337–344; see also

("… das Recht muß stets von realen Tatbeständen ausgehen, weil es, wie immer es beschaffen sein mag, stets den Zweck hat, auf reale Tatbestände angewendet zu werden." Durch Rechtsbegriffe aber werde niemals ein reales Sein erkannt, "sondern immer nichts anderes als Normen, die durch menschliche Tat verwirklicht zu werden bestimmt sind.").

[16] To the previous paragraph see Lepsius (2000), pp. 314–320.

[17] Jellinek (1900), p. 334: "wenn die motivierende Kraft seiner Vorschriften durch sozialpsychologische Mächte derart verstärkt ist, daß jene Normen sich gegen widerstrebende individuelle Motive als Bewegungsgründe des Handelns durchzusetzen imstande sind.". For Jellinek's theory of validity see Landau (2000).

Albert 1988, pp. 193–201; Anter 1998, pp. 520–523) According to Jellinek, facticity does not seamlessly turn into normativity. He is not a theorist of the authoritarian state. The transformation from the factual to the normative rather requires a normative level on which it is determined that a fact receives legal validity. Rules need to be acknowledged; and this acknowledgement would be impossible without taking into account the factual circumstances.[18] In the end, it is a human act of recognition that determines the normative force. Since human beings are unable to fully differentiate the world into norms and facts, and since their evaluation of situations will always be affected by factual circumstances, these circumstances exercise a normative force. The notion of the normative force of the factual rephrases the idea that something factual is valid—and not the fact that facticity generates law. In Jellinek's words:

> The transformation of the initially entirely factual power of the State into legal authority is always effected by means of the joining belief that this factual is of a normative kind, that it should be like it is.[19]

Facticity influences normativity by way of a psychological operation of acknowledgement. Besides, there is also a reverse influence for Jellinek, that is, the influence of normativity on facticity. Jellinek refers to the psychological notion of a sort of normativity that ranks above positive law demanding the alteration of the given legal situation (1900, 344–353). This notion does not belong to the sphere of what is genuinely legal. It rather is important for the explanation of the law. Both psychological notions, the normative force of the factual and the legal idea of the alteration of facticity, do not belong to the legal side of the State. Jelllinek discusses them as parts of the social theory of the State. He employs psychological operations in order to explain the validity of the law. These operations are not of legal nature can therefore not be adequately dealt with by employing juridical methods.

This is proof of Jellinek's conviction that, when explaining legal issues, one cannot do without taking into account factual circumstances. This does not imply that factual circumstances are of interest per se. They rather have an explanatory value in a legal context.

Therefore, Jellinek's social theory of the State is not to be interpreted as a theoretical attempt of a legal sociologist. It should be taken as an approach that detects historical and social facts which are considered important from a legal point of view. Thus, one should not expect the social theory of the State to be particularly fertile from a sociological point of view. On the contrary, Jellinek does not provide sociological explanations, but supplies his juridical approach with sociological facts. The social side of the State fulfils an indispensable complementary function for Jellinek's juridical approach. The topics of the "General Theory of State" can be

[18] Jellinek (1900), p. 337, Jellinek refers to a psychologically caused behavior of the human in regard to the factual processes that are not only perceived as something actual but also as standard of assessment.

[19] Jellinek (1900), p. 342: "Die Umwandlung der zunächst überall rein faktischen Macht des Staates in rechtliche erfolgt stets durch die hinzutretende Vorstellung, daß dieses Faktische normativer Art sei, daß es so sein solle, wie es ist."

only understood correctly when taking into account this complement. This also explains why Jellinek (1900), pp. 182–183 introduces the legal concept of the State within the framework of his social theory. The Two-Sides-Theory is neither the expression of an equal relation between the juridical a sociological method nor a division of labor between law and sociology. This prompts the question of how Jellinek conceives the relation between these two disciplines from his genuinely juridical point of view.

3.2 Interdisciplinary Issues

Not only does Jellinek's general theory of the State presuppose a specific theoretical conviction regarding the relation between facts and norms. It also rests on the notion that different disciplinary approaches produce different epistemological objects. Jellinek, writing in 1900, is one of the pioneers of modern interdisciplinary research within his own discipline. In his book, Jellinek discusses intensively the demarcation of the two disciplines law and sociology.[20] Which discipline is competent for devising a general social theory of the State? Here Jellinek faces a dilemma. In principle, the social theory only serves to detect legally relevant facts—hence it plays an ancillary role in the epistemology of law. At the same time, Jellinek maintains that those facts, despite being legally relevant, could not be detected by legal methodology. Thus, the social theory of the State takes on a bridging function. Because the legal epistemology will produce a different "State" as sociology would do. While the methodological boundaries are clear-cut with regard to the legal side of the State, they are more open within the area of the social theory.

In the end, Jellinek's general theory of the State is a distinctly legal approach. It opens itself for epistemic purposes, remains however firmly grounded on juridical methodology and does not integrate the methodology of other disciplines. Therefore, Jellinek's social theory of the state may not be measured against sociological expectations. It will always be embedded in a juridical epistemological interest, even though its object of investigation is the State as a multidisciplinary phenomenon. Therefore, it would have been more consistent, had Jellinek put alongside the legal side of the State a number of other "sides" and not just a social side, depending upon the question whether the historical, psychological, sociological or political facticity of the state is relevant for the respective legal issue. Instead of proposing two sides of the State, Jellinek should better have spoken of the multivalence of the state. (See closer Lepsius 2000, pp. 329–331) Reducing the state to only two sides implies that virtually anything which is non-legal belongs to the field of sociology. Thus, the legal concept of the State faces a convolute of characteristics, an accumulation of historical, psychological, political, philosophical and other criteria. Anything that is non-legal is taken under the common roof of a "General Theory of the State",

[20] To the relation of the theory of state and social sciences see Jellinek (1900), pp. 82–99, regarding the importance of sociological special disciplines for the theory of state (99–125).

although different disciplines would be competent for these aspects. Based on Jellinek's methodological premises, this only makes sense because it is juridical epistemology that ultimately decides which social facts are legally relevant.

Therefore, the fundamental problem with Jellinek's social theory of the State is that his theory investigates a non-legal epistemological object only from a juridical point of view. In the end the "interdisciplinarity" created by this very object is confined by the boundaries of the law. The guiding principle of Jellinek's approach is not an academia based on the division of labor, but rather the historically, psychologically and sociologically learned jurist who, despite his learnedness, does not intermingle the disciplines. Legal dogmatics are complemented, but not replaced.[21] This also holds true for the social theory of the State. It instructs the jurist to take into account the social circumstances that are necessary from his juridical epistemological interest; but it does not invite someone who is not a jurist to deal with legal issues. Just as little is it inclined to compete with the historian or the sociologist for the historical or sociological investigation of the State. It is the jurist who has to decide if and to which extent he or she should resort to sociological insights against the background of his own epistemological interests.

3.3 *Political Issues*

The legal and the social side of the State relate to one another. Jellinek conceives them as a corollary of a genuinely legal interdependence between facticity and normativity. Normative aspects affect the factual side, and factual aspects affect the normative side. Hence, the Two-Sides-Theory does not make a static claim. Its task is to diagnose as well as to explain social and normative changes. Jellinek strives neither for an objective recognition nor for an ultimate justification of the State. His theory of the State remains relative and dynamic as to its content for the very reason of its basic categories being of methodological, rather than substantial nature. His content-related statements therefore are to be seen as exemplary applications of his methodological criteria, not as substantial interpretations.

[21] This fundamental interdisciplinary understanding of Jellinek can be found in his earlier methodological fundamental work "System der subjektiven öffentlichen Rechte" ("System of the Subjective Public Rights"), Jellinek (1892), pp. 18–19: "Now it is obvious that the jurisprudent should explore the legal substance of law being only unilaterally educated in dogmatic. There is not any human field of knowledge that does not require the knowledge of others for its fruitful treatment; the broader the view of a researcher, the more comprehensive his knowledge is causing the knowledge of his subject to be more solid and in depth. The knowledge and importance of other disciplines that approach the law will be of importance for the form and result of the work of a jurisprudent. The combination of the knowledge of different fields of knowledge should not result in telescoping these areas in each other. The dogmatic of law should be supplemented by economic and cultural history as well as by social sciences, but not be supplanted." On Jellinek's theory of subjective rights see also Jouanjan (2004a).

Already in the first chapter, Jellinek (1900), pp. 13–19 emphasizes the importance of politics for the theory of the State. Both the social and the juridical theory of State require a complementary political perspective. In reality, the State is in a constant movement, and both the social and the juridical theory may take only snapshots of it (1900, 45–46). Abstracting the State from politics produces nothing, at best the recognition of a skeleton of the State. "In the theoretical juridical theory of the State (*theoretische Staatsrechtslehre*) as a conceptual discipline everything is abstract; the concrete is inherent in the flow of political life."[22]

For Jellinek, taking into account political influences is a manifestation of the theoretical dualism between facticity and normativity. Political ideas connect both sides of the State. In the social theory that focuses on causal relations, they are part of the ground of legal validity that, in turn, reconnects to the factual. Political ideas are rendered "subjective" and owe their factual status to a mass psychological process of acknowledgement. Moreover, politics have an influence on the "normativistic" exploration of the State that is conducted by juridical State theory. On Jellinek's account, political recognition is what continuously generates the demand for new law. "But this demand requires a profound knowledge of the prevailing law. That is why the juridical theory of State law is of great importance for politics because politics cannot fulfil its tasks without it."[23] In other words: The law, being a product of the normative force of the factual, is affected by politics but it also affects the room for maneuver of politics.

Thus, considering political influences is not just an epistemological claim, but also accounts for the constitutional situation of the German Empire of 1871. Jellinek clearly distances himself from Gerber's and Laband's[24] *staatsrechtlichem Positivismus* (verbatim: "state law" positivism) by rejecting the notion that the content of legal norms could be determined by pure logic. Jellinek is adamant that especially the principles of State law elude a purely logical approach. The contrast to Laband could have hardly been starker. Laband contended self-assuredly that "all historical, political and philosophical contemplations of the State law" were "without any relevance".[25] Jellinek maintained by contrast that "criticizing the extant institutions of public law" was a task of the theory of constitutional law: "Jurisprudence would surrender the more noble part of its profession, if it only looked backwards and did not assist the powers of the future in carving their way."[26]

[22] Jellinek (1900), p. 6: "In der theoretischen Staatslehre als einer Begriffswissenschaft ist alles abstrakt; das Konkrete wohnt dem Strom des politischen Lebens inne." (See also pp. 358–359).

[23] Jellinek (1900), p. 19: "Solche Forderung setzt aber gründliche Kenntnis des herrschenden Rechts voraus. Daher hat die Staatsrechtslehre große Bedeutung für die Politik, die ihre Aufgaben ohne jene nicht erfüllen kann."

[24] To this point see Sinzheimer (1953), p. 161; Koch (1977), pp. 61–67; Albert (1988), pp. 66–67, 74; Friedrich (1997), pp. 277–278, 285 ss.; Schönberger (1997), p. 216 ss.

[25] Laband (1911), p. VIII: "Alle historischen, politischen und philosophischen Betrachtungen [...] ohne Belang".

[26] Jellinek (1900), p. 19: "Die Rechtswissenschaft würde den edleren Teil ihres Berufes gänzlich aufgeben, wenn sie nur nach rückwärts gewendet wäre und nicht auch nach vorwärts den Mächten der Zukunft den Weg bahnen mithülfe."

The "General Theory of the State" aims at establishing a theoretical model which does not only facilitate a general understanding of the State, but whose fundamental categories are also useful for solving specific issue of policy and conflicts of constitutional law. Jellinek alludes to the issues discussed in the legal theory of the state during the German Empire. Around 1900, the German Empire's constitution could no longer cope with the political development which was geared towards a continuous parlamentarization of powers. The 1871 Constitution with its still limited role of the *Reichstag*, became outdated and needed a progressive interpretation. Contemporary scholarship, however, with its commitment to a positivistic methodology that strictly focused on the wording of the constitution could not provide such an interpretation. It was less and less able to grasp the reality of state. (See also Jellinek 1906) The institutional change of the Empire called for a dynamic, forward-looking theory which, at the same time, did not question the State as a uniform entity. The specific interdependence between social and juridical theory should therefore also be seen as a consequence of the political situation of late German Constitutionalism.[27]

4 The Context of the Two-Sides-Theory

4.1 Neo-Kantianism and Epistemology

We have seen that the Two-Sides-Theory is based on specific epistemological premises, interdisciplinary presuppositions and political circumstances. It is not by chance that the theory was born in 1900. At the very latest since 1880, the philosophy of Neo-Kantianism had not only dominated professional philosophical discussions in Germany, but had become a fundamental epistemological attitude to the humanities in general.[28] Neo-Kantianism aimed at pushing back scientific positivism and its causal-empirical ideal of accuracy, without falling behind the scientific standard that had been achieved by the natural sciences. On the basis of the Kantian differentiation between "Is" and "Ought", a primarily epistemologically oriented philosophy evolved that provided an overarching theory of all sciences. Its fundamental tenet is that methodology determines the object of investigation. This reversed the common conception of the relationship between object and method, namely that the task of methodology was to adequately recognize the extant object. Towards the end of the nineteenth century the notion gained acceptance that the object of investigation depended upon the chosen method and that the object changes according to the chosen point of view. Methodological issues began to

---

[27] Cf. Schönberger (2000), p. 3, who considers Jellinek's major works as a "differentiated answer to the crisis of Laband's theory of constitutional law."

[28] Regarding Neo-Kantianism instead of many others Orth and Holzhey (1994), Holzhey (1994), Müller (1994), and Pascher (1997).

replace discussions focusing on the respective object as essential questions of science.

What is more, Neo-Kantianism stimulated the creation and differentiation of new scientific disciplines around the year 1900. (See Hübinger 1988; Duve 1998, pp. 232–282) Disciplines that focused on the object of investigation, rather than on their methodology, as did the General Theory of State, got under the pressure to "modernize" themselves. A methodological approach that created the very object of investigation inevitably ran afoul with the presuppositions of the General Theory of State and called into question the whole discipline. Instead of a "general" theory of State "specific" theories of State appeared to be the order of the day. In fact only differentiated sociological, historical and juridical approaches satisfied the scientific criteria of preciseness of that time.

The epistemological categories of Neo-Kantianism enabled the respective disciplines to engage in epistemological considerations regarding isolated phenomena of their field, without being compelled to resort to philosophy. Thanks to the very fact that Neo-Kantianism provided an epistemology that was independent of specific philosophical tenets, it was able to catalyze methodological discussions within the respective disciplines and to back up their differentiation methodologically. It should be noted that, by 1900, German academia found itself in a position of global dominance. It owed this rank to methodological reflections that were detached from temporarily contingent substantial issues and, in connection with that, to the formulation of novel research questions within the respective disciplines. This is the merit of Neo-Kantianism.

4.2 *Jellinek's Juridical Implementation of Neo-Kantianism*

The importance of Jellinek's theory of State is equal to the importance of German academic culture around the year 1900. Not only does Jellinek apply the epistemological postulates of Neo-Kantianism to the theory of State, but he also develops those postulates on the basis of the issues of State law.[29] Jellinek's "General Theory of the State" as well as his "System of the Subjective Public Rights" may be interpreted as an exemplary juridical implementation of the methodological reorientation that started around 1900 (see Jouanjan 2004a, 2008): Jellinek does not presuppose an extant object "State" that only needed to be explored by employing multiple methods. His concept of the State is no longer determined by the object "State", rather it is created by employing these very methods. Jellinek asks (1892, p. 16f., 21; 1900, p. 163): How should we conceive the concept of State in order to comprehend the State as an entity? As a scholar, influenced by Neo-Kantianism, he proceeds by creating the object of investigation. Yet, he retains the notion of a uniform object of the State, the "State as such". In the background of the "creating

[29] On the influence of Neo-Kantianism on Jellinek, and on Jellinek as an independent Neo-Kantian intellectual Albert (1988), pp. 45–51, 70; Lepsius (2000), pp. 331–343.

approach", remains a conception that is determined by the object itself. This causes the conundra and tensions in Jellinek's work. Jellinek is halfway stuck in the development of Neo-Kantianism: On the one hand, he recognized the importance of the method for the recognition of the object, but on the other hand, he holds on to a conception of the object "as such". It is the task of the Two-Sides-Theory to solve this tension.

Neo-Kantianism was not a uniform, self-contained trend. It had changed during its heydays (1870–1910) from an approach that was object-determined to one that emphasized the creation of the object itself. Jellinek's theory of State marks this change, which explains his mediating epistemological interest (differentiated disciplines and epistemological processes with a uniform object of investigation). Because Jellinek still follows the older, object-determined approach, he is able to attribute two sides to the epistemological object "State". He uses the State as an incident to which a epistemological approach was to be applied that maintained the notion of an object as such, while simultaneously recognizing the object's methodological creation.

4.3 *Epistemological Reasons for the Criticism of Jellinek*

Jellinek's book is not only a treatise on the general epistemology of the State, but it also proposes a methodology for public law. Jellinek uses the State as an example for the formulation and discussion of fundamental methodological questions. Therefore, his critics often argue epistemologically than from a perspective of constitutional theory. This holds true in particular for the critique by Hans Kelsen and Leonard Nelson.[30] Kelsen faults that Jellinek combined two conceptions of the State although it was epistemologically impossible to recognize the same object by two different conceptions.[31] He criticizes Jellinek for clinging to the notion of a uniform epistemological object of the State despite acknowledging the different modes of creating the object by the respective disciplines.

[30] Kelsen (1911), pp. 480–490; Kelsen (1922), pp. 114–120; Nelson (1917), pp. 6–50. Nelson criticizes that in Jellinek's work law becomes a psychological phenomenon. But law was independent from all factual and the reason for the validity of a legal norm could only be due to another legal norm. Jellinek confuses the legal relevance of a fact under the law with the power of a fact to create law.

[31] Kelsen (1922), p. 117: "Der Versuch, eben dasselbe Objekt: den Staat, zum Inhalt zweier verschiedener Begriffe, eines sozialen und eines Rechtsbegriffs zu machen und dabei die Identität des Erkenntnisgegenstandes aufrechtzuerhalten, muß natürlich zu den schwersten Widersprüchen und Verrenkungen führen." Translation: "The attempt to make the same object, the "state", the subject of two different terms, a social and legal term of law, while maintaining the identity of the epistemological object, has to result in the most severe contradictions and sprains." Concerning Kelsen's criticism on Jellinek, see Koch (1977), pp. 67–76; Lepsius (1994), pp. 156–161; Pascher (1997), pp. 155–156; Kersten (2000), pp. 169–178; Lembcke (2016).

If one accepts the idea that epistemology creates the object of investigation Kelsen's criticism is warranted. Such an epistemology is no longer able to accept uniform objects once the methodologies are differentiated from one another. However, Jellinek wrote his work 20 years earlier, during a time of epistemological change. He applied the "creating approach" to the differentiation of disciplines, not to the objects of investigation in general. Thus, he assumed that each disciplined had to apply its own methodology while maintaining that it was not impossible to explore a uniform object like the State from different disciplinary perspectives. For Jellinek, it was clear that the disciplines were determined by their methodology. Yet he was not convinced that different methodologies would create different objects of investigation, as it was clear for Kelsen some 20 years later.

Jellinek did not want to violate the postulate of a "purity of methods", that is, to engage as a legal scholar in historical or sociological investigations. Including facticity is mainly due to his legal epistemology. It is prompted by the necessary reconnection of law (and therefore also the State in its legal dimension) and fact. Jellinek's problem is that he intends to approach a non-legal object from the viewpoint of legal epistemology.

This, in turn, explains the more recent criticism offered by social scientists. According to Stefan Breuer, Jellinek's social conception of the State does not have "a substance of its own". He criticizes that Jellinek was not able to get rid of the constraints of his discipline and that he remained stuck in the normative investigation of the State (Breuer 1999, pp. 14, 17). Like Kelsen's, this criticism is warranted, but it is based on the particular methodological issue Jellinek faced.

Neither legal scholars nor social scientists therefore agree with the Two-Sides-Theory (see Lembcke 2016) and passed on warranted criticism that ultimately concerns Jellinek's methodological premises which again should not be condemned, but rather be praised as an implementation of the epistemology of his time. Hence, one should justifiably call Jellinek a theorist of the "sowohl-als-auch", the "as well as" (Möllers 2000b, p. 155) or a great "synthesist",[32] even a communitarian (Brugger 2016). His "General Theory of the State" owes its lasting impact as a classical text less to the fundamental substantial discoveries regarding the State's nature, but to the fact of being an epistemological and interdisciplinary examination of the State as an example. Beyond its concrete substantial output, it is to be seen as a role model for methodology.

5 The Categorical Impact of the Two-Sides-Theory

Jellinek's theory is a starting point for further investigation to which one can resort up until the present day. It may count as a classical text in the sense of the "final summary of 19th century State theories" (Kelsen 1925, p. IX) because almost every

[32] Stolleis (1992), pp. 450, 454: the conveyance of something that eventually is not-conveyable.

line of thinking may refer to it in formulating its own positions. In three particular aspects, Jellinek represents fundamental consent the theory of State.

5.1 *Interdisciplinary Fundamental Conceptions*

Many disciplines deal with the entity "State", and the conception of the State they employ does not have to be identical with its juridical conception.[33] It was the Two-Sides-Theory that, for the first time, addressed this problem and gave it a fundamental expression. It freed constitutional theory (*Staatslehre*) from its normative biases and it opened it for political, sociological and historical developments. Jellinek's opening of the legal studies for non-legal topics that, at the same time, retained the juridical method, left its mark on German State law theory. Among a number of possible interdisciplinary approaches Jellinek's prevails: It is the model of the intellectual jurist who is able to detect and process those factual circumstances from sociology, history, psychology or politics which appear relevant to him. This is not a division of labor.[34] The legal scholar is rather trusted with multi-dimensional tasks and with solving methodological issues by employing juridical methods. The interdisciplinary model rests on the jurist who is educated in social sciences. Yet this comes with the danger that the "opening" of jurisprudence, in fact, will result in an extension of the law beyond its province, hence not being an actual opening towards different subjects. Jellinek conveys his interdisciplinary perspective with juridical professionality. He integrates the different perspectives in the sense of a "Theory-Interdisciplinarity" beneath the same juridical roof. This makes an interdisciplinary sharing of results dispensable for jurisprudence.

Until the present day, in German constitutional theory a collaborative and interdisciplinary understanding is underdeveloped that is not only directed at the exploitability of non-legal topics, but equally to the exploitability of legal results for neighboring disciplines. This results in a remarkable resistance of constitutional theory when it comes to empirical insights. Jellinek's own sociological perspective had already not been empirical and little has changed until today. Likewise, economics, neglected by Jellinek, until the present day, has been of marginal importance to German legal scholars. Conversely, the inclusion of a "reality" that stands beyond the law, gets attributed a disproportional amount of importance, and this reality is predominantly considered historically, philosophically and sociologically. A certain hybris of legal scholars that focus on "reality" and a corresponding ignorance of other rationalities beside the law (for instance, political or economic controlling and sanctioning) stands in the same tradition. This conception of

---

[33] From a historical point of view Reinhard (2000); from a sociological Breuer (1998); from a political Anter (1996); Vorländer (2016); from the philosophy of history van Crefeld (1999).

[34] For a different interdisciplinary understanding that is based on the division of labor of different disciplines, see Kelsen (1925), pp. 7–19, 314–315, 344.

interdisciplinarity cannot only be blamed on Jellinek. His theory rather expresses a self-conception that prevails until now.

5.2 *Basic Epistemological Insights*

Both in law and social sciences, the State has a double meaning with regard to its factual and normative importance. It characterizes the result of a normative construct and a factual description. The concept of "state" simultaneously describes a condition and an idea; it serves as a descriptive and attributive category. For instance, the concept of "constitutional democracy" does not only express the contemporary constitutional situation of the German Basic Law, but it also contains a normative program of how one should conceive the constitutional reality. Current characterizations such as the "informal state", "cooperative state" or "small government/state" typically connect the condition as such and its evaluations. Hence, they provide mixed statements on the actual and the desired state. The State is an epistemological object that is typically associated with the "Is" as well as to the "Ought". Not uncommonly, the attractiveness of the State as an epistemological object is due to the fact that one can amalgamate statements on the status quo and the desired status.

Therefore, in jurisprudence we do not only encounter fundamental discussions of the concept of the "State",[35] but also ideal expectations. The category of the State is capable of conceptionalizing the political goal of territorial, mental and personal integrity or an institutional order. For instance, constitutional theory (*Staatslehre*) is able, by analyzing the concept of the State, to put itself into the position of gathering ideas of the State that have no positive legal validity and that are nonetheless used for juridical investigation and for giving them a normative and determining power. Constitutional theory is able to meet the needs for an immaterial enrichment as well as for a social reconnection of the law. Here we see the reverse side of the factual and the normative, the double-nature of the term "state", which furnishes both a realistic and an immaterial object of research. Until today this epistemological issue is immaculately conveyed by the theory of the two sides of state. Jellinek's theory of the state symbolizes the feasibility of a mediation between being and what is ought to be, facticity and normativity by maintaining epistemological standards.

[35] Regarding the exploitability of different perceptions of the state for doctrinal purposes see, from a critical distance, Möllers (2000a).

5.3 *The Concept of State as an Expression of Scientific Political Expectations*

The theory of the two-sides of the State does not only denote a principal issue of interdisciplinarity and epistemology. There is a third point that is uniquely German: The Two-Sides-Theory scientifically shelters political expectations. Hardly in any other country or other legal system the concept of the state benefits from a similarly prominent position. As a legal term it is rather neglected in some places. For instance, the Anglo-Saxon legal terminology does not contain a translation for *Staatsrecht* or *Staatslehre* (which is why this text oftentimes had to resort to the term "constitutional theory" to refer to the latter). The term state law and the term "state" only describe the federal member state: a meaning that is far cry from the dignity of the German term. Also in the Romanic countries it does not mean "droit de l'État" or "diritto dello stato" but "droit constitutionnel" or rather "diritto costituzionale", hence constitutional law, and not "state law"; hence constitutional theory and not "state theory".

"State law" and the "theory of the state" as objects of research are a peculiarity of the German tradition.[36] In international comparison the "state" is at least in the end of the nineteenth and the twentieth century a distinctly German issue. Therefore, it is not surprising that a discipline called "General Theory of the State" is unknown to other countries. This finding contrasts the scientific perception of the general theory of state in Germany. According to its standard the theory of the state is a "general" one, but in reality, it is just a German one.

This difference between its own standard and reality is due to the political circumstances in Germany at that time. The absence of a theory of the state in other countries primarily accounts for the fact that countries such as France, Great Britain or the United States of America, had already established a national political order or even a nation state—in contrast to Germany where the nation state only was permanently established with German unification in 1990. Neither the German Empire of 1871 nor the Weimar Republic can be considered a nation state with Austria having been excluded from the German territory. In 1990, however, Austria was not considered a part of Germany any longer. Unification only applied to East and West Germany. Throughout the nineteenth and twentieth century Germany suffered from not forming a stable political unity. The concept of "state", hence, was able to host the political expectations because, legally, there was no single state in Germany (but only a number of states). Moreover, the categories of political organization in Germany—unlike in France for instance—were historically primarily linked to the term of empire ("Reich") not to the state. In Germany the term "state" did not match to the legally composed statehood. Thereby it was able to preserve a peculiar openness in terms of content, while having its own demand of simultaneously being compulsory. The state remained the goal, whereas the Empire and the constitution were reality.

[36] See Schönberger (1999), p. 122; Jouanjan (2004b), both in comparison to France.

Hence, Germany as a “State” could remain a category that evaded the respective reality of state law. In that manner it could liaise as the catch basin for different expectations towards ideal and formal orders. In that manner it provided an academic phenomenon at which, beyond the reality of the constitution of the Empire, specific issues could be discussed: fundamental methodological issues (interdisciplinary and epistemological issue) as well as substantive issues (e.g. the tasks and purposes of the State). The theory of the state had been the scientific refuge for issues that lacked legal validity. Jellinek’s service of mediation is one of theory and practice. It includes political ideas in legal theorems and therefore conversely has the demand of being able to intervene creatively in the political life as a scientist.

These three aspects, interdisciplinarity, epistemology and normative expectations make the term “state” scientifically attractive, and they explain the continuing importance of the theory of the Two Sides of the State. Georg Jellinek’s Two-Sides-Theory provides inventive answers to all of the three questions. They outlasted the time in which they were written, even though they remain connected to the objective, methodological and political situation of the late German Empire.

Acknowledgments A previous version of this article was published in German as: Die Zwei-Seiten-Lehre des Staates, in: Andreas Anter (ed.), Die normative Kraft des Faktischen. Das Staatsverständnis Georg Jellineks, Baden-Baden: Nomos Verlag 2004, pp. 63–88. The text was revised by the author. I owe many thanks to Jonas Sillmann and Fabian Michl for the translation.

References

Albert H-P (1988) Der Staat als “Handlungssubjekt”. Interpretation und Kritik der Staatslehre Georg Jellineks, Diss. Phil. Heidelberg

Anter A (1996) Max Webers Theorie des modernen Staates. Herkunft, Struktur und Bedeutung, 2 edn. Berlin

Anter A (1998) Georg Jellineks wissenschaftliche Politik. Positionen, Kontexte, Wirkungslinien. Politische Vierteljahresschrift 39:502–526

Boldt H, Conze W, Haverkate G (1990) Staat und Souveränität I-V. In: Brunner O, Conze W, Koselleck R (eds) Geschichtliche Grundbegriffe, vol 6. Stuttgart, pp 4–98

Breuer S (1998) Der Staat: Entstehung, Typen, Organisationsstadien. Reinbek

Breuer S (1999) Georg Jellinek und Max Weber. Von der sozialen zur soziologischen Staatslehre. Baden-Baden

Brugger W (2016) Georg Jellinek als Staatstheoretiker und Kommunitarist. In: Brugger W, Gröschner R, Lembcke O (eds) Faktizität und Normativität. Georg Jellineks freiheitliche Verfassungslehre, Tübingen, pp 5–37

Draht M (1987) Staat. In: Evangelisches Staatslexikon, Band II, 3. Aufl., Stuttgart, pp 3305–3353

Duve T (1998) Normativität und Empirie im öffentlichen Recht und der Politikwissenschaft um 1900. Historisch-systematische Untersuchung des Lebens und Werks von Richard Schmidt (1862–1944) und der Methodenentwicklung seiner Zeit, Ebelsbach

Friedrich M (1997) Geschichte der deutschen Staatsrechtswissenschaft, Berlin

Holzhey H (ed) (1994) Ethischer Sozialismus. Zur politischen Philosophie des Neukantianismus, Frankfurt/Main

Hübinger G (1988) Staatstheorie und Politik als Wissenschaft im Kaiserreich: Georg Jellinek, Otto Hintze, Max Weber. In: Maier H et al (eds) Politik, Philosophie, Praxis. Festschrift für Wilhelm Hennis, Stuttgart, pp 143–161
Jellinek G (1892) System der subjektiven öffentlichen Rechte, Tübingen
Jellinek G (1900) Allgemeine Staatslehre, Berlin, 3rd edn. 1914
Jellinek G (1906) Verfassungsänderung und Verfassungswandlung, Berlin
Jouanjan O (2004a) Les fondations de la théorie des droits publics subjectifs dans la pensée de Georg Jellinek. Revue universelle des droits de l'homme 16:6–16
Jouanjan O (2004b) Braucht das Verfassungsrecht eine Staatslehre? Europäische Grundrechtezeitschrift 31:362–370
Jouanjan O (2008) Georg Jellinek als Philosoph. In: Rechtstheorie in rechtspraktischer Absicht. Festschrift für Friedrich Müller, Berlin, pp 135–153
Kelsen H (1911) Hauptprobleme der Staatsrechtslehre. Entwickelt aus der Lehre vom Rechtssatze, Tübingen
Kelsen H (1922) Der soziologische und der juristische Staatsbegriff. Kritische Untersuchung des Verhältnisses von Staat und Recht, Tübingen
Kelsen H (1925) Allgemeine Staatslehre, Berlin
Kempter K (1998) Die Jellineks 1820–1955. Eine familienbiographische Studie zum deutschjüdischen Bildungsbürgertum, Düsseldorf
Kersten J (2000) Georg Jellinek und die klassische Staatslehre, Tübingen
Kersten J (2015) Georg Jellinek (1851–1911). In: Häberle P, Kilian M, Wolff H (eds) Staatsrechtslehrer des 20. Jahrhunderts, Berlin, pp 59–68
Koch H-J (1977) Seminar: Die juristische Methode im Staatsrecht. Über Grenzen von Verfassungs- und Gesetzesbindung, Frankfurt/Main; teilweise abgedruckt als: Die staatsrechtliche Methode im Streit um die Zwei-Seiten-Theorie des Staates (Jellinek, Kelsen, Heller). In: Paulson SL, Schulte M (eds) Georg Jellinek. Beiträge zu Leben und Werk, Tübingen, pp 371–389
Laband P (1911) Das Staatsrecht des Deutschen Reiches, Band 1, 5th edn. Tübingen und Leipzig (1888)
Landau P (2000) Rechtsgeltung bei Georg Jellinek. In: Paulson SL, Schulte M (eds) Georg Jellinek. Beiträge zu Leben und Werk, Tübingen, pp 299–307
Lembcke O (2016) "Das mag in der Praxis richtig sein, taugt aber nicht für die Theorie": Zum Verhältnis zwischen Faktizität und Normativität bei Jellinek und Kelsen. In: Brugger W, Gröschner R, Lembcke O (eds) Faktizität und Normativität. Georg Jellineks freiheitliche Verfassungslehre, Tübingen, pp 63–107
Lepsius O (1994) Die gegensatzaufhebende Begriffsbildung. Methodenentwicklungen in der Weimarer Republik und ihr Verhältnis zur Ideologisierung der Rechtswissenschaft im Nationalsozialismus, München
Lepsius O (2000) Georg Jellineks Methodenlehre im Spiegel der zeitgenössischen Erkenntnistheorie. In: Paulson SL, Schulte M (Hg.) Georg Jellinek. Beiträge zu Leben und Werk, Tübingen, pp 309–343
Matz U (1974) Staat. In: Krings H, Baumgartner HM, Wild C (eds) Handbuch philosophischer Grundbegriffe, vol 5. München, pp 1403–1419
Möllers C (2000a) Staat als Argument, München
Möllers C (2000b) Skizzen zur Aktualität Georg Jellineks. Vier theoretische Probleme aus Jellineks Staatslehre in Verfassungsrecht und Staatstheorie der Gegenwart. In: Paulson SL, Schulte M (eds) Georg Jellinek. Beiträge zu Leben und Werk, Tübingen, pp 155–171
Müller C (1994) Die Rechtsphilosophie des Marburger Neukantianismus, Tübingen
Nelson L (1917) Die Rechtswissenschaft ohne Recht. Kritische Betrachtungen über die Grenzen des Staats- und Völkerrechts insbesondere über die Lehre von der Souveränität, Göttingen
Orth EW, Holzhey H (eds) (1994) Neukantianismus. Perspektiven und Probleme, Würzburg
Pascher M (1997) Einführung in den Neukantianismus, München
Reinhard W (2000) Geschichte der Staatsgewalt, München

Sattler MJ (1993) Georg Jellinek (1851–1911). Ein Leben für das öffentliche Recht. In: Heinrichs H et al (eds) Deutsche Juristen jüdischer Herkunft, München, pp 355–368

Schönberger C (1997) Das Parlament im Anstaltsstaat. Zur Theorie parlamentarischer Repräsentation in der Staatsrechtslehre des Kaiserreichs (1871–1918), Frankfurt/Main

Schönberger C (1999) Der "Staat" der Allgemeinen Staatslehre: Anmerkungen zu einer eigenwilligen deutschen Disziplin im Vergleich mit Frankreich. In: Beaud O, Heyen EV (eds) Eine deutsch-französische Rechtswissenschaft? Baden-Baden, pp 111–137

Schönberger C (2000) Ein Liberaler zwischen Staatswille und Volkswille. Georg Jellinek und die Krise des staatsrechtlichen Positivismus um die Jahrhundertwende. In: Paulson SL, Schulte M (eds) Georg Jellinek. Beiträge zu Leben und Werk, Tübingen, pp 3–32

Sinzheimer H (1953) Jüdische Klassiker der deutschen Rechtswissenschaft, Frankfurt/Main

Stolleis M (1992) Geschichte des öffentlichen Rechts in Deutschland, vol 2, 1800–1914. München

Thoma R (1926) Staat (Allgemeine Staatslehre). In: Handwörterbuch der Staatswissenschaften, Band VII, 4th edn. Jena, pp 724–756

van Crefeld M (1999) Aufstieg und Untergang des Staates, München

Vollrath E (1998) Staat, II. 19. und 20. Jh. In: Historisches Wörterbuch der Philosophie, vol 10. Basel, pp 30–50

Vorländer H (2016) Statuslehre und Staat bei Georg Jellinek. In: Brugger W, Gröschner R, Lembcke O (eds) Faktizität und Normativität. Georg Jellineks freiheitliche Verfassungslehre, Tübingen, pp 145–160

Sein and *Sollen*, "Is" and "Ought" and the Problem of Normativity in Hans Kelsen

Nicoletta Bersier Ladavac

Abstract Hans Kelsen's Pure Theory of Law is a theory that seeks to draw a clear distinction between the object of study and the methods of inquiry within legal science. Its object of study is the knowledge of valid—i.e. existing—legal norms. Therefore, legal science according to Kelsen is a science that deals with the validity and not the efficacy of norms, and it is therefore a normative science, a science of the ought that is premised on the principle of imputation, which seeks to gain knowledge of and to describe the provisions that indicate the way in which people must behave and the sanctions that must be imposed on those who fail to act in the manner required. Legal science can, thus, be distinguished in terms of both its object and its method from other empirical and naturalist sciences, namely sciences based on the principle of causality. For Kelsen, validity is the prerequisite for the existence of positive law, the *Sollen*, while value is the foundation for natural law, the *Sein*.

1 The Is/Ought Distinction: An Ontological Distinction

One of the most important aspects on which Hans Kelsen built his theory of law, known as the Pure Theory of Law, is the philosophical—and most of all ontological and epistemological-dualistic distinction between *Sein* and *Sollen*, that is the Is and the Ought, also called the fact-value distinction. This distinction is a fundamental one in order to understand the meaning and purpose that Hans Kelsen sought to give to his legal enterprise. The Is is the domain of nature, facts, of the physical world, the world of things, in short, the natural and material reality of being and existence, the world of science and natural science (*Wissenschaft* and *Naturwissenschaft*); the

Translation of the manuscript by Thomas Roberts.

N. Bersier Ladavac (✉)
Thémis, Centre de Philosophie du droit, de Sociologie du droit et de Théorie du droit, Geneva, Switzerland
e-mail: nbersier@iprolink.ch

N. Bersier Ladavac et al. (eds.), *The Normative Force of the Factual*, Law and Philosophy Library 130, https://doi.org/10.1007/978-3-030-18929-7_3

Ought on the other hand is the opposite of the Is and represents what ought to be done (*Sollen*) or not to be done. It is the domain of the ideas, of the immaterial and spiritual dimension, and it is impossible to derive an Ought from an Is. The two dimensions are completely and absolutely separated, and also cannot contradict each other. On that distinction Kelsen based his concept of law and his theory of law, the Pure Theory of Law, *Reine Rechtslehre* (Kelsen 1934; Paulson and Litschewski Paulson 1992). The *Reine Rechtslehre* has a normativist dimension. It is a theory of legal cognition, the knowledge of its object, and the key to that normativist dimension is the Kantian argument. Kelsen already introduced the Kantian distinction between Is and Ought into his first important work *Hauptprobleme der Staatsrechtslehre* (Kelsen 1911), a distinction that remained fundamental and constant throughout his legal thought, and that he developed in most of his theoretical works, especially in his theory of law. Kelsen derived this ontological distinction between Is and Ought from Kant's distinction between the noumenal and phenomenal realms, although he did not follow Kant completely in adopting the rigorous metaphysical categories of the *Critique of Pure Reason* (Kant 1998). Kelsen is concerned with Kant's purity when distinguishing descriptive Is statements from prescriptive Ought statements of Is. Statements of Is and statements of Ought should not be mixed. The difference between Is and Ought is evident and the same subject cannot be considered at some times in terms of Is (whether it exists or does not exist) and at other times in terms of Ought (whether it ought or ought not to be). Is and Ought cannot be mixed together.

Undoubtedly Kant's philosophy represents the philosophical dimension to Kelsen's theory, although not in the sense of logical positivism, but rather as an expression of the methodological dualism developed by Kelsen. This dualistic distinction between Is and Ought (Stewart 1990) radically excludes any theoretical or factual link between facticity and normativity, between human reality and the legal dimension, i.e. between the *Sein/Sollen* distinction that marks out "two completely independent spheres that are epistemologically unbridgeable – the external, physical world and a normative or ideal sphere" (Paulson 1996, p. 801). To recall it in Kelsen's words "[T]he opposition between *Sein* and *Sollen*, between 'is' and 'ought', is a logico-formal opposition, and, in so far as the boundaries of logico-formal enquiry are observed, no path leads from the one world to the other; the two are separated by an unbridgeable gap.

From the point of view of logic, enquiring into the why of a concrete 'ought' can only lead to another 'ought', just as the answer to the why of an 'is' can only be another 'is'" (Paulson 1996, p. 802, note 37) *Sein* and *Sollen* are in a radical opposition and therefore the dimension of facticity and that of normativity are straightforwardly separated. This formal-logical antagonism also has the consequence of an inevitable division between the sciences and the related epistemological problem of the scientific knowledge, the object of research of each being different. The 'Is' relates to actual facts, that is to the dimension of concrete reality, nature and empirical experience, whereas the 'Ought' relates to the dimension of ideality and spirituality, values and the non-empirical dimension, or in other words—in terms of philosophy of law—to legal science, norms and normativity. A *Sein* statement refers to natural entities or social facts as objects of investigation whereas a *Sollen* statement develops an entity that does not exist in nature, being a human creation. Since it does not describe any natural events or social behaviour, Ought statements express duties and are aimed at fulfilling certain prescriptive circumstances. In Kelsen's view, Ought statements make it possible to interpret without recurring to meta-legal authorities the meaning of certain facts as a system of objectively valid legal norms so that a legal statement can be prescriptive rather than descriptive because the statement about a duty prescribes how one ought to behave. And the Ought of a norm involves acting a certain way in the empirical dimension, the *Sein*-dimension.

This illustrates the practical character of a norm. A norm is an Ought because it cannot express an arbitrary personal desire that comes from an Is and it posits a concept (legal positivism) in a particular desired direction. It is posited in the Is and the addressee must behave as the posited Ought prescribes. Thus, a legal statement is an Ought duty that is a mere concept logically connected to the factual world of Is. A legislative act is a fact that can be described but it is not yet a norm. A norm is a statement about the legislative act and gives meaning to the legislative fact. One is a fact, the other is the meaning of that particular fact. Legal validity refers to the meaning of the empirical legislative fact. The content of the legislative concept is represented by a term and is the intended signification of the concept. Thus, the norm is a representation of a concept even if the prescription within the concept has not actually taken place. A norm does not prescribe a fact as if it were empirically perceivable. Thus the norm, even if it is an Is that occurs and exists, is a prescription with a substantive Ought content. This means that legal authority is prescriptive rather than descriptive. Laws are Ought statements describing norms that prescribe the conduct that an addressee ought to engage in. An Ought statement is actually a statement about a legal Is. The Ought statement is an act of meaning. It prescribes, authorises and regulates an object that can be perceived, and that is addressed as an Ought to an addressee directing him how to behave. The Ought is a category that relates to the empirical legal material (Kelsen 1934, pp. 20–21). This means, that any given human behaviour must coincide with the norm that decreed that this particular behaviour should be obligatory. The Is/Ought distinction means that the Ought statement relates to a fact (the behaviour) and that this fact is the "legal Is". The Ought statement is not a fact but is expressed and connected with factual language, a verbal expression and means of communication that incorporates a value-indifferent meaning (Kelsen 1991, p. 62).

2 The Distinction Between Causal and Normative Sciences

The radical distinction between Is and Ought particularly concerns what is admissible as science (*Wissenschaft*) if science is defined as a rational enterprise dealing with questions of what is. Accordingly, what is rational can be analysed in science while questions of what ought to be, being irrational, cannot. Is belongs to science, while Ought belongs to ideology and since science must be kept pure of ideology Is and Ought cannot be confused. Sciences of nature are concerned with Is, whereas sciences of Ought are—in Kelsen's scheme—concerned with norms and are called normative sciences. The normative sciences are pure because they describe Oughts without subscribing to or evaluating them. Therefore the Pure Theory of law is a normative science concerning law. Through the category of Ought, which operates through the scheme of norm, it is possible for Kelsen to describe a science of norms without engaging in any form of evaluation, and this can be defined as normative science. On the contrary, all other sciences (sociology, history, psychology and so on) are concerned with problems of causality. Kelsen's purpose was to emancipate his theory from both, the traditional natural law theory and the traditional legal positivism, in other words from both natural law theory and empirical positivist theory.

By developing the Is/Ought distinction Kelsen drew out, probably to its farthest limit, the process of purifying formal legal structures of empirical and metaphysical content, namely elements falling within the scope of the *Sein*. As a consequence our knowledge relates to two fundamentally distinct sciences, first the causal sciences encompassing the traditional theory of natural law, and secondly the normative sciences, distinguishing between logical-gnoseological knowledge and phenomenological and deontological knowledge of the law. The *Sein* dimension is expressed in causal or natural laws, and the *Sollen* dimension in norms. Moreover, in describing as normative those sciences that have an Ought as their subject matter he aimed "to stress as strongly as possible the fact that the normative sciences need not create norms but simply now them, for science is never prescriptive, creative will, but descriptive, perceptive intellectually" (Ebenstein 1945, pp. 6–7) At this point we should chiefly notice that for Kelsen the term 'normative' means not setting up the norm but knowing the norm. In that sense, legal science, normative science does not relate to the reality of actual facts and events, the world of is, and is therefore not an explicative discipline; on the contrary, it is concerned with norms, "i.e., actual legal materials from which it must deduce its specific legal concepts" (Ebenstein 1945, pp. 6–7), and from a legal point of view it is a positive science, that is the foundation of legal positivism. In fact, according to the natural law theory, a positive law is valid because its content conforms to natural law *qua* norm, but "[A]ccording to the Pure Theory of Law as a positivistic legal theory, the validity of positive law is altogether independent of its content; a positive law is valid not because it has a definite, namely a just content, but because it was created in a particular way…" (Paulson 1975, p. 771, note 11) In fact, the point of departure of legal positivism is the idea that law is conventional, a human creation, a pure work of man (Paulson 1975, p. 772, note 17), whereas natural law theory affirms that law does not depend on human will, but creates itself.

Thus, Kelsen's aim was to base his theory of normativity on a scientific footing. Kelsen's theory was therefore able to purify in the most radical manner the formal structure of the law of its empirical and evaluative content. Kelsen set out his theory in full as early in the first edition of the *Reine Rechtslehre* (Kelsen 1934) drawing a clear distinction between *Sein* and *Sollen* as well as the legal consequences this entails. In fact, his entire legal theory along with his normativism is based on the distinction between *Sein* and *Sollen*. He thus distinguishes between the law, understood as a specific object of the pure theory of law, and natural facts (i.e. anything from the world of *Sein*) as well as moral values and justice, on the grounds that such phenomena belong to the realm of Is, while the law belongs to the realm of Ought. As for Kelsen, the values of morals and justice are in fact irrational ideals, which therefore cannot be accessed through rational thought, while the law is by its very nature knowable and rational.

In the part of the *Reine Rechtslehre*, the Pure Theory of Law, where Kelsen addresses problems related to the so-called static nature of the law (Kelsen 1934) he elaborates above all his normative conception by rigorously releasing the pure forms of law from any external contaminant concepts. His conception of the legal norm lacks any empirical content, whether psychological or voluntaristic; moreover the distinction between validity and efficacy is used in order to delineate better the law as *Sollen*, as a discipline that belongs exclusively to the realm of Ought, and to set it apart from the actual behaviour of individuals, which by contrast belongs to the realm of *Sein*.

3 The Ontological Function of the Norm

Kelsen clearly explains in various passages of the Pure Theory of Law the function of the norm within the structure of law and also in relation to human behaviour. Kelsen affirms that the norm is not an empirical fact but is related to factual reality in the sense that it gives legal sense to a factual event conferring legal meaning upon it. The event can thus be interpreted according to the norm because the norm operates as a scheme of interpretation. Epistemologically, interpretation of norms means legal cognition because it is directed at norms, more specifically at legal norms. Kelsen goes further regarding the function of the norm explaining that norms classify material facts and events as legal or illegal acts in accordance with what is to be considered to be legal or illegal. Accordingly, the purpose of the Pure Theory of Law is to comprehend whether an event or a material fact is legal or illegal, and for Kelsen if it is legal it can only be comprehended as law. So the norm is not just a term, a material entity, and does not exist in nature, and is not a fact of nature, but acts as an epistemological category, a scheme of interpretation for the legal dimension in order to determine whether something is legal or not. Moreover, a material fact can be interpreted as legal only if the content of the material fact can be cognised as the content of a norm. However, Kelsen says that the content of a norm is about the same even if not the same, or may be compared, as the content of an event because the norm refers to the event, that is to the human behaviour implied in the event.

And because Kelsen's Pure Theory of Law is a theory that seeks to draw a clear distinction between the object of study and the methods of inquiry within legal science on the one hand and other fields such as sociology, psychology, religion or politics on the other, the object of study of Kelsen's science of law is therefore a clearly delineated object, namely the knowledge of valid—i.e. existing—legal norms. And this legal science analyses norms within their constituent elements and in terms of their reciprocal relations, organising them according to particular structures. Therefore, legal science as cognitive science of norms is different from all other cognitive sciences that refer to and explain natural events in terms of causal laws. The Pure Theory of Law is in that sense a legal science that encompasses material facts only and the question as to whether these facts are the content of legal norms. Accordingly, another characteristic of the *Reine Rechtslehre* is to refer to the specific autonomy of a realm of meaning.

4 Is and Ought and Legal Proposition (*Rechtssatz*)

The Pure Theory of Law as legal science, in the sense of positive law, subsumes the norm as Ought. It is the Ought that confers normativity. Seeking to free law from all ideological elements, the *Reine Rechtslehre* draws an absolute distinction between the legal norm and the moral norm because legal law is autonomous from moral law. Therefore, the legal norm cannot be considered as an imperative or a command as under the traditional theory but must rather be a hypothetical judgement, i.e. a link between a conditioning material fact and a legal consequence. The legal proposition is hypothetical in form, in that the satisfaction of the condition specified in the 'if' clause will assure the legal result specified in the 'then' clause. Legal norms prescribe certain behaviour; legal propositions concern the eventuality that a person may not follow these prescriptions. Norms are created by legal officials, while legal propositions are created by legal theorists. The legal norm as legal proposition, or to say it with Stanley Paulson, the reconstructed legal norm (*Rechtssatz*) is the basic form of positive law.

Positive laws link a legal condition with a legal consequence. In the causal sciences, the empirical sciences, the mode of linking between material facts is causality, whereas according to the Pure Theory of Law legal facts are linked to events by imputation (*Zurechnung*). Moreover, the reduction of the concept of person as a center for the imputation of norms is used by Kelsen in order to eliminate both psychological and naturalistic elements in addition to the metaphysical ones. Within the causal sciences the legal consequence depends on the empirical-material legal condition whereas under the theory of the *Reine Rechtslehre* the legal consequence is linked to the legal condition by imputation. Hence the normativity originating from Ought is nothing other than the connection through imputation between an unlawful fact and a legal condition, and it is the Ought that gives validity to the positive law. This means that according to the system of law based on the Ought the material facts are posited within their reciprocal relations, whereas under natural law theory the Must is the expression of the law of causality. In fact, according to the laws of nature if A is then B must be, whereas according to the relevant applicable positive law if A is then B ought to be.

It is not only a mere verbal difference because under positive law it is a legislator which establishes links between material facts, between the offence caused by certain behaviour and punishment that is the consequence of that behaviour, a linkage that is different from the linkage of causality. It is an idiosyncratic parallelism between *Sein*-fact and the norm. That means that the Ought represents the specific sense in which the legal condition and the legal consequence belong together within the legal proposition, or reconstructed legal norm (*Rechtssatz*), and hence that which ought to be (*Sollende*) done constitutes a basic concept within legal thought. And if a norm, which is characterized by an Ought, is deprived of its proper meaning, then there is no legal meaning at all in the assertions concerning either permitted or prohibited behaviour. However the nature of the relationship between legal norms and legal propositions is problematic, as Paulson points out (Paulson 1975, p. 774).

The Ought in the legal norm is different from the Ought in the legal proposition. The Ought in the legal norm represents the will of the law-creating agent and is a command, a permission or an authorisation, and the Ought of the legal norm is a generic term. The Ought of the legal proposition that if the condition of the if-clause is satisfied then a sanction must follow is valid because the then-clause is imputed to the subject that is liable for non-compliance with the if-clause. As Paulson explains, "If through some act an individual expresses his intention that another individual is to behave in a particular way… the meaning of this act cannot be accounted for by saying that the other individual will behave in the prescribed way, but only by saying that he ought so to behave" (Paulson 1975, p. 776, note 35) the generic Ought is for Kelsen merely subjective and expresses the intention of an agent issuing a prescription. In other cases the generic Ought has for Kelsen an objective meaning independent from the prescribing agent's intention. However as Paulson points out, "it is difficult to distinguish legal norms from prescriptions that have only a subjective meaning. Kelsen sees the resolution of this problem as an important task for the Pure Theory. His solution is the doctrine of legal validity, which provides conditions for determining the validity of legal norms. … The doctrine of legal validity includes two analytical constructions of legal science: first, the concept of authorization in a normative hierarchy and, second, the concept of the basic norm" (Paulson 1975, p. 777).

A law has a specific meaning of its own, and the philosophical meaning and importance of the Kelsenian idea of ought is to purify the Ought of positive law of its metaphysical and ideological value and the characteristics of traditional law. Since the traditional theories—natural law and the empirical theories—are not exhaustive, Kelsen introduces his alternative theory. As the *Reine Rechtslehre* is a theory free of the ideology and foreign elements that were typical and characteristic of traditional theories, it preserves its anti-ideological function by seeking to isolate the representations of the positive law from every natural law ideology. The Pure Theory of Law, in confining and limiting itself to the positive law, is for Kelsen the theory of legal positivism. As it concerns the dimension of norms, law is normative and is opposed to what is descriptive, which on the contrary deals only with the *Sein*-dimension. Since for Kelsen the normative dimension, the only one that really counts, represents a system of legal norms prescribing certain modes of conduct, he endorses a strict normativism (*Normativismus*), asserting that the normative dimension of law accounts for the nature of the Ought. This involves the notion of obligation, the authority of and justification for the law, that is what makes law obligatory, and how people must acknowledge the authority of law, as well as reasons for action.

5 The Function of the Basic Norm

Legal norms belong to the sphere of Ought and are norms intended to guide human conduct. Thus in order to infer an Ought conclusion from an Is premise it is necessary to draw on an Ought premise that gives normative meaning relating to an Is. Since the chain of validity for legal norms has to end somewhere, it is necessary to point to an Ought that must be presupposed, and Kelsen defines this presupposed Ought as the 'basic norm'. The basic norm performs the following theoretical functions in Kelsen's theory of law: to establish a non-reductive explanation for legal validity and for the normativity of law, and to explain the systematic character of legal norms. Moreover, authorisation is a central idea within Kelsen's concept of legal validity. The authorising norm confers the power to create law and also establishes the conditions for the exercise of that power. Thus, a norm is legally valid due to its authorising norm, which itself is a positive norm. Thus legal validity depends upon whether positive norms exist within a normative hierarchy. However, this identification of legal norms by appeal to their authorising norms cannot go on indefinitely and must end somewhere. Kelsen defines this original norm as the basic norm (*Grundnorm*) which is simply presupposed and points to the historically first constitution beyond which there are no further authorising norms in the positive legal order.

This binding norm must according to Kelsen be presupposed. As Paulson explains, Kelsen thus sees "the doctrine of legal validity as an analytical doctrine of legal science, a complete statement of the conditions for the legal validity of norms" (Paulson 1975, p. 778). As Kelsen for himself asserts: "A norm is legally valid if and only if (1) it has been created in accordance wih the conditions specified by its authorizing norm, and the authorizing norm has, in turn, been created in accordance with the conditions specified by *its* authorizing norm, and so on, for each level of authorizing norms in the hierarchy; and (2) the norm is generally efficacious" (Paulson 1975, pp. 778–779). With his doctrine of legal validity Kelsen aims to explain the creation of norms. As Paulson points out, "Kelsen's doctrine of legal validity is, in the end, a doctrine of the creation of norms" (Paulson 1975, p. 779).

The importance of the distinction between Is and Ought lies in the fact that for every normative statement (e.g., what one ought to do) there must be a normative premise. In a normative system like law, every statement about what one ought to do or ought not to do needs to be justified from a more general or more basic Ought statement, which leads upwards in the hierarchy to an ultimate statement until reaching a foundational normative premise, that is an act that has been authorised by the historically first constitution. Kelsen defines this foundational norm on which legal normative systems are based as the basic norm (*Grundnorm*). The separation between Is and Ought statements and the hierarchical structure of normative systems leading to an ultimate norm must be necessarily grounded on a foundational norm that is itself subject to no requirement of direct proof. One must simply accept or not accept this ultimate norm. For Kelsen legal science, and every Ought claim, implies the presupposition of the foundational norm of the normative system which means that each normative system is independent of every other normative system. Thus the normative system that relates to law and its foundational norm is necessarily independent from any other normative system, whether religious or moral. However, this does not exclude the possibility that legislators or lawmakers may be influenced by the content of another normative system—be it a moral or a religious one—because it is necessary to distinguish between the logical structure of each normative system and the empirical, historical or causal reasons that influenced the way in which lawmakers promulgated the legal norms that they did.

6 Natural Law, Positivism and Rational Choice

Natural law and positivism are legal doctrines that conceive of the normative system in diametrically opposed terms. Natural law represents the doctrinal view that there is an enforceable natural law, which pre-dates any political and social institutions. This system of norms is different from that endorsed by positivism, for which the law is solely and exclusively positive law, a coercive order of norms within which they are posited by acts of human intention, which can be modified depending upon the particular requirements of the time. Essentially, the two doctrines differ in terms of the way in which they justify the validity of the normative system. For legal positivism, the validity of law must not be sought in a different system, which is considered to be superior to positive law. On the other hand, while asserting its superior status to any other type of law, natural law does not deny validity to positive law, also considering that it is valid and backed up by coercion. It thus calls for compliance with the law, provided that the content of its norms reflects the content of natural law, which is considered to be superior, being immanent within nature and man, and its provisions being inferable from nature. Since these norms do not result from human acts of will, they are unchangeable, absolute and valid in all places and at all times. Legal positivism proposes a legally valid law, while natural law on the other hand seeks to construct a just law.

Within a free socio-political system, if they are both considered as prerequisites for rational choices, natural law and legal positivism both operate on the same level. And as free choices, they are premised on values that are all deemed to be valid. Amongst scholars however, it would appear that legal philosophers tend more towards natural law, while lawyers come down decisively in favour of legal positivism. As it is not possible to revisit here the entire history of the debate between the two doctrines, we have chosen to set out the thinking of Hans Kelsen (1881–1973). While having analysed the two doctrines in particular detail (Kelsen 1927/28a, pp. 221–250; Kelsen 1927/28b, pp. 71–94; Kelsen 1949, pp. 481–513; Kelsen 1961, pp. 8–45; Kelsen 1963a, b, 1965, pp. 465–469), he made the choice, in keeping with his legal positivist vision, in favour of legal positivism. Why? Because natural law is considered to be superior to positive law, is absolute in nature and considers itself to have absolute validity. For its part positive law asserts that the only valid law is positive law. It does not regard norms emanating from a supra-human authority to have any relevance, thereby excluding from the domain of legal science not only divine law, as the law supposedly created by God and posited by him within nature, but also the law considered to be immanent within nature, even if not necessarily created by God.

However, Kelsen sees a link between the two doctrines thanks to a common aim. According to Kelsen, natural law sets out the dictates of absolute justice with which man should comply; consequently, positive law is valid insofar as it reflects natural law and insofar as it presents itself as a just system. This begs the following question: must positive law be complied with if it is not consistent with natural law? For natural lawyers, explains Kelsen, the answer is no as this would entail complying with a law that was not always just. The validity of positive law must therefore be sought within natural law, as the only law that is capable of providing a criterion for distinguishing between what is just and was is not, or in other words what is valid and what is not. But why therefore should legal positivism reject the viewpoint of natural law? If, as is asserted by natural law, there are norms that can be inferred from nature then, in constituting the decisive criterion, nature takes on the role of lawmaker. This means attributing a primary role to nature, which is characterised by a (divine or supernatural) will or an intention that is capable of creating norms. Natural law is therefore rooted in religious belief or in any case belief in a superhuman entity. Thus, in taking as a point of reference a transcendent will, whether divine or not, it is automatically possible to infer the absolute criterion for establishing the justice or injustice of positive laws.

Kelsen sees the force of natural law and, considering the issue of its foundation, finds it to lie in religion. He then asks whether it is possible to separate natural law from religion. This however appears to be impossible because only a superhuman and divine entity can serve as a model for determining what is just and what is not, in doing so enabling positive law to posit adequate positive laws in accordance with an unimpeachable model of justice. Without the divine or superhuman attribute, natural law would lack its principal function and could not impose itself. The norms of justice, which natural law identifies in nature and infers from divine authority, can only be those norms that natural lawyers presuppose within human beings, asserting them to have been inferred from nature. However, Kelsen says, it can be demonstrated that nature cannot be the true source of natural law by the fact that contradictory norms have been inferred. This is because, if it is divine, nature cannot be contradictory. Therefore, as nature cannot be contradictory if it is divine, it is impossible for any law to be immanent within nature; this becomes all the more evident if it is attempted to infer natural law from the nature of man since also human behaviour is contradictory, or changeable depending upon the circumstances and not always compliant with the dictates of justice. If this were possible on the other hand, then nature would contradict itself, essentially being a non-natural nature. Thus, due to the changeable nature of human conduct, it is not possible to infer criteria from nature that can tell us how to act in accordance with the dictates of justice.

Nevertheless, Kelsen seeks to find a justification for natural law. In order to avoid conflicts between natural law and positive law, it is necessary to ensure that positive law does not feel under threat from, or excluded by, natural law. In order to establish whether a norm of positive law is consistent with natural law, and is thus valid, it cannot be posited by simply anyone at all. In fact, if this were possible, then anybody could at his or her absolute discretion refuse to obey positive law, which must however be observed as it is backed up by coercion within a system of positive law. In order to avoid this conflict, as the strict positivist and normativist that he was, Kelsen argued that a doctrine founded on natural law must argue that the dilemma can only be resolved by positive law itself, thus accepting the overriding force of positive law. This is because when the lawmaker issues a law it claims that it is just, and if it is always the lawmaker that decides in relation to this matter then positive law must always be considered to be valid. Having thus endorsed and accredited positive law in recognising its authoritativeness, natural law can thereby always reinforce positive law by offering the opportunity to justify and reinforce any positive law in a sense that is even absolute (because natural law presents itself as an absolute truth) and not merely relative due to the contingent nature of positive law. However, natural law will only be able to provide a credible justification for positive law if the former presents itself as an eternal and invariable realm of justice. And this can only be possible if that system is based on a transcendent, divine and religious authority.

At this stage Kelsen has to clarify the concept of nature by asking: What is nature? What therefore is natural law? There is a range of opinion regarding this matter and it has been seen that natural law can differ in content depending upon the circumstances. If in legal terms one of the ideals of society is certainty, a society that is based on natural law will however give rise to the utmost uncertainty. It is thus proper to ask which rights are natural and which rights are not. However, it would appear that it is not possible to draw up such a catalogue of rights, as each natural right could correspond to an opposing right; it is not therefore possible to establish which rights are rooted in absolute values. In any case, rights are relative for Kelsen as they refer to absolute values. Value relativity thus constitutes the watershed between natural law and positive law. In fact, from the viewpoint of values the distinction between facts and values, and between *Sein* and *Sollen*, locates values within an area that is devoid of certainty, where each value claims its own truth without being able to attain the status of an absolute principle. However, the resulting relativism, in particular ethical relativism, does not entail the creation of an ethical and moral void, but rather gives equal certainty to each system of ethics. On the other hand, from the viewpoint of the law the distinction between facts and values enables a distinction to be drawn between legality and justice. In this way it is possible to achieve that certainty within the law that, as factual and not ethical certainty, presents itself as a distinctive prerequisite of the state governed by the rule of law.

For Kelsen, due to its universal and absolute claim to validity, natural law has always operated above positive law on the strength of the idea that positive law is only a relative law. But is it possible to infer what is just and what is not just from natural law? Just law, or unjust law, is based on a value judgment. Is it therefore possible to infer a value judgment from a factual judgment, namely a natural event, or in other words an Ought from an Is? The natural lawyers disregard this question and engage in a two-stage operation in order to avoid it: first they infer values from nature, i.e. from fact, attributing a positive value to that fact, which they subsequently assert to be a prescription. But is it possible to infer a prescription from a description, or a value from a fact? Natural law should normally be inferred from value judgments and not from factual judgments. This results, Kelsen explains, in the so-called naturalistic fallacy. Put simply, nature is considered to have evaluative significance, and not to consist simply in facts. Nature thus *is*, but also gives rise to a judgment based on the assertion that everything that happens in nature is good. Nature is thus vested with an evaluative rather than a mere factual role, and is charged with either positivity or negativity, whereas nature in itself and of itself is neutral. Having inferred a value from a fact, a *Sollen* from a *Sein*, the natural lawyer then performs a methodological leap in inferring a value from another value, attributing positive or negative value to everything that happens, thereby transforming a factual judgment into a value judgment. In order to assert that something is good or bad, the natural lawyer thus does not invoke nature *tout court*, but rather a system of values premised in nature, which is believed to be inherent within in. However, if a given fact is natural this does not necessarily mean that the event is good; there may be disagreement as to whether an event is positive or negative (a natural event is a fact, while the issue as to whether it is positive or negative implies a value judgment). However, people disagree regarding the values that are to be attributed to facts, which means that the evaluations of natural facts, whether good or bad, cannot be absolute and must be relative.

What therefore can be used as a basis for natural law, given its complex and ambiguous definability? It is necessary to reach agreement over how to attribute value judgments to facts. We have seen how natural law draws force from the notion that nature is good: from this it infers an ethical and ideological conception of nature, giving rise to the myth of its goodness which for the natural lawyer is the ultimate value, whilst everything else represents a negative value. For the natural lawyer, an ethics that conforms to reason is an ethics that conforms to nature, it is a positive ethics.

This raises the question of the relationship between nature and history along with the related shift of the value system, and one must ask whether it is man that should guide nature or by contrast nature that should guide the choices of men. Is there dominion over nature or of nature? Is history created by man or is it a product of nature? Is it possible to revive a doctrine in the present day and age, namely natural law, that is rooted in a different system of values with a world view different to that of modernity? Is it possible today to propose a natural law? How can the relationship between natural law and positivism be reconsidered in the light of current problems? It is also clear nowadays that the problem of law is in part a problem of legal values. It is thus necessary to clarify the relationship between legal values and practical human values. There is no doubt that in the modern age natural law has transformed, detaching itself from Christianity and from any other religious faith, presenting itself as a strictly rational doctrine that investigates and elaborates the rules of human cohabitation. The rationalist nature of natural law has resulted in the emergence of a secular aspect to natural law. In seeking to act as a means for supplementing and interpreting positive law, natural law exercises an undoubted influence over positive law, in particular on constitutional law, seeking to infer general principles from the law of nature. Today, as in the past, legal values are objective values for natural law; they are substantive and not formal, and thus are universal values of justice that are nothing other than ideal principles rooted in reason and in the spirit of man. The general principles of natural law are thus general principles of law, to which positive laws must refer. However, many contemporary discussions demonstrate the limit, or one might say the natural limit, to natural law, namely that it has never elaborated a definitive hermeneutic methodology. In fact, for modern natural law it is inconceivable to use natural law in order to interpret positive law. The question arises as to what principles, in particular in relation to justice, should be applied to actual contemporary cases.

For positive lawyers, now more than ever, positive law claims its complete unquestionable autonomy and independence from natural law. In fact, for them positive law posits historically conditioned values, which are distinct from the ideal values of natural law. For the lawyer, but also for the man on the street, ideal values can only be taken into account to the extent that they reflect the values of positive law. There is a clear opposition between natural law and positive law because positive law excludes natural law. Conflicts concerning values are not legal conflicts but belong to moral philosophy. For the secular thinker, natural law is part of ethics and a rigorous form of legal positivism will exclude any type of ethical awareness. However, a conflict nonetheless arises because the concept of justice is implicit within the concept of law. This means that, in terms of ethics, a legal system cannot be considered to be a true legal system unless it is rooted in the notion of justice. In fact, a rule that is not founded in justice cannot be valid, and cannot have binding force. Consequently, a legal order that is premised on the notion of justice is valid and thus has binding force.

It is finally necessary to clarify the meaning of coercion. According to the positivist view, there is no validity *a priori* within natural law. There is only a duty to act in a particular manner according to the applicable law. For the natural lawyers on the other hand, the duty to obey the law is not only a legal one but also a moral one in the sense that the moral duty must be modelled on the principles of natural law, which vest the legal order with validity and coercive force. The duty to obey positive law is thus also a moral duty towards the legal system and not only a legal duty to act according to the dictates of that system. This is because the duty towards the system is not derived from the system alone, but is also dependent upon rules and principles that are external to the system. This means therefore that validity is not inherent only within the legal system itself, but is also dependent upon principles of natural law. Natural law can therefore admit legal positivism and recognise that a legal order is a social and political fact without making any reference to validity, even though validity presupposes the positivist viewpoint, namely that a legal order can be determined and described independently according to natural law principles. Thus, contemporary natural law can quite comfortably admit that positive law is a social and political fact; from its standpoint—that of moral philosophy—when the validity of a factual order is a matter for discussion this begs the question as to whether there is a moral duty to comply with the rules of this system. And the answer to this question is yes because natural law does not in fact have any reason to reject social facts.

7 Conclusion

There is no doubt that the dualism between *Sein* and *Sollen* is a source of ethical relativism and that the law must be "ethicised" in order to overcome it (Ghezzi 1996). In fact, an ethical-political assessment implies a choice concerning values, which being relative create uncertainty. It is in the light of all of the above that the core question therefore arises, namely as to which choice is preferable in the name of rationality. If it is accepted that we live in a world of ethical relativism, which proclaims the relativity of values—of all values, including absolute values—from a perspective of evaluative pluralism, it is not possible to support any ethics or bioethics that has absolute status. If according to the dictates of freedom of conscience and in a spirit of tolerance we cannot admit a state philosophy or religion, then we also cannot endorse a state ethics or bioethics, even within a state governed by the rule of law. The force of a state, above all of a state governed by the rule of law, lies in its ability to operate as an institution that guarantees pluralism and diversity. This implies the defence of the values of freedom, pluralism and the inviolable and inalienable rights of the individual. The points of contrast have become particularly sharp in the areas of ethics and bioethics. When confronted with a truth that is not (or no longer) absolute, we must at this stage rely on reasonableness. This reasonableness must defend the freedoms of man, his fundamental freedoms, but not through the utopia of a natural law metaphysics, though by the same token not through a legal positivism devoid of ethics. As current legal philosophy has convincingly argued, fundamental rights include both ethical foundations as well as legal elements, and adapt themselves both to the moral significance of an idea that protects human dignity and moral autonomy as well as to legal significance. This means that rights transform into fundamental norms of the legal order as a necessary instrument for the development of man's full potential within society. Fundamental rights, as an expression of equal opportunity for choice within freedom, express at the same time a fundamental morality and legality in the face of which, in the words of Max Weber (Rossi 2007, p. 187), only an ethic of responsibility can show the individual the sense of the world and of his own choices.

References

Ebenstein W (1945) The pure theory of law. The University of Wisconsin Press, Madison

Ghezzi ML (1996) Diversità e pluralismo. Raffaello Cortina, Milano

Kant I (1998) Critique of Pure Reason (1781). In: The Cambridge edition of the works of Immanuel Kant (Edited and trans: Guyer P, Wood AW). Cambridge University Press, Cambridge

Kelsen H (1911) Hauptprobleme der Staatsrechtslehre entwickelt aus der Lehre vom Rechtssatze. J. C. B. Mohr (Paul Siebeck), Tübingen

Kelsen H (1927/28a) Die Idee des Naturrechts. Zeitschrift für öffentliches Recht VII:221–250

Kelsen H (1927/28b) Naturrecht und positives Recht. Internationale Zeitschrift für Theorie des Rechts II:71–94

Kelsen H (1934) Reine Rechtslehre. Einleitung in die rechtswissenschaftliche Problematik. Franz Deuticke, Leipzig & Wien

Kelsen H (1949) The natural law Doctrine before the tribunal of science. West Polit Q II:481–531

Kelsen H (1961) Naturrechtslehre und Rechtspositivismus. Revista Juridica de Buenos Aires 4:8–45

Kelsen H (1963a) Grundlage der Naturrechtslehre. Das Naturrecht in der politischen Theorie. Springer, Vienna

Kelsen H (1963b) Positivisme juridique et doctrine du droit naturel. In: Mélanges en l'honneur de Jean Dabin. Sirey, Brussels-Paris

Kelsen H (1965) Was ist juristischer Positivismus? Juristenzeitung 15/16:465–469

Kelsen H (1991) General theory of norms (Edited and trans: Hartney M). Clarendon Press, Oxford

Paulson SL (1975) Constraints on legal norms.: Kelsen's view in the essays (reviewing Hans Kelsen: essays in legal and moral philosophy by Hans Kelsen, O. Weinberger, P. Heath). Univ Chicago Law Rev 42(4):Article 7

Paulson SL (1996) Hans Kelsen's earliest legal theory: critical constructivism. In: Paulson SL, Paulson BL (eds) Normativity and norms. Critical perspectives on Kelsenian's themes. Clarendon Press, Oxford

Paulson SL, Litschewski Paulson B (1992) Introduction to the problems of legal theory. A translation of the Reine Rechtslehre or pure theory of law. Clarendon Press, Oxford

Rossi P (2007) Una idea di Occidente. Donzelli, Rome

Stewart J (1990) The critical legal science of Hans Kelsen. J Law Soc 17(3):273–308

Law as Fact and Norm. Georg Jellinek and the Dual Nature of Law

Matthias Klatt

Abstract The history of legal scholarship is full of one-sided views that undervalue either the factual or the normative dimension of the law. This article develops a well-balanced account of law's relation to both fact and norm by discussing two elements of Georg Jellinek's theory of law. First, it discusses his thesis of the 'normative force of the factual', in the light of Kelsen's critique and the problem of an Is-Ought-Fallacy. This article argues that we should better label this thesis the 'regarded-as-normative force of the factual'. Second, the article focuses on Jellinek's two-sided theory of the state and its modern variant, the dual nature thesis. It identifies the bridge problem as the main challenge to these accounts, and answers this problem by pointing to the dual nature of legal argumentation and to a dynamic theory of legal discourse.

1 Introduction

To arrive at a well-balanced account of law's relation to both fact and norm is a difficult enterprise. The history of legal scholarship is full of one-sided views that undervalue either the factual or the normative dimension of the law. The extreme positions in this history display two paradigmatically opposing views on the nature of law. According to one view, the law is essentially factual. Karl Olivecrona's (1971) realistic theory of 'Law as Fact' is an example for this position. Lassalle's (1899, p. 68) claim that 'constitutional questions are primarily not questions of law but questions of power' is another. The opposing pole sees law as essentially and purely ideal. A representative of this view is classical natural law doctrine, maintained by Blackstone (2016, p. 41).

In contrast to these partial accounts, which focus on either the factual or the normative dimension alone, I will explore the 'and' of this paper's title. In other words,

M. Klatt (✉)
University of Graz, Graz, Austria
e-mail: matthias.klatt@uni-graz.at

N. Bersier Ladavac et al. (eds.), *The Normative Force of the Factual*, Law and Philosophy Library 130, https://doi.org/10.1007/978-3-030-18929-7_4

I will defend the view that law is, in essence, both factual and normative. My starting point for this integrative enterprise is Habermas' (1996, p. 6) lamentation that

> tossed to and fro between facticity and validity, [...] legal theory today [is] disintegrating into camps that hardly have anything more to say to one another. The tension between normative approaches, which are constantly in danger of losing contact with social reality, and objectivistic approaches, which screen out all normative aspects, can be taken as a caveat against fixating on one disciplinary point of view.

I will begin with an analysis of Jellinek's famous thesis of the 'normative force of the factual' (Sect. 2). Next, I will address whether this thesis exhibits, as Kelsen has argued, an Is-Ought-Fallacy (Sect. 3). I will then move to a different and in a certain way more promising part of Jellinek's work, his two-sided theory of the state and its modern variant, the dual nature thesis (Sect. 4). Subsequently, I will challenge these integrative accounts of the nature of law with the problem of how to bridge Is and Ought. I will reject Jellinek's psychological bridge theory in favor of a discursive bridge theory (Sect. 5).

2 The Normative Force of the Factual

In order to gain a clear and precise account of Jellinek's much discussed thesis of the normative force of the factual, I will first elaborate on his intellectual-historical background (Sect. 2.1). Into this context, I then place Jellinek's psychological account of the nature of law (Sect. 2.2) which attracted critique from Kelsen (Sect. 2.3).

2.1 The Intellectual-Historical Background

In German public law scholarship at the turn of the twentieth century, the legal theorist Georg Jellinek (1851–1911) stands out by creating an innovative level of methodological sophistication (Klatt 2019). His works on the problematic relation between law and state had great impact upon two then emerging new academic disciplines, sociology of law and political science. No lesser scholar than Max Weber (1990, p. 149; see also Groh 2016) acknowledged Jellinek's achievements in that regard. Jellinek (Ehrenberg and Jellinek 2005, p. 278) himself stressed his wish to contribute to the founding of sociology, which he described as 'a science of the future which possesses the closest contact with the study of law and politics'. His lasting influence lies predominantly in his unique combination of stressing both the facticity of law and state, clearing the way for social sciences, *and* law's normativity, thereby preserving the independent standpoint of legal studies. We owe Jellinek firm and sustainable solutions to epistemological core problems of legal studies.

They inform the self-conception and methodological approaches of legal scholarship to date (Klatt 2015, pp. 489–499).

Jellinek's first major monograph already lays down some of his main methodological theses (cf. Klatt 2019). On the one hand, he clearly identifies the field of legal scholarship as a normative one, distinct from the factual world. On the other hand, he (Jellinek 2011, pp. 16–17) stresses that the abstract concepts and rules of law are intelligible only if one knows 'the buzz and ado of the world, in which the practical human being finds himself, a world of human interests and passions, which ought to be restrained and set into harmony'. Jellinek (2011, p. 18) concludes: 'The knowledge and observance of the other academic disciplines that address the law is relevant for both the nature and the result of the work of legal scholars.'

This fundamental idea is central also to his main treatise, in which Jellinek contradicts the strict formal positivism of public law scholars of his time. Gerber and Laband, in particular, had narrowed legal scholarship towards pure juristic construction during the second half of the nineteenth century. They eliminated all philosophical, historical, political, and social perspectives from legal studies. Legal decisions, the dominant view claimed, should be justified without such perspectives, 'discarding all alien approaches' (Gerber 1848, p. VII). In sharp contrast to this positivistic constriction, Jellinek pleads for broadening the perspective of legal scholarship. He avoids, however, the frequent mistake to lapse into the opposite extreme that completely devalues the juristic construction in favor of those other perspectives. Jellinek grants a methodological value to doctrinal construction. Precisely this combination represents Jellinek's main achievement.

Jellinek's famous thesis of the normative force of the factual, however, can easily be misinterpreted. It is hence useful to take a closer look at this particular element of his rich and complex work.

2.2 *Jellinek's Psychological Account of the Nature of Law*

Jellinek develops his thesis in the context of identifying the relation between the law and the state. The question of the nature of the law is merely a preliminary question for him. It needs clarification in order to answer the main problem he is concerned with, namely the relation between the law and the state.[1] Several points of Jellinek's account of the nature of the law are entirely unproblematic. He characterizes the law as a system of rules on human behavior. In contrast to similar systems like custom or religion, the law has the specific aim of protecting human goods and interests. Legal norms concern the outer conduct of humans; they are given by external authority; and they are guaranteed by coercive power.

Furthermore, according to Jellinek, we can examine the nature of the law, thus characterized, in two distinct ways. The first way seeks an objective explanation that

[1] This is clear from the first sentence in the 11th chapter of his Allgemeine Staatslehre, see Jellinek (1966, p. 332).

is independent of human beings. Jellinek disapproves of this way, since it would amount to metaphysical speculation on transcendental values. Jellinek characterizes the remaining, second way as 'subjective' since it seeks to explain the law as a psychological phenomenon. It understands the law as existing 'in our heads', in the beliefs and convictions of human beings (Jellinek 1966, p. 332).

Based on this psychological approach, Jellinek (1966, pp. 338–339) assigns a normative quality to factual events:

> The recognition of the normative force of the factual is of the greatest importance if we are to gain an insight into the development of the law and of morality. Initially the commands issued by the authorities of priesthood or state are simply complied with – be it from fear or from other motives; and, as a result, the belief grows that the frequently repeated command in itself and in isolation from its source constitutes – by virtue of its inner obligating power – a norm to be fulfilled per se, in other words, a moral norm.

Jellinek (1966, p. 338) is eager to stress that this normative force of the factual does not depend on any reasonable test at all:

> It would be entirely wrong to locate the normative force of the factual in its conscious or unconscious reasonableness. The factual can be rationalized at a later date, but its normative quality lies in the feature of our nature, which is not derivable further, in virtue of which the already Practiced is physiologically and psychologically much easier reproduced than the New.

In accordance with this general approach, Jellinek (1966, p. 342) characterizes the evolution of legal authority as an internal psychological process:

> The transformation of the power of the state, which is initially purely factual everywhere, into a legal power results always from the added belief that this factual has a normative quality, that it ought to be such as it is. Thus, this process takes place purely internal, in the heads of the people.

On the face of it, this argument seems to derive an Ought from an Is. It is hence not surprising that one of the most frequently raised objections against Jellinek's thesis is that it was exhibiting an Is-Ought-Fallacy. Notably Kelsen criticized Jellinek in that respect.

2.3 *Kelsen's Critique*

The categorical distinction between Is and Ought figures as one of the most important fundaments in Kelsen's pure theory of law, as he (Kelsen 1953, p. 146) himself underlines:

> The logical distinction between Is and Ought as well as the impossibility to arrive from the one area to the other by means of a logical deduction are core positions of the pure theory of law.

It sounds almost like a comment addressed to Jellinek when Kelsen (1953, p. 147) stresses that social psychological and sociological approaches cannot take part in normative legal scholarship. Kelsen (1941, p. 52) insists

> upon clearly distinguishing [sociological jurisprudence from normative jurisprudence], in order to avoid that syncretism of methods which is the cause of numerous errors. What must be avoided under all circumstances is the confounding [...] of cognition directed toward a legal 'ought', with cognition directed towards an actual 'is'.

Kelsen (2010, pp. 28–29) explicitly comments that Jellinek's theory in particular completely failed to address the proper object of legal science, namely the legal Ought:

> For whereupon answers the insight into the normative force of the factual, what alone is *explained* by it? Factual incidents, of external or internal nature. [...] the real psychological acts of will of people who subject themselves to the commands of the law and make them guidelines of their conduct; and finally: these norm-corresponding actions themselves. All this will and action, however, is not an Ought [...] but only an Is, an actual psychological or physical event, the content of an Ought, but not this Ought itself, which is only a form.

Kelsen bases his objection to Jellinek upon a classic philosophical argument, the Is-Ought-Fallacy, which warrants closer inspection.

3 The Is-Ought-Fallacy

In order to understand the core of Kelsen's critique, I will first concentrate on the problem of the Is-Ought-Fallacy as discussed by Searle and von Wright (Sect. 3.1). This will allow me to revisit Jellinek's thesis in order to assess whether it actually commits this fallacy (Sect. 3.2). I will conclude that it does not (Sect. 3.3).

3.1 Searle and von Wright on Is and Ought

The view that it was impossible to derive an Ought from an Is, so that there is no logical bridge over the gap between facts and values, goes back to Hume (2009, Sect. III.1.1). Moore (1993, pp. 89–110) later used this view to develop the argument that it was impossible to define the ethical concept 'good' by means of a different, non-ethical concept. Any attempt to define such value concepts by recourse to natural concepts commits the naturalistic fallacy. Hare (2003) followed upon this by stressing that one cannot draw prescriptive conclusions from descriptive premises.

Therefore, overall, Kelsen's objection against Jellinek is in eminent philosophical company. This objection, however, would still fail from the outset if it actually *were* possible to derive an Ought from an Is. Several philosophers have attempted to demonstrate this possibility. Most notably Searle (1964) tried to demonstrate that the incriminated deduction was possible by an institutional act within systems of constitutive rules (see also Weinberger 1991, p. 27). We can explain the core of Searle's argument with the example of a person giving a promise. If *A* promises to do *p* (first premise), and by promising to do *p*, A has placed himself under an obligation to do *p* (second premise), then it follows that *A* ought to do *p* (conclusion). Both premises, that is, both the performance of actions and the existence of obligations, are facts. The conclusion, however, is a prescriptive statement. Hence, Searle seems to have demonstrated that one can derive a normative statement from factual statements, at least in the context of constitutive rules.

Searle's argument, however, rests on a couple of mistakes. The most lucid account of these mistakes stems from Georg Henrik Von Wright (1985), pp. 273–275). Precisely three different considerations disprove Searle's argument. First, it is vital to see that Searle's example of promise giving builds upon a specific normative context that includes an implicit norm of promise keeping. According to that norm, someone who promises something ought to fulfill this promise. Searle does not mention this norm explicitly in his list of premises. Nonetheless, it constitutes the practice of promise giving in the first place, so that this practice cannot exist without presupposing this norm. Hence, one could object to Searle's argument in this way: The conclusion that *A* ought to do *p* is not deduced from the factual statement that *A* gave a promise, but rather from this factual statement in combination with the norm of promise keeping. In other words, the conclusion is not derived from an Is, but from an Is in combination with an Ought.

Second, one could challenge Searle's view that the conclusion was normative in the first place. The conclusion could be interpreted as a factual statement to the effect that there *is* an obligation for *A* to do *p*. Searle's conclusion would then not be a norm, but a descriptive proposition about a norm or, in other words, about the existence of a certain obligation. Von Wright (1985, p. 274 n. 19) quite lucidly points out that Searle himself states that the Ought in the conclusion of his argument was 'relative to the *existence* of the obligation'.[2] On this interpretation, the conclusion is a purely factual statement, and hence the argument does not prove the possibility to derive an Ought from an Is.

The third, and most important, consideration von Wright raises against Searle analyses the specific normative nature of the conclusion. For it is not, as Searle assumes, the strong and genuine deontic or normative Ought of moral and legal norms. Rather, it uses a merely technical sense of an Ought. A technical Ought demonstrates a practical necessity which stems from a certain means-end-relation. On this interpretation, *A* ought to do *p* (means) because otherwise he would fail to satisfy the obligation constituted by the norm of promise keeping (end). In other words, by giving a promise to do *p*, *A* has for himself created a practical necessity of doing *p*, or else he would fail to fulfill his obligation. This practical necessity, however, is a fact, not a norm. The technical 'Ought' is really an Is. Again, we are left with the result that Searle's example does not prove a deduction of an Ought from an Is.

The above analysis demonstrates that Kelsen's objection against Jellinek's thesis of the normative force of the factual does not fail simply for the reason that it was actually possible to derive an Ought from an Is, and that the accusation of exhibiting a fallacy is, for this reason, mistaken. On the contrary, our discussion of the three

[2] Quoting Searle (1969, p. 182), italics by von Wright.

considerations von Wright raised against Searle's argument demonstrated that deriving an Ought from an Is indeed constitutes a fallacy.

To demonstrate that it is a fallacy in general to derive an Ought from an Is, however, does not suffice to establish that Jellinek's thesis in fact does exhibit this fallacy, as Kelsen argues. So let us take a closer look on Jellinek's thesis again.

3.2 Jellinek Revisited

Jellinek himself presents his theory as if it were a theory on the validity of legal norms. In fact, he stresses that all law has the necessary property of being valid.[3] Jellinek's concept of legal validity, however, is imprecise, and this impreciseness explains very well why Kelsen could have thought that Jellinek's thesis was vulnerable to the objection from the Is-Ought-Fallacy. Jellinek (1966, p. 333) defines legal validity as follows:

> A [legal] norm is valid if it is capable of taking effect qua motivation, of determining the will.

From a non-positivist and legal-theoretical perspective, however, this definition is not concerned with the validity, but rather with the efficacy of norms. Validity is a broader concept that embraces the efficacy of a norm as a necessary element, but also includes two additional criteria, namely the authoritative issuance and the correctness of the norm.[4] Hence, in relation to validity, as Jellinek claims, the definition is incomplete; it lists only one of the three elements required for legal validity. This incompleteness then causes the impression that Jellinek committed an Is-Ought-Fallacy, by deducing law's validity (an Ought) from its efficacy (an Is).

Read in relation to the concept of efficacy, however, Jellinek's definition is perfectly sensible. This revised definition would read: 'A legal norm is efficacious if it is capable of taking effect qua motivation, of determining the will.' The efficacy of a legal norm comprises two fundamentally different aspects (cf. Alexy 2002, pp. 14–16). The first aspect is external efficacy. This is concerned with the questions whether the people actually comply with a norm in their outer behavior, by and large, or whether an observable sanction is imposed for non-compliance. The second aspect is internal efficacy. It regards the will-related, motivational aspects of why people believe in the validity of a certain norm and direct their behavior accordingly. Psychological dispositions and normative expectations are what matters here.

We can now see clearly that Jellinek's definition perfectly grasps the internal aspect of law's efficacy. Interpreted in that way, the thesis of the normative power of the factual is nothing else than a description of the fine psychological mechanisms

[3] 'Alles Recht hat als notwendiges Merkmal das der Gültigkeit'. Jellinek (1966, p. 333).

[4] I follow legal non-positivism's connection thesis here, cf. Alexy (2002, p. 4); Klatt (2012, pp. 11–14, 22–23).

bringing about compliance in the actual behavior of people, both on the individual and the social level.[5] Jellinek's thesis explains the efficacy of a legal norm.

This understanding of Jellinek's thesis is actually supported by Jellinek (1966, p. 334, emphasis original) himself:

> Law's positivity thus rests eventually always on the *conviction* that it is valid. The whole legal system is built upon this purely subjective element. This truth results necessarily from the insight that the law is placed inside us, that it is a function of human society and thus must rest on purely psychological elements.

Jellinek clearly states here that he is not writing on law's validity per se, but on people's *convictions* of validity. We should take him by his word. The question Jellinek seeks to answer here is not when the law is valid, but rather when people *believe* that it is valid. The answer that his thesis of the normative power of the factual gives—namely, that people believe that a norm is valid when they witness that something repeatedly occurs in the factual world (cf. Jellinek 1966, pp. 337–338)—is an answer precisely to the question where these *convictions* of validity stem from. It is not and does not purport to be an answer to the distinct question of when law is valid. Hence, the ascription of a thesis of the 'normative force of the factual' to Jellinek is in a certain sense misleading. It would be more accurate to label his thesis the 'regarded-as-normative force of the factual' thesis. In the present context, it is vital to realize that in this more precise version Jellinek's thesis loses all resemblance of an Is-Ought-Fallacy.

Why is it that Jellinek's definition is imprecise? Why does he seem to confuse validity and efficacy? The answer may lie in his limited cognitive interest. In the relevant paragraphs of his work, he (Jellinek 1966, p. 337) is simply interested to 'advance into the last psychological sources of the law'. In fact, Jellinek (1966, p. 339, emphases added) could not possibly stress this specific cognitive interest more, as becomes clear also in the following passage:

> The relation of the factual to the normative emerges even more sharply in the *genesis* of the law. Originally, all law is nothing else than pure factual habit. The continuous routine generates the *conviction* that this habit is norm-corresponding, and the norm itself *appears* therefore to be an authoritative command of the polity, hence it appears as legal norm.

All phrases of this quotation set in italics clearly demonstrate Jellinek's limited cognitive interest. In modern, legal-theoretical terms, however, we would ascribe these thoughts to law's social efficacy, and not (as Jellinek himself) to its validity.

This rather benevolent interpretation of Jellinek's imprecise definition seems to presuppose that he accepts that efficacy is merely a necessary, rather than a sufficient element of the concept of law. Accepting that efficacy is a necessary, but not a sufficient element of the law is tantamount to adopting a non-positivist position on the concept of law. Therefore, we still must rule out the possibility that Jellinek simply adopts a narrow, positivist concept of the law, like, e.g., Bierling. For Bierling

[5] On the two levels of psychological effectiveness of the law, see Jellinek (1966, p. 334).

(1894, p. 19) the concept of law rests on the psychological element of people's internal dispositions to recognize a norm as legal:

> Law in the juridical sense is generally everything that human beings who live together in some community or another mutually recognize as norm and rule of their life together.

Read in this way, Jellinek would simply *identify* law's validity with the internal grounds for its psychological efficacy, and my benevolent interpretation above that Jellinek *mixes up* validity and efficacy due to his limited cognitive interest would be difficult to maintain.

There are some indications, however, that speak against assigning such a narrow, positivist definition of law to Jellinek. A couple of pages after the passages on the psychological elements cited above, Jellinek (1966, p. 344) introduces a second element of the law:

> The criticisms of positive-legal settings by means of using the standard of an aspired aim can perfectly be distinguished from situations that are not yet sensed to be in accordance with the norms.

By the 'standard of an aspired aim' Jellinek (1966, p. 345) refers to natural law, as becomes very clear from the context of this quotation and by his remark that 'the positive law is contrasted with a different law which claims to have a higher rank'. It would be mistaken, though, to assume that with this second element, Jellinek introduces law's ideal dimension, following a non-positivist definition of the law, and making the validity of the law dependent upon its moral correctness. For natural law, in turn, is only invoked by Jellinek insofar as it is relevant for the efficacy of law, understood as the inner psychological disposition to accept norms as valid. This becomes clear in the following passage (Jellinek 1966, p. 353):

> The convictions of a natural or reasonable law contribute forcefully to legalize even drastic, quickly executed changes in the situation of state and law.

Again, 'convictions' of natural law and reasonableness are what count for Jellinek, and not natural law or reasonableness per se. Jellinek (1966, p. 354) characterizes not only the disposition to transform the factually practiced into something normative, but also the idea of a critical, reasonable higher-order law as 'psychological elements'. His account of the law, therefore, does not amount to a fully-developed ideal dimension of the law, but persists entirely in a realistic, social-psychological concept of law. Stanley Paulson (2007, p. 838) has seen this most clearly:

> Jellinek's concept of law proves to have been factual rather than normative in character, a construction based on psychological processes. [...] Thus, far from insisting on a hard and fast distinction between 'is' and 'ought', Jellinek reverted ultimately to factual explanations of the ostensibly normative.

So in the end, it still seems to be the case that Jellinek deflates law's connection to the ideal world of moral values and follows a purely realist and positivist concept of law. Ultimately, Jellinek seems to tend towards a monistic assertion of a psychological-sociological method (cf. Murkens 2013, p. 20). This tentative conclusion, however, may still be premature since Jellinek's (1966, p. 344) analysis of the 'second element' is also limited by his cognitive interest, which is to explain the 'genesis and development' of the law. Hence, from the fact that the second element is also limited to the psychological dimension nothing follows regarding Jellinek's approach to law's validity. He is, again, merely making a point on the psychological effectiveness of the law. He is not at all concerned with the reasonableness of the law, but only with the factual development of convictions of reasonableness. Once more, I would like to underline that, contrary to the appearance of Jellinek's definition of the 'validity' of law cited above, he is not concerned with validity here but with efficacy or, in other words, with mere psychologically determined convictions of validity.[6]

3.3 Conclusion on Kelsen Versus Jellinek

My conclusion is that Jellinek's thesis of the 'regarded-as-normative force of the factual' is a thesis about the genesis of psychological efficacy of the law—and not a thesis about law's validity or its moral quality or reasonableness (Jellinek 1951, p. 348; cf. Klatt 2019; Landau 2000, pp. 302–303). In consequence, Kelsen's objection against Jellinek is insofar mistaken.[7] Jellinek does not, as Kelsen claims, derive an Ought from an Is. He merely derives a psychological disposition to regard something as normative from an Is—which is hardly problematic.[8]

4 Law's Dual Nature

I would now like to leave Jellinek's thesis of the 'regarded-as-normative force of the factual' and turn to a different element of his theory of law. This element is far more promising when we seek to understand law as both fact and norm. I will first develop upon Jellinek's two-sided theory of the state (Sect. 4.1). I will then discuss the modern variant of Jellinek's groundbreaking work, the dual nature thesis (Sect. 4.2). Lastly, I will attend to the main problem of the dual nature account of law, which I label the 'bridge problem' (Sect. 4.3).

[6] This point has been misunderstood by many scholars, including Stolleis (1992, p. 452): 'question of the validity of law'.

[7] In the context of the Is-Ought-Fallacy, there is a second argument Kelsen brings forward against Jellinek, namely that the distinct methods of *Kausalwissenschaft* and *Normwissenschaft* created two distinct objects of inquiry, and that it was a mistake to refer to them by the same predicate. I do not consider this argument here, but see Klatt (2015, pp. 493–494).

[8] Weinberger, however, has challenged the explanatory strength of Jellinek's thesis even in this regard by pointing to the freedom humans have in creating institutions and forms of life and thereby making changes to what ought to happen. Weinberger (1991, p. 27).

4.1 Jellinek's Two-Sided Theory of the State

Jellinek's two-sided theory of the state is based on a neo-Kantian doctrine of methodological dualism, which in turn stems from the fundamental distinction between the two modalities of Is and Ought (Paulson 2007, p. 838). According to Jellinek, these two modalities are reflected in the juridico-normative and socio-factual sides of the state respectively. This theory (Jellinek 1966, pp. 50–51) distinguishes between a social, factual, empirical side of the state, which captures the state as a social phenomenon, and a juristic, normative theory of the state, which addresses the state as a normative order. Jellinek stresses that we must address both sides in order to get a full picture of the state. He (Jellinek 1966, p. 12) ultimately aims at a comprehensive theory that embraces both sides.

The comprehensive character of his theory becomes particularly clear when he discusses the necessary connection between the two elements. Jellinek (1966, p. 354) stresses that the conservative element, which transforms the factually Practiced into the Normative, and the rational, evolutionary, propulsive, change-directed element, which stems from the convictions of a natural law, must both collaborate with each other. It is a mistake, according to Jellinek, to render absolute one of the two elements alone. Ignoring, e.g., the historical-conservative element and following exclusively the rational ideal may lead to a destructive, subjective criticism and, ultimately, to anarchism (Jellinek 1966, p. 355).

Most interestingly, Jellinek (1966, p. 355) does not elaborate on the opposite mistake to the same degree. He merely briefly mentions it, by referring to the 'one-sided historical thinking' and to the conviction of the state as 'brute power'. He makes it clear that the law is not identical with the factual situation, because otherwise it could not be used to assess this situation in the first place. This sentence distinctly demonstrates the relevance of the ideal-rational in Jellinek's theory. Nevertheless, his discussion displays a certain asymmetry, because he addresses the two extreme positions with such different degrees of elaborateness. This again may indicate that ultimately his focus is, as Paulson (2007, p. 838) has argued, solely on the factual.

Jellinek's two-sided theory of the state has provoked severe criticism that mostly misses the point of his groundbreaking approach.[9] Jellinek's theory has been misdiagnosed with a 'structural aporia' that only led to 'perplexity' (Möllers 2000, pp. 156, 170). Others have criticized the two-sided theory for being limited to only two sides. According to this criticism, given the plurality of different scientific perspectives on the state, Jellinek should rather have developed a polyvalent theory of the state (Lepsius 2000, p. 330; Lepsius 2004, p. 76). This suggestion is, however, unconvincing for two reasons. First, a multi-coloured potpourri of disordered topoi is necessarily inferior to the categorical power of the two fundamental modalities of Is and Ought. Second, Jellinek by no means denies the polyvalence. On the contrary, he himself stresses the plurality of disciplinary perspectives on the law and

[9] I have addressed this criticism previously in Klatt (2019).

state: Jellinek (1966, p. 15, 74) postulates 'polydirectional knowledge'. He (Jellinek 1882, p. 9) underlines that when researching the state, 'nearly all sciences must participate'. This is precisely one of the most important legacies of Jellinek to date: Only if the various disciplines act together in an integrative way, while at the same time preserving their respective identity, legal scholarship can attain a comprehensive picture of the law (Kersten 2000, p. 187; Klatt 2015, pp. 498–499; Stolleis 1992, pp. 451–454).

Heirs to Jellinek's two-sided theory of the state in contemporary scholarship are non-positivist positions, firstly, on the concept of law and, secondly, on the theory of legal science and legal argumentation. These approaches are the modern variants of Jellinek's two-sided theory of the law and state, and it is to them I will now turn.

4.2 The Dual Nature Thesis

Alexy (2010) developed the dual nature thesis with regard to the concept of law and the classical problem of the connection or separation of law and morality. I (Klatt 2015, 2016) have recently transferred this thesis to the two areas of legal argumentation and to the methodology of legal scholarship.

According to the dual nature thesis (Alexy 2010), law has a dual nature, comprising both a real or factual dimension and an ideal or critical dimension. The main justification for an ideal dimension is law's claim to correctness (Alexy 1998; Klatt 2012, pp. 5–6, 11–13, 15–16). Since this claim is open towards moral correctness, the ideal dimension of law implies non-positivism. To be sure, it is contested whether moral correctness and, what is the same, whether the ideal dimension really is a dimension *of law* and not simply provided to the law from an external world of morality. John Mackie's objection from moral irrationalism is a representative of the main challenge against the ideal dimension of the law: Practical propositions, Mackie (1977, p. 35) argues, are necessarily subjective, relative, and instances of pure decisionism. To a certain extent, legal non-positivists (Alexy 2013, pp. 101–102; Klatt 2012, p. 6) can counter this challenge by pointing to the possibility of engaging in rational practical discourse.

The argumentative strength of this optimistic answer, however, has its limits. The limits of rational discourse and procedural theories of practical rationality are defined by rational disagreement and moral pluralism (Rawls 1993, p. 55). The forms and procedures of rational discourse often help us to evaluate a certain outcome as either discursively necessary or, alternatively, as discursively impossible. In these two scenarios, legal discourse determines a definite result. Nevertheless, now and again legal discourse leads to an outcome that is merely discursively possible. That is why the ideal dimension is overall insufficient, and that is why we have the real dimension of law as its complement.

The real dimension of law consists in the positivity of law. It is defined by the two elements of authoritative issuance and social efficacy (Alexy 2010, p. 173).

Law's real dimension helps solving the problems of practical knowledge and social coordination the ideal dimension leaves us with. It provides legally established procedures and authorities that guarantee the achievement of decisions and their enforcement. It is vital to see that the real dimension of the law ultimately rests on the ideal dimension. This is so since the real dimension of law originates from the need to legal certainty (Radbruch 1990, p. 50). Since 'the nurture and development of legal order are important moral aims' (Allan 2016, p. 82; see also Finnis 1982, pp. 231–233; Finnis 1987, pp. 376–377), the real dimension thus originates in the ideal dimension. Precisely in this sense the ideal dimension is analytically prior to the real dimension of the law. This asymmetry is, arguably, just the opposite way round than the asymmetry I have identified above[10] in Jellinek, which favours the factual over the ideal dimension.

This insight also leads way to another crucial difference between the dual nature thesis and Jellinek's theory. Jellinek's thesis of the 'regarded-as-normative power of the factual' addresses the ideal, rational, evolutionary, and critical dimension of the law merely as a psychological element. In contrast, the dual nature thesis upgrades the ideal to a distinct dimension of its own that stands at parity with the real dimension.

Irrespective of a symmetry or asymmetry between Is and Ought, any account of law's dual nature must solve the problem of how exactly the two dimensions are integrated with each other. I label this the 'bridge problem' and address it in the following section.

4.3 *The Bridge Problem*

The bridge problem is one of the main challenges directed against any theory that maintains a dual nature of the law. This challenge argues that even if law had an ideal and a real dimension, these two dimension were only added to one another (cf. Klatt 2016, p. 37). Mere addition is far less than full integration. The critic could argue that the mere addition of real and ideal elements in the law gives rise to all sorts of inconsistencies. The vital question the bridge problem poses is, therefore, this: How can we achieve integration, rather than mere addition, of real and ideal elements in our account of the law?

The bridge problem is not merely a theoretically possible thought. It features prominently among legal realists and scholars endorsing skeptical views. A contemporary to Jellinek, Ludwig Gumplowicz (1907, p. 450), himself engaging in purely sociological analysis of the state, sneered at attempts to construct the state 'juristically' by comparing these attempts to 'eating a Beethoven sonata with spoons'. The modern variant of this critique is the objection from incommensurability (cf. Murkens 2013, p. 20).

[10] See Sect. 3.2 above.

The bridge problem is one of the most prominent puzzles in legal philosophy, and many eminent scholars struggle with coming to terms with this enigma. Even Kelsen (2010, p. 28), who originally most forcefully pointed to the 'insurmountable gap' which divided the two worlds of Is and Ought, took a more harmonizing view towards the end of his career. Kelsen (1941, pp. 52–53) then argued that sociological and normative jurisprudence stood 'side by side', that they had 'a definite relation' and could 'complement' each other. There is a clear tension between the early and the late Kelsen in that respect.

I would like to start my discussion of the bridge problem by underlining two requirements that any theoretical answer must fulfill. The first requirement is that the relation between Is and Ought must be well-balanced.[11] Neither the ideal nor the real dimension of the law must be overrated or downplayed. The second requirement is that we must preserve the distinctiveness of each dimension in order to avoid a syncretism of methods. This is actually a point accentuated by both Jellinek (1905, p. 17) and Kelsen (1941, p. 52). Their concurrence on this requirement, despite their disagreement in other respects, should remind us of its importance. Clearly distinguishing factual and ideal approaches to the law, notwithstanding their relations, is a general requirement of a rational application of cognitive methods (Dreier 1981, p. 232). This requirement is grossly neglected, e.g., by Lind's (2018, pp. 266, 286–287) fusion thesis, which completely denies the distinctiveness of Is and Ought due to their 'entanglement', as well as by Loughlin's (2010, p. 220) concept of political practice which deliberately 'blurs any clear distinction between fact and norm'.

To stipulate these two requirements, however, does not amount to a demonstration of how a bridge theory can actually fulfill them. Jellinek has his own answer to the latter problem. His bridge theory tries to integrate Is and Ought by means of psychology. Stolleis (1992, p. 452) has most lucidly put this point by remarking that for Jellinek 'human convictions are the bridge between Is and Ought'. While Jellinek's bridge theory arguably does fulfill the second requirement by maintaining the distinctiveness of different methodological approaches, it does not comply with the first requirement. To make the ideal dimension dependent upon psychological facts is not a well-balanced account of the interplay between Is and Ought. In fact, it is not even a bridge theory, since the distinct quality of the ideal dimension is ultimately simply extinguished: As we have seen, Jellinek downsizes the ideal dimension of the law to something 'regarded-as-normative'. His bridge theory does not bridge Is and Ought, but different aspects of law's real dimension.

There is a second, more crucial problem with Jellinek's bridge theory: It has a purely internal character. Jellinek's bridge is nothing else than an internal psychological process, inside our heads. There are strong arguments, however, to prefer an external bridge theory. For reasons of transparency and democratic legitimacy, the bridge between Is and Ought, between law's real and ideal dimensions, has to be visible from the outside. Jellinek chooses the wrong forum, so to speak, by anchoring his bridge theory in an internal rather than in an external, public forum.

[11] I explore the idea of balancing Is and Ought in legal argumentation in Klatt (2016, pp. 37–41).

This criticism leads way to constructing an appropriate bridge theory that fulfills the two requirements and provides a public rather than a psychological forum. As Loughlin (2010, p. 219) reminds us, '[t]he concept of practice is of particular value here because it blends empirical and normative considerations.' While this statement provides a robust fundament for further thoughts, we must pose a crucial question here: Which type of practice exactly is suitable for the bridge theory we are looking for?

Loughlin follows a particular notion of practice that is inspired by Carl Schmitt and French existential philosophy. In sharp contrast to Loughlin, I would like to adopt a different concept of practice that is more suitable. This is the concept of discursive practice as developed, most notably, by Dworkin (1986, pp. 13–14) and Alexy (1989). This concept best accounts for the 'argumentativeness of legal practice' (Allan 2016, p. 60; cf. Finnis 1987, p. 358). The practice of legal argumentation provides the appropriate forum in which we may hope to bridge the two dimensions of the law.

5 Legal Discourse Bridging Is and Ought

The two dimensions of the law interpenetrate in legal discourse. This is why I coined the thesis of the 'dual nature of legal argumentation' (Sect. 5.1). I will exemplify this thesis with regard to the canons of interpretation (Sect. 5.2) and to the further development of the law (Sect. 5.3).

5.1 The Dual Nature of Legal Argumentation

The dual nature of law is omnipresent in legal argumentation (Klatt 2012, p. 22; Klatt 2016). Legal argumentation is connected to the real, authoritative, institutional dimension of law. It takes place in an institutional setting bringing about decisions that are enforced, if necessary, by coercion. We can refer to the role of courts to underline this point. Courts enjoy practical and not merely theoretical authority (Raz 1986, p. 54). They create coercive 'institutional settlement' of a legal dispute (Waldron 2003, p. 56).

At the same time, legal reasoning is connected to the ideal dimension of law. It implies moral reasoning, according to the special case thesis (Alexy 1999, p. 375). The discourse theory of legal argumentation analyses the conditions of rational practical argumentation in law by reference to rules and forms of discourse. It thereby also explicates the limits of rationality in legal discourse: These rules and forms do not always lead to a single correct answer, and the discourse then ends, for the time being, with rational disagreement. This realm of discursively merely possible (as opposed to discursively necessary or impossible) conclusions is the reason why we have laid down positive, formal legal rules on how to reach and enforce binding decisions. The positivity of the law, in other words, makes up for the limits of legal discourse.

The omnipresence of law's dual nature in legal discourse implies that legal argumentation comprises both real and ideal elements. It is hence too narrow a position to claim that the application of law consists only in mere interpretation of authoritative norm texts (cf. Finnis 1987, p. 358, 363). Such an account would overplays law's real dimension; it is not well-balanced and therefore violates the first requirement stipulated above. Due to law's ideal dimension, legal discourse requires practical moral reasoning irrespective of whether principles of justice are source-based in the positivist sense (cf. Allan 2016, p. 63; Perry 1987, p. 215).

5.2 The Canons of Interpretation

The 'dual nature of legal argumentation' is clearly reflected in the various canons of interpretation (Klatt 2016, pp. 31–34). To give but two examples: The semantic argument draws to the wording of a norm. It establishes how the legal terms are actually used by competent speakers in a given language community (Klatt 2008, pp. 45–46, 52–54). Therefore, the semantic argument belongs to law's real, factual dimension (cf. Alexy 1989, p. 239: 'special case of empirical reasoning'). The objective-teleological canon, in contrast, opens legal interpretation for moral argument, and it thus belongs to law's ideal dimension (cf. Alexy 1989, pp. 241–244). Similar considerations are true for all remaining canons of interpretation (see Klatt 2016, pp. 32–33). Quite importantly, this understanding of the interrelatedness of the canons and the dual nature of law allows to solve the old puzzle of the hierarchy of the canons. The solution (Klatt 2016, pp. 33, 37–38) lies in determining the correct weight of both the 'real' canons and the 'ideal' canons in a given case by means of a balancing exercise.

5.3 Further Development of the Law

Another area that demonstrates how Is and Ought are intertwined in legal discourse is the classical problem of further development of the law. Further development of the law (Klatt 2008, pp. 5–7, 240–241, 274–275) is a special legal method which is to be distinguished from interpretation by the fact that it transgresses the limits of the wording of a legal norm. It can occur in two different forms. If a norm is applied to a case despite the fact that the case does not fall within the scope of its wording, then the norm is extended by means of analogy. If, in contrast, a norm it not applied to a case despite the fact that the case does fall within the scope of its wording, then the norm is restricted by means of teleological reduction. The methodological instrument of further development of the law shows that the limits of the wording of a statute are the limits of interpretation, but not of argumentation. Argumentation continues beyond the wording.

Whether or not courts have the competence to engage in these forms of further developing the law is a heavily contested issue in many jurisdictions. What matters in the present context is that any such competence cannot be legitimate unless law comprises an ideal dimension (see Klatt 2016, pp. 34–35). Further development necessarily transgresses law's real dimension, outweighs the authoritative limits of wording and original intent. As the German Federal Constitutional Court (BVerfGE 34, 269 (287)) has clearly stated in *Soraya*: 'Where written law fails, the judge's decision fills the existing gap by using common sense and general concepts of justice [...].'

In England, by contrast, Lord Sumption (2016) recently delivered a much-discussed account of the limits of law that denied the courts a competence to further develop the law. He included a fierce conservative attack on the so-called evolutive interpretation employed by the European Court of Human Rights that is a form of further development of the law. Juxtaposed with the richer and more complex theory of the dual nature of legal argumentation maintained in this article, Lord Sumption's position overplays the real dimension of the law at the cost of devaluing its ideal dimension, and it thus fails to meet the first requirement stated above.[12] Most notably, Jellinek (1966, pp. 356–357) himself defends the court's competence to further develop the law in the course of his discussion of the complementary relation between Is and Ought.

6 Conclusion

In order to clarify law's relation to both norm and fact, I have discussed Georg Jellinek's thesis of the normative force of the factual. I have placed this thesis in the context of his psychological account of the nature of law, which received severe critique from Kelsen because of the categorical distinction between Is and Ought. This led to the problem of an Is-Ought-Fallacy. I have first discussed Searle's eventually failing attempt to demonstrate the possibility of deriving an Ought from an Is by institutional acts in the context of constitutive rules. Second, I have demonstrated, contra Kelsen, that Jellinek does not commit this fallacy. Jellinek is not concerned, despite deceptive appearances, with a full account of law's validity, but rather with the much narrower project of explaining how internal psychological processes and convictions contribute to the genesis and development of the efficacy of the law. He focusses not on validity, but on convictions of validity. Hence, I have argued, we should better label his thesis the 'regarded-as-normative power of the factual'. This thesis remains entirely in the realistic, social-psychological sphere.

I have then moved to a more promising element in Jellinek's theory, namely his neo-Kantian two-sided theory of the state. Promising and comprehensive as it is, I

[12] On the two requirements for an appropriate bridge theory, see Sect. 4.3 above.

nevertheless have identified the same asymmetric tendency towards law as fact as in his thesis of the 'regarded-as-normative force of the factual'. I continued this discussion by addressing a modern variant of Jellinek's account, the dual nature thesis. A comparison between the two theories revealed important differences. While the dual nature thesis analytically favors the ideal over the real dimension, Jellinek tends towards the factual side. Furthermore, Jellinek's theory downsizes law's ideal dimension to a psychological element, whereas it stands at genuine parity with the factual in the dual nature thesis.

Subsequently, I have turned to the bridge problem. This problem is concerned with how legal scholarship could actually move away from merely adding the two dimensions and instead arrive at fully integrating them. Building upon the two requirements of balancing the two dimensions while keeping their cognitive approaches distinct, I have rejected Jellinek's internal, psychological bridge theory. Instead, I have argued for an external, open, and public forum for bridging Is and Ought. This forum is ultimately available in legal discursive practice. Is and Ought interpenetrate in legal discourse, and the dual nature of the law is omnipresent in legal argumentation. I have labelled this the 'dual nature of legal argumentation' and demonstrated it by referring to the canons of interpretation and to the further development of the law.

While my analysis justifies that it is indeed possible to develop a well-balanced account of law's relation to both fact and norm, it also highlights that the two dimensions do not stand in complete harmony. Rather, we can better characterize their relation as a dynamic tension. There is no higher norm from which we could derive the preference of the factual over the ideal dimension—or, indeed, the reverse. As Radbruch (1990, p. 50) reminded us, this preference may only be determined by the 'responsible decision' of changing eras. I would like to add to Radbruch that these responsible decisions must take place in open and public discourse, rather than in Jellinek's internal psychological forum. Moreover, once these decisions have been made, they remain to be subject to further discourse. Precisely in this sense our discursively justified decisions about the correct relation between the factual and the ideal dimension of the law have at any one time a preliminary character.

References

Alexy R (1989) A theory of legal argumentation: the theory of rational discourse as theory of legal justification. Oxford University Press, Oxford

Alexy R (1998) Law and correctness. Curr Leg Probl 51:205–221. https://doi.org/10.1093/clp/51.1.205

Alexy R (1999) The special case thesis. Ratio Juris 12:374–384

Alexy R (2002) The argument from injustice: a reply to legal positivism. Oxford University Press, Oxford

Alexy R (2010) The dual nature of law. Ratio Juris 23:167–182

Alexy R (2013) Some reflections on the ideal dimension of law and on the legal philosophy of John Finnis. Am J Jurisprud 58:97–110. https://doi.org/10.1093/ajj/aut009

Allan TRS (2016) Interpretation, injustice, and integrity. Oxf J Leg Stud 36:58–82. https://doi.org/10.1093/ojls/gqv014

Bierling ER (1894) Juridische Prinzipienlehre: Band 1. Freiburg (Breisgau)

Blackstone W (2016) Commentaries on the laws of England: of the rights of persons. Oxford University Press, Oxford

Dreier R (1981) Sein und Sollen. Bemerkungen zur Reinen Rechtslehre Kelsens (1972). In: Dreier R (ed) Recht, Moral, Ideologie: Studien zur Rechtstheorie. Suhrkamp, Frankfurt am Main, pp 217–240

Dworkin R (1986) Law's empire. Fontana, London

Ehrenberg V, Jellinek G (2005) Victor Ehrenberg und Georg Jellinek: Briefwechsel 1872–1911. Klostermann, Frankfurt am Main

Finnis J (1982) Natural law and natural rights. Oxford University Press, Oxford

Finnis J (1987) On reason and authority in "Law's Empire". Law Philos 6(3):357–380

Gerber CF (1848) System des deutschen Privatrechts. Mauke, Jena

Groh K (2016) Human rights and subjective rights: affinities in Max Weber and Georg Jellinek. In: Bryan I, Langford P, McGarry J (eds) The reconstruction of the Juridico-political: affinity and divergence in Hans Kelsen and Max Weber. Routledge, London, pp 140–159

Gumplowicz L (1907) Allgemeines Staatsrecht, 3rd edn. Wagner, Innsbruck

Habermas J (1996) Between facts and norms: contributions to a discourse theory of law and democracy (trans: Rehg W). Polity Press, Cambridge

Hare RM (2003) The language of morals. Clarendon Press, Oxford

Hume D (2009) A treatise of human nature. Oxford University Press, Oxford

Jellinek G (1882) Die Lehre von den Staatenverbindungen. O. Haering, Berlin

Jellinek G (1905) System der subjektiven öffentlichen Rechte, 2nd edn. Mohr Siebeck, Tübingen

Jellinek G (1966) Allgemeine Staatslehre: Unveränderter Nachdruck der dritten Auflage (1921). Gehlen, Berlin

Jellinek G (2011) System der subjektiven öffentlichen Rechte (1905), 2nd edn. Mohr Siebeck, Tübingen

Jellinek W (1951) Über die normative Kraft des Faktischen: Zu Georg Jellineks 100. Geburtstag am 16. Juni 1951. Juristenzeitung 6(11):347–348

Kelsen H (1941) The pure theory of law and analytical jurisprudence. Harv Law Rev 55:44–70. https://doi.org/10.2307/1334739

Kelsen H (1953) Was ist die Reine Rechtslehre? In: N.N. (ed) Demokratie und Rechtsstaat: Festgabe zum 60. Geburtstag von Zaccaria Giacometti. Polygraphischer Verlag, Zürich, pp 143–162

Kelsen H (2010) Über die Grenzen zwischen juristischer und soziologischer Methoden: Vortrag gehalten in der Soziologischen Gesellschaft zu Wien. In: Jestaedt M (ed) Werke 3: Veröffentlichte Schriften 1911–1917. Mohr Siebeck, Tübingen, pp 22–55

Kersten J (2000) Georg Jellinek und die klassische Staatslehre. Mohr-Siebeck, Tübingen

Klatt M (2008) Making the law explicit: the normativity of legal argumentation. Hart, Oxford

Klatt M (2012) Robert Alexy's philosophy of law as system. In: Klatt M (ed) Institutionalized reason: the jurisprudence of Robert Alexy. Oxford University Press, Oxford, pp 1–26

Klatt M (2015) Integrative Rechtswissenschaft: Methodologische und wissenschaftstheoretische Implikationen der Doppelnatur des Rechts. Der Staat 54(4):469–499

Klatt M (2016) The rule of dual-natured law. In: Feteris ET, Kloosterhuis H, Plug HJ, Smith CE (eds) Legal argumentation and the rule of law. Eleven International Publishing, The Hague, pp 27–46

Klatt M (2019) Georg Jellinek. In: Acham K (ed) Die Soziologie und ihre Nachbardisziplinen im Habsburgerreich: Ein internationales Handbuch zur Geschichte der Kulturwissenschaften in Zentraleuropa. Böhlau, Wien (forthcoming)

Landau P (2000) Rechtsgeltung bei Georg Jellinek. In: Paulson SL (ed) Georg Jellinek: Beiträge zu Leben und Werk. Mohr Siebeck, Tübingen, pp 299–307

Lassalle F (1899) Über Verfassungswesen. In: Blum E (ed) Ferdinand Lassalle's politische Reden und Schriften. Pfau, Leipzig, pp 40–69

Lepsius O (2000) Georg Jellineks Methodenlehre im Spiegel der zeitgenössischen Erkenntnistheorie. In: Paulson SL (ed) Georg Jellinek: Beiträge zu Leben und Werk. Mohr Siebeck, Tübingen, pp 309–343
Lepsius O (2004) Die Zwei-Seiten-Lehre des Staates. In: Anter A (ed) Die normative Kraft des Faktischen: Das Staatsverständnis Georg Jellineks. Nomos, Baden-Baden, pp 63–88
Lind D (2018) Fact/value complexes in law and judicial decision. In: Marchetti G, Marchetti S (eds) Facts and values: the ethics and metaphysics of normativity. Routledge, London
Loughlin M (2010) Foundations of public law. Oxford University Press, Oxford
Mackie JL (1977) Ethics: inventing right and wrong. Penguin, Harmondsworth
Möllers C (2000) Skizzen zur Aktualität Georg Jellineks: Vier theoretische Probleme aus Jellineks Staatslehre in Verfassungsrecht und Staatstheorie der Gegenwart. In: Paulson SL (ed) Georg Jellinek: Beiträge zu Leben und Werk. Mohr Siebeck, Tübingen, pp 155–171
Moore GE (1993) Principia Ethica. Cambridge University Press, Cambridge
Murkens JEK (2013) From empire to union: conceptions of German constitutional law since 1871. Oxford University Press, Oxford
Olivecrona K (1971) Law as fact, 2nd edn. Stevens, London
Paulson SL (2007) Jellinek, Georg. In: Clark DS (ed) Encyclopedia of law and society: American and global perspectives, vol 2: F-O. Sage Publications, Los Angeles, pp 837–838
Perry SR (1987) Judicial obligation, precedent, and the common law. Oxf J Leg Stud 7:215–257
Radbruch G (1990) Der Zweck des Rechts (1937). In: Kaufmann A (ed) Rechtsphilosophie III. C.F. Müller, Heidelberg, pp 39–50
Rawls J (1993) Political liberalism. Columbia University Press, New York
Raz J (1986) The morality of freedom. Clarendon Press, Oxford
Searle JR (1964) How to derive 'ought' from 'is. Philos Rev 73:43–58. https://doi.org/10.2307/2183201
Searle JR (1969) Speech acts: an essay in the philosophy of language. Cambridge University Press, Cambridge
Stolleis M (1992) Geschichte des öffentlichen Rechts in Deutschland, vol. 2: Staatsrechtslehre und Verwaltungswissenschaft 1800–1914. C.H.Beck, München
Sumption (2016) The limits of law. In: Barber NW, Ekins R, Yowell P (eds) Lord Sumption and the limits of the law. Bloomsbury Publishing, London, pp 15–26
Von Wright GH (1985) Is and ought. In: Bulygin E, Gardies JL, Nilniluoto I (eds) Man, law and modern forms of life. Reidel, Dordrecht, pp 263–281
Waldron J (2003) Authority for officials. In: Meyer LH, Paulson SL, Pogge TW (eds) Rights, culture and the law: themes from the legal and political philosophy of Joseph Raz. Oxford University Press, Oxford, pp 45–69
Weber M (1990) Gesamtausgabe, vol. 5: Briefe 1906–1908. Mohr, Tübingen
Weinberger O (1991) Law, institution and legal politics. Fundamental problems of legal theory and social philosophy. Kluwer, Dordrecht

The 'Normative Force of the Factual': A Positivist's Panegyric

Christoph Bezemek

Abstract Georg Jellinek's concept of a 'Normative Force of the Factual' offers a powerful explanation as to how normality and normativity interrelate. This essay discusses the problems underlying the transition from fact to norm and shows how this phenomenon may be aligned with Kelsensenian positivist theory; notwithstanding the strict separation of "Is" and "Ought" essential to it.

1 Sub-Standard

To refer to the 'Normative Force of the Factual' means to invoke a standard-feature of the repertoire that shapes legal discourse. Or so it may seem. At the same time, however, it attests to the fact that legal doctrine oftentimes simply is not able to elucidate a given state of affairs.

To refer to the 'Normative Force of the Factual' in this perspective, typically obscures a lawyer's inability to account for a certain outcome using the tools of her trade. Put bluntly: It means to rely on a euphemism that merely embellishes ulterior mechanisms at work in instances which ought to be assessed from a legal perspective (and thus differently); diverse mechanisms, to be sure, still mechanisms that share the smack of dubiousness: the element of retardation, the power of persistency; the fait accompli…[1]

To refer to the "Normative Force of the Factual", thus, means to accept a sub-legal efficacy that is not decried as arbitrary only in want of alternatives. Alternatives (blatantly) wanting, necessity bursts through the well-regulated channel shaped by the norm: Wherever the 'Normative Force of the Factual' applies, the force of the normative becomes a negligible factor, in a single instance as well as in a multitude

[1] For a closer analysis *see* Grimmer (1971), pp. 11–12.

C. Bezemek (✉)
University of Graz, Graz, Austria
e-mail: christoph.bezemek@uni-graz.at

N. Bersier Ladavac et al. (eds.), *The Normative Force of the Factual*, Law and Philosophy Library 130, https://doi.org/10.1007/978-3-030-18929-7_5

of instances or, in extremis, concerning the normative order of a political community as a whole.

To refer to the 'Normative Force of the Factual' then means to accept that, sometimes, the legal order is overwhelmed, and legal doctrine with it. Scholars who invoke the concept often do so in bad faith (or at least with a bad conscience): as it is, rather the "pragmatic minds", as Jürgen Habermas emphasizes, that "affirm the 'Normative Force of the Factual'" (2003, p. 365). Thus, rather than being part of the *legal* discourse, this affirmation turns out to be part of a sub-discourse among *lawyers* who shrug their shoulders in the face of what seems inevitable.

To refer to the "Normative Force of the Factual", finally, rather than being a standard-feature of legal discourse, seems to resort to the sub-standard of the lawyer's repertoire.

2 The Original Understanding

Based on this (widely, if not commonly, accepted) understanding of the "Normative Force of the Factual", it may seem enticing to give in to the temptations of academic finger-wagging and to rattle on about the need of careful doctrinal analysis and intellectual honesty in lieu of 'pragmatic affirmation'. This (in and by itself possibly commendable) undertaking, is, however, not what this essay aims at; not least as the understanding underlying it (as widely accepted as it may be), is quite distant from the meaning that Georg Jellinek, the original author of the phrase, intended it to convey when he introduced it in his 'Allgemeine Staatslehre' in 1900.

As it oftentimes happens with catchy phrases, the 'Normative Force of the Factual' fell victim to its own success, or perhaps rather: to a sequence of intended and unintended distortions (Kersten 2000, p. 365). These distortions, however, may at least partly have been caused by the fact that only a few among us would subscribe to the statement of Georg Jellinek's son, Walter, on the occasion of his father's 100th birthday, that

> this fortunate linguistic impression allows at once to see what it means – that what actually is, is imbued with the tendency to be perceived as what ought to be. (1951, 348; my translation)

Be that as it may. Walter Jellinek sure is correct that "a winged word easily escapes the cage of the thoughts surrounding it." (1951, p. 348; my translation) To inspect the cage of the thoughts surrounding the 'Normative Force of the Factual' (and to pay some attention to the relation of facts and norms in general) is what I would like to undertake in this contribution. Still, already at this point, this requires an important caveat: Georg Jellinek's concept of a 'Normative Force of the Factual' describes a phenomenon at the intersection of sociology, ontology and law. It asks, as Oliver Lepsius emphasizes, to perceive a non-legal object of cognizance from a legal perspective,[2] as it has decisive implications for questions of law and state, in particular for legal and political theory.

These implications are at the core of the following essay as it intends to analyze the essential functionality of the phenomenon Jellinek describes. In order to do that, Jellinek's concept of a 'Normative Force of the Factual' will be decontextualized as well as marginalized.

To trace the tendency of the 'Is' to be perceived as an 'Ought' in such a distorted manner may seem unsatisfactory to those closely acquainted with Jellinek's work, as this approach has to neglect important questions of constitutional theory.[3] I ask the experts to be lenient, while, at the same time, I rest assured that the task ahead will still prove to be challenging due to the multifaceted phenomenon it has to address.

To adequately face this challenge requires to employ an appropriate method: The essay will, therefore, overall resort to transdisciplinary eclecticism (paired, in some instances, with rabulistics). This, however, may seem to be a questionable endeavor at first glance, in particular for an orthodox Austrian scholar (as I of course, strive to be): Thinking back on my student days in Vienna when I was taught (time and again) to strictly separate 'Is' and 'Ought' under reference to Hans Kelsen's pure theory of law,[4] 'the 'Normative Force of the Factual'' hardly seems to be a suitable topic for an academic endeavor grounded in positivist theory.

3 An Olive Branch

Luckily, however, it seems that (as often) Kelsen himself may have assessed the issue more generously than some Kelsenians: In an article published in 1965 titled 'What is Legal Positivism?' Kelsen explains:

> [T]he validity of a legal order in general and of a single norm in particular depends on [two] facts. [The first] being that law has to be posited in a qualified manner, the [second] being that law has to be efficacious to a certain degree. In this sense *alone*," Kelsen emphasizes in italics, one can speak of a "normative force of the factual". (Kelsen 1965, p. 465; my translation)

This doesn't seem like much at first glance. The olive branch extended over the gulf that separates 'Is' and 'Ought' appears to be rather short. Whether it is sufficient to bridge it, will depend on how wide the gulf proves to be. To examine this, requires to accept Kelsen's reservation as a 'working assignment' and to focus on the *emergence* as well as on the *persistence* of norms and the order these norms constitute.

---

[2] *See* Lepsius's essay in this volume.

[3] I.a the "Two-Sides"-Theory, questions of the state's self-imposed commitment or the constitutional law perspective, in general.

[4] For this position *see* i.a. Gálvez (2014), p. 43. For a closer analysis of Kelsen's position *see* Nicoletta Bersier's contribution to this volume.

This is not to say that the emergence and the persistence of norms are separate problems in Jellinek's understanding. Much rather, according to Jellinek, both incidents exhibit common roots in an approach that perceives norms "only as a psychological, that is an internal phenomenon", as "part of human imagination", as something that "exists in our heads" (1900, 332; my translation); something "which is valid only by means of its motivational capacity, its capacity to determine the will" that springs from the "original conviction that we are obligated to follow it" (1900, 333; my translation).

It is important to emphasize this, as it helps to correctly assess the relation of motivation and motive for the purpose at hand: Already on this level it suggests that, according to Jellinek's approach, it is not 'the Factual' in itself, but rather our relation to 'the Factual'[5]; that it is the *force* springing from this relation which is at the origin of his endeavor to, as he calls it, 'advance towards the last psychological sources of law'; to find an answer to the 'great principal question': 'how does non-law become law?' (Jellinek 1900, p. 320; my translation).

4 A Fallacy

Jellinek's walk with the emotive wiggle stick soon leads him towards the human "tendency to elevate the factual to the normal" and to deduce *normative* implications from the *normality* so defined; to transform *regularity* into *ruleness*.

'Man', he explains,

> perceives his constant surroundings, his perpetual perceptions, his continual practice not only to be a mere fact but to be an evaluative norm that helps him to detect deviations. (Jellinek 1900, p. 307; my translation).

To be sure: At first glance, this approach hardly seems to be reconcilable with Kelsen's position; in particular as his posthumously published treatise, 'The General Theory of Norms' explicitly (albeit not too sympathetically) discusses the interplay of norm and normality.

Because, as Kelsen explains, "in so far 'norm' is expressed in the adjective 'normal', it means not an 'Ought' but an 'Is'.

> 'Normal' is what regularly happens in fact. To assume that because something is happening on a regular basis, it ought to happen would be a fallacy; logically an Ought cannot be derived from an Is." (Kelsen 1979, p. 3; my translation).

The argument from a logical impossibility to transform an 'Is' into an 'Ought' has deep roots in the history of philosophy (*see* i.a. von der Pfordten 1993); roots which, as is well known, run back to David Hume's 'Treatise of Human Nature' (1739). Countless, even if prominent (just *see* Searle 1964), undertakings to refute it were only moderately successful (*see* i.a. Augsberg 2008, pp. 470–471); in particular as

[5] For this point also *see* Klatt in this volume who introduces the 'regarded-as-normative power of the factual'.

they often met with the allegation to employ crypto-normative propositions unable to redeem their argumentative presupposition (*see*, in particular, von Wright 1985).[6]

5 Thousandfold Norms

However, it would be unfair to accuse Jellinek of being taken in by the deductive fallacy Hume, among others (*see*, in particular, Moore 1993), denounced: Jellinek's approach is not about the *logical deduction* but about the psycho-*logical emergence* of ruleness from regularity in, as he puts it, 'ontogenetic' and 'phylogenetic perspective' (1900, 322)—concerning the individual as well as the group.

And, evidently, he was onto something: The examples he uses to illustrate his point, already concerning those "thousandfold norms on which our daily life is built", (1900, 307; my—not quite literal—translation) are not merely impressive because of their anecdotic evidence but may also be (relying on the benefit of hindsight) furnished with further studies on the respective subject:

That to most people, as Jellinek writes, their "native preparation of nourishment tastes pleasantly" (1900, 337; my translation), that, to put it in simple terms: we do not eat what we like but we like what we eat, seems nowadays sufficiently established by dietological and sociological accounts (*see*, from various perspectives, Rozin 1997; Numark-Sztainer and Perry 1999; Hirschfelder and Pollmer 2018 and, of course, Simmel 1910).

And if the childless among us doubt that the tendency to generate rules from regularities may be observed, as Jellinek states, "in its utmost purity in the child" (1900, 307), a multitude of studies in the field of behavioral science may be pointed at to suggest just that (just *see* Bear and Knobe 2017 with further references). Parents, of course, would have been aware of that anyhow.

The same applies to Jellinek's statements on the normative force of fashion, social customs and rules of common decency (1900, 307): Whoever finds his depiction of fashion to be too superficial may be satisfied studying the 'imitation-drive' outlined in Georg Simmel's 'Philosophy of Fashion' (Simmel 1905). And whoever finds Simmel's account of fashion to be outmoded or too exhausting may be referred to a current meta-study on the topic (Aspers and Godart 2013).

Evidence on how social customs are derived from common practice within a given group is to be found in Adam Smith's 'Theory of Moral Sentiments' first published in 1759 (Smith 1774, p. 207). Nearly 200 years later Martin Heidegger cut to the chase when discussing "averageness […] as an existential character of the they":

> we enjoy ourselves and have fun the way *they* enjoy themselves. We read, see, and judge literature and art the way *they* see and judge. But we also withdraw from the 'great mass' the way *they* withdraw, we find 'shocking' what *they* find shocking. That *they*, which is

[6] For a careful analysis of von Wright's critique of Searle's approach *see* Klatt in this volume.

> nothing definite and which all our, though not as a sum, prescribes the kind of being of everydayness. (Heidegger 1996, p. 119)

Roughly another 100 years later, the disburdening function of this "kind of being of everydayness" may be amply observed in what is currently referred to as the 'norm-core-phenomenon' (Rowan 2014).

And finally, concerning the rules of common decency, it may suffice to point to the advice Eugen Ehrlich gives in the 'Fundamental Principles of the Sociology of Law';

> that whoever inquires as to the origin and effects [of norms] should first try to answer the easier question why he doesn't see a man on the street in bourgeois clothes doesn't wear a necktie. (Ehrlich 1967, p. 63)

Of course: bourgeois clothes themselves may have fallen victim to the 'Normative Force of the Factual', but, it is to be assumed, the point still may be well-understood.

6 Animal Computans

Jellinek's selection of examples, their structure, their relation to another, and in particular the rather erratic conclusion he draws concerning individual and community may fall short of current standards in social science. Still, his pioneering achievement can hardly be denied: Jellinek, at the dawn of the twentieth century, admirably tilled a field that should be in the academic limelight only decades later[7] because of concepts such as George Canguilhem's discussion of normality and pathology (Canguilhem 1978) or Michel Foucault's survey of normalization as instrument of power in modernity (Foucault 1995).

At the core of the issue at hand, however, Jellinek's concept makes the grandest impression by the intuitive conciseness that helps to reconstruct what Friedrich Nietzsche described as the "paradox of a task which nature has set itself in regard to man": "The breeding of an animal which can make promises"; an animal that can think causally, an animal that can act in anticipation based on that causal thinking,[8] an animal that, as Nietzsche puts it, has "the power to calculate" and thus has itself become

> *calculable, disciplined, necessitated* even for himself and his own conception of himself, that, like a man entering into a promise, he could guarantee himself *as a future*. (Nietzsche 1887, pp. 61–63)

[7] Academic honesty, of course, requires not to leave Emile Durkheim's seminal contribution to the concept of normality unmentioned (Durkheim 1895; for a concise introduction *see* Horwitz 2008).

[8] Sellars (1980), p. 138 hit the nail right on the head by stating: "To say that man is a rational animal is to say that man is a creature not of habits, but of rules. When God created Adam, he whispered in his ear, 'In all contexts of action you will recognize rules, if only the rule to grope for rules to recognize. When you cease to recognize rules, you will walk on four feet'"

This capacity of the individual holds the precondition of society: "[W]ithout the intentional or unintentional application of rules of calculation", as Hermann Heller puts it in his Theory of the State, "it is impossible for mankind to live and work together." (Heller 1934, p. 251; my translation).

Against this backdrop it becomes clear that Jellinek not only develops a theory of the emergence of norms, but, overall, lays out the foundation of a theory as to the emergence of normative consciousness (as he puts it: "the fundamental psychological facts on which the possibility of a legal order depends" Jellinek 1900, p. 322; my translation); normative consciousness that allows to confront a complex and contingent environment based on past experience. The aptitude to infer rules from regularity makes man *calculable*; shaping the precondition (Forst 2015, p. 38) for being "bound by commitments that are not subjected to our discretion" (Jellinek 1900, p. 352), the precondition for establishing, one step after another, what John Searle, writing more than 100 years after Jellinek, called "deontic power" based on status functions (Searle 2011).

It has to be admitted: This presentation simplifies a complex process to infer *deficiency* from *difference* and *dues* based on this assessment (a process at the intersection of *average*, *typicality* and *ideal-type*). However, for the purpose at hand, it makes sufficiently plausible, how the 'Normative Force of the Factual', based on the prognostic capacity of cognitive expectability (Möllers 2015) constitutes norms as counter-factually (or rather: *a*-factually) stabilized expectations (Luhmann 1969, p. 37). And it makes plausible how a *rule*—as a result of this process—may become detached from *regularity* and thus allows for frustrated expectations, without itself being necessarily put into question.[9]

7 Lawless Irregularity

The addendum "necessarily" in the preceding paragraph is important: It may well be argued that ruleness which originates from regularity finds a twofold prerequisite in this regularity; not only as its foundation but also as its condition: The norm needs to resonate in normality, thereby ensuring that the lifeline connecting normality and normativity is not severed.

This is easily demonstrated by pointing to extreme cases like the disruptive scenarios discussed by Carl Schmitt: Evidently "there is no norm that would apply to chaos." (Schmitt 2004, p. 19; my translation). As Hermann Heller remarked:

> the validity of the norm presupposes the normal state of affairs for which the norm is *calculated*; exceptional and thus unpredictable circumstances are withdrawn from any normative evaluation. (Heller 1934, p. 255)

---

[9] The norm's emancipation from the fact, thus taking effect within the individual, allows Jellinek—without contradiction—to exhibit factual recurrences at one point as actuality and at another—close to Kelsen's understanding—as an interpretative scheme by observing that "[a]ll law is an evaluative norm, and thereby never coincides with the state of affairs that is being evaluated."

Jellinek, of course, was well aware that normativity was destined to erode along with the normality it was based on. Consistently he emphasized that "law never ha[d] the power to determine the course of the state in times of crisis" (Jellinek 1900, pp. 258–259; my translation); an observation which, even if only in extreme cases, leads back to the common understanding of the concept of a 'Normative Force of the Factual', discussed at the beginning of this essay.

Going beyond that, at this point, we may conclude that—in general—no *expectability* that is to be solidified into an *expectation* may be derived from contingency. And if—contrarily—contingency massively, with irresistible force, breaks down on an existing normality, the expectations calculated based on this normality do not (and cannot) provide any stability. In these cases, the safeguards of the political (and thus: normative) sphere (Arendt 2003, pp. 9–10) have been surmounted.

The 'Normative Force of the Factual' at the same time aids in diagnosing this form of crisis that cannot be averted by the means provided by the normative order *and* to overcome it; still without lending justification to any reality just because of its efficacy.

And yet, it has to be admitted: even as presented in the given context, the capacity, in particular the evolutive capacity, of the approach is limited (*see* Loughlin 2010, pp. 219–221). Grand theories of social ontology like John Searle's 'Making of the Social World' (Searle 2011) rest on a broader foundation. Still, to judge Jellinek by that standard is neither expedient, nor is it appropriate: as the 'Normative Force of the Factual' (even if slightly supplemented) does have the power to construct normative alternatives to the state of affairs from which they originate (*see,* in particular, Heller 1934, pp. 253–254); towards a normativity that allows, as Christoph Möllers put it in his latest book, "[t]o distance oneself from the world while in the world" (Möllers 2015). The emergence of the normative in its specific manifestation harbors the 'possibility of norms' which to seize is up to us.

Of course, diligent students of Robert Musil may have already been aware of that, knowing that "[i]f there is a sense of reality, there must also be a sense of possibility" (Musil 1953, p. 12). Still, Jellinek, who unlike us did not have a chance to study the 'Man without Qualities', indeed shows himself to be the "Great Synthetisist" (Stolleis 1992, p. 450) by tracing back the 'sense of possibility' to the 'sense of reality', thereby dissolving the antithetical relation of fact and norm within the individual.

8 Watching Television

Still, even if we were to accept this, the question remains how this is related to the emergence of legal norms in a positivist perspective; aside, of course, from the option to enact a normative practice generated by the mechanisms of the 'Normative Force of the Factual' into law, or by referring to it in positive law, thus ensuring the resonance of the normative in normality.

Jellinek would reply that the relation between the factual and the normative "becomes [even clearer] in the emergence of law" (my—not quite literal—translation) when compared to the other examples like culinary taste, fashion, social custom and rules of common decency.[10] As "all law in a people", Jellinek emphasizes, was

> "originally nothing but factual practice, the continuity of which caused the perception of its normative character; which is why the norm itself appears to be an authoritative command of the community, i.e. a legal norm; whereby", so he ends, "also the problem of customary law is solved." (Jellinek 1900, p. 339; my translation)

This "solution" may seem appealing. However, at the same time, it comes with far more prerequisites than Jellinek would make us believe, starting with Jellinek's anthropologically untenable 'original' position which already Heller cynically dismissed as "fanciful romanticism of the communal spirit" (Heller 1934, p. 252).

Still: Far more important than to discuss the accuracy of Jellinek's anthropological assumptions is to point to the fact that they are hardly extraordinary at the time he writes (*see* i.a. Jhering 1866, p. 119): Also, and in particular Hans Kelsen, emphasizes in the first edition of the 'Pure Theory of Law' that "in the primitive legal community the creation of general legal norms follows from custom, i.e. practice of the members of the community." (Kelsen 1934, p. 118; my translation).

For a start, the only thing remarkable about this may be the (questionable) empirical claim Kelsen's and Jellinek's concept have in common. The instance, that the 'Pure Theory' is capable of accepting custom as a norm-creating moment and thus as objectively valid (Kelsen 1960, pp. 231–232; my translation) is not. Far more interesting is how this creation is bound to happen, how, according to Kelsen's first condition introduced above,[11] it is to be "posited in a qualified manner" (Kelsen 1965, p. 465; my translation).

The first edition of the 'Pure Theory' falls silent when it comes to this. And the 'General Theory of Norms' contents itself to refer to the second edition (Kelsen 1979, p. 114). Here Kelsen hints to a "collective will" (Kelsen 1960, p. 9; my translation) as law making entity. As this is to imply an actual and intentional act of positing law, this view has drawn substantial criticism namely by Ota Weinberger (Weinberger 1981, pp. 28–29; for a detailed discussion *see* Jabloner 2013, pp. 12–14).

Against this backdrop it is quite remarkable that Kelsen in his final discussion of the topic, in the article referred to above, abstains from pointing to the "collective will", describing the origin of customary law simply this way:

> "if people who live together in society conduct themselves under certain conditions in a certain manner, in each individual arises the will that one ought to act this way. This [so he concludes] is the psychological foundation of customary law." (Kelsen 1965, p. 466; my translation)

[10] *Supra* § 5.

[11] *Supra* § 3.

This psychological foundation, however, is strikingly similar to the mechanisms at work behind the capacity discussed by Jellinek "to elevate the factual to an evaluative norm"; specifically to the "general mental property" he refers to "which perceives the ever recurring fact as a norm" (Jellinek 1900, p. 309; my translation); or, to put it more precisely: the capacity to generate normativity from normality.

To make good use of this capacity by underpinning Kelsen's position would also help to reveal that some of the criticisms of his are uncalled for, like Norbert Hoerster's in asserting that Kelsen was wrong to assume that "any random habit that lasts for a certain period of time automatically becomes a norm", as there were many habits, "like the habit of watching television" on a daily basis that were not tied to any normative claim (Hoerster 2006, p. 73): Following the approach outlined above, Hoerster not only underestimates the transformative potential of the 'Normative Force of the Factual'. He also resorts to an ill-chosen example: I for one, as a small boy, was taught by my dear mother not to call other people on the phone (a time when landlines still were in use) between 7:30 p.m. and 8 p.m. because at that time, my mother explained, one was supposed to watch the news (and thus not to be disturbed).

9 A Suitable Cross-Check

Of course, the fourth revolution may have invalidated this rule (bringing down the landlines as well as the evening news). This, however, leads to the second point: the importance of the 'Normative Force of the Factual' when it comes to the *persistence* of legal norms. This question may be dealt with briefly as Kelsen regards custom in its law-creating and in its law-destroying varieties as functionally opposing but still as structurally concurrent phenomena. *Desuetudo* [to abstain from a certain practice], so we read in the second edition of the 'Pure Theory of Law',

> is quasi a negative custom; its essential function consists in repealing the validity of an existing norm. If however, so he continues, efficacy is a condition of validity not only for the legal order as a whole but also for a specific legal norm, the law-creating function of custom cannot be excluded by means of positive law as the negative function of desuetudo is concerned. (Kelsen 1960, p. 220; my translation)

Kelsen's view on the abstention from a custom may serve as a quite suitable cross-check for the argument made above: if it is not completely off the mark in view of the *emergence* of legal norms in terms of Kelsen's theory, it cannot be completely off the mark as the *persistence* of legal norms is concerned. Then, of course, the 'Normative Force of the Factual', as Jellinek, put it "provides the right understanding not only for the *emergence* but also for the *existence* of the legal order." (Jellinek 1900, p. 339; my translation). Jellinek's perception of the 'Normative Force of the Factual' as a coherent phenomenon concerning the *emergence* as well as the *persistence* of legal norms completes this impression: in the given context the interplay of fact and norm presents itself in its degenerative rather than its generative capacity.

10 Both Sides of the Dichotomy

Not to be misunderstood: this is not to say that the central differences between Kelsen's and Jellinek's approach are to be discarded; in particular when it comes to the important point of the persistence of legal norms: The 'Pure Theory of Law', in accepting efficacy only as a condition of validity, has little sympathy to offer to Jellinek's "psychologism" (*see* Paulson 2005, p. 193). This, however, does not bar from seeing the "psychological phenomenon of recognition" Kelsen discusses in the 'General Theory of Norms' (Kelsen 1979, p. 33) mirrored in the mechanisms at work behind the 'Normative Force of the Factual': Against the backdrop of a validity conditioned by efficacy "the state and its order [necessarily] appears rational to the overwhelming majority of people", as Jellinek (1900, p. 324; my translation) put it. It *has* to appear rational one may add if the condition of validity is not to erode. So, in this perspective, even if with a grain of salt, it has to be concluded that "what is actual [indeed] is rational" (Hegel 2008, p. 14); with all the implications that come along with such a view.

This, however may finally lead to questions that are not to be addressed in this essay. And by far it is more important to emphasize that in the marginalized (in any case functional) perspective on the 'Normative Force of the Factual' introduced here, this concept may also be put to good use within the frame of the 'Pure Theory of Law'; that it allows to better understand that even in a positivist perspective of the Kelsenian variety 'Is' and 'Ought' are not to be understood as separated but as dichotomous phenomena; as phenomena that they are to be grasped in their interrelation and that, indeed, no olive branch is needed to bridge the gulf between 'Is' and 'Ought'.

Of course, one may argue, that a close reading of Kelsen's writings may have been sufficient to understand that and to counter misperceptions in academic writings. But such an objection would not be justified: The 'Pure Theory of Law', according to its very object,[12] is not designed to shine its light on both sides of the dichotomy. Touching on, as Jellinek puts it, "a deep-reaching doctrine of the law-creating [and I would like to add: the law-destroying] forces" (Jellinek 1900, p. 320; my translation) we may be well advised to pay close attention to concepts like his.

Acknowledgements This essay is based on the author's inaugural lecture at University of Graz on May 12th 2017. Many thanks to my team: Myriam Becker, Christa Pail, Jürgen Pirker, Renate Pirstner-Ebner, Susanne Rufer and Hannah Schöffmann for their support in organizing the event and for immensely facilitating my transition to University of Graz, Faculty of Law.

[12] *See* Lepsius in this volume.

References

Arendt H (2003) Was ist Politik? Piper, München
Aspers P, Godart F (2013) Sociology of fashion: order and change. Annu Rev Sociol 39:171–192
Augsberg S (2008) Der "naturalistische Fehlschluß" als juristische Argumentationsfigur. Archiv für Rechts- und Sozialphilosophie 94:461–476
Bear A, Knobe P (2017) Normality: part descriptive, part prescriptive. Cognition 167:25–37
Canguilhem G (1978) [1966] On the normal and the pathological. Reidel, Dordrecht
Durkheim E (1982) [1895] The rules of sociological method. The Free Press, New York
Ehrlich E (1967) Grundlegung der Soziologie des Rechts, 3rd edn. Duncker & Humblot, Berlin
Forst R (2015) Normativität und Macht: Zur Analyse sozialer Rechtfertigungsordnungen. Sukrkamp, Berlin
Foucault M (1995) [1975] Discipline and punish: the birth of the prison, 2nd edn. Vintage Books, New York
Gálvez J (2014) Der Positivismus von Kelsen. In: Aliprantis N, Olechowski T (eds) Hans Kelsen: Die Aktualität eines großen Rechtswissenschafters und Soziologen des 20. Jahrhunderts, pp 39–51
Grimmer K (1971) Die Rechtsfigur einer "Normativität des Faktischen". Duncker & Humblot, Berlin
Habermas J (2003) Interpreting the fall of a monument. Constellations 10:364–370
Hegel GWF (2008) [1820] Outlines of the philosophy of right. Oxford University Press, Oxford
Heidegger M (1996) [1927] Being and time. State University of New York Press, New York
Heller H (1934) Staatslehre. Sijthoff, Leiden
Hirschfelder G, Pollmer P (2018) Ernährung und Esskultur: Kulturwissenschaftliche Perspektiven. Aktuelle Ernährungsmedizin 43:41–55
Hoerster N (2006) Was ist Recht? Beck, München
Horwitz A (2008) Normality. Contexts 7:70–71
Jabloner C (2013) Kein Imperativ ohne Imperator. In: Olechowksi T, Zeleny K (eds) Methodenreinheit und Erkenntnisvielfalt. Manz, Wien, pp 1–22
Jellinek G (1900) Allgemeine Staatslehre. Häring, Berlin
Jellinek W (1951) Über die normative Kraft des Faktischen. Juristenzeitung, 347–348
Kelsen H (1934) Reine Rechtslehre. Franz Deuticke, Wien
Kelsen H (1960) Reine Rechtslehre, 2nd edn. Franz Deuticke, Wien
Kelsen H (1965) Was ist juristischer Positivismus? Juristenzeitung:465–469
Kelsen H (1979) Allgemeine Theorie der Normen. Manz, Wien
Kersten J (2000) Georg Jellinek und die klassische Staatslehre. Mohr Siebeck, Tübingen
Loughlin M (2010) Foundations of public law. Oxford University Press, Oxford
Luhmann N (1969) Normen in soziologischer Perspektive. Soziale Welt 20:28–48
Möllers C (2015) Die Möglichkeit der Normen. Suhrkamp, Berlin
Moore GE (1993) Principia Ethica. Cambridge University Press, Cambridge
Musil R (1953) [1943] The man without qualities, vol I. Secker & Warburg, London
Nietzsche F (1913) [1887] The geneaology of morals: a polemic. In: Levy O (ed) The complete works, vol XIII. Noulis, Edinburgh
Numark-Sztainer D, Perry S (1999) Factors influencing food journal of the choices of adolescents: findings from focus-group discussions with adolescents. J Am Diet Assoc 99:929–937
Paulson S (2005) Zwei radikale Objektivierungsprogramme in der Rechtslehre Hans Kelsens. In: Paulson S, Stolleis M (eds) Hans Kelsen: Staatsrechtslehrer und Rechtstheoretiker des 20. Jahrhunderts. Mohr Siebeck, Tübingen, pp 191–220
Rowan R (2014) So now!: On Normcore. e-flux 58:01/16
Rozin P (1997) Why we eat what we eat, and why we worry about it. Bull Am Acad Arts Sci 50:26–48
Schmitt C (2004) Politische Theologie: Vier Kapitel zur Lehre von der Souveränität, 8th edn. Duncker & Humblot, Berlin

Searle JR (1964) How to derive ‘ought’ from ‘is’. Philos Rev 73:43–58
Searle JR (2011) Making the social world: on the structure of human civilization. Oxford University Press, Oxford
Sellars W (1980) Language, rules and behavior. In: Sichatascerado J (ed) Pure pragmatics and possible worlds: the early essays of wilfrid sellars. Ridgeview, Atascerado
Simmel G (1995) [1905] Philosophie der Mode. In: Behr M, Krech V, Schmidt G (eds) Georg Simmel Gesamtausgabe, vol X. Suhrkamp, Berlin
Simmel G (1910) Soziologie der Mahlzeit, Der Zeitgeist, Beiblatt zum Berliner Tageblatt 41 vom 10 Oktober 1910
Smith A (1774) The theory of moral sentiments, 4th edn. Straham, London
Stolleis M (1992) Geschichte des öffentlichen Rechts in Deutschland, vol 2. Beck, München, pp 1800–1914
von der Pfordten D (1993) Sein, Werten, Sollen. Archiv für Rechts- und Sozialphialosophie 79:48–69
von Jhering R (1866) Der Geist des römischen Rechts auf den verschiedenen Stufen seiner Entwicklung, vol I, 2nd edn. Breitkopf & Härtel, Leipzig
von Wright GH (1985) Is and ought. In: Bulygin E, Gardies JL, Nilniluoto I (eds) Man, law and modern forms of life. Reidel, Dordrecht, pp 263–281
Weinberger O (1981) Normentheorie als Grundlage der Jurisprudenz und Ethik. Duncker & Humblot, Berlin

The Effectiveness-Legitimacy Conundrum in the International Law of State Formation

Andreas Th. Müller

Abstract According to the traditional textbook account, the coming into existence of States is a fact, depending on the realization of effective government over territory and people (so-called three-elements doctrine). Against this background, the present contribution argues that while the formation of States is a predominately fact-based phenomenon, it is not limited to a mere test of effectiveness. The formation of States has always incorporated elements of legitimacy and even more so by virtue of the development of international law in the wake of World War II. Issues of legitimacy become relevant in particular in extreme situations, i.e. in the event that the foundational principles of the contemporary international legal order as manifested in the concept of peremptory norms of general international law (*jus cogens*) are at stake.

The textbook account of State formation, as it is authoritatively set out in Georg Jellinek's *Allgemeine Staatslehre*, appears to be as straightforward as simple: The coming into existence of States is a fact. International law cannot produce this fact, but ties legal consequences to it.[1] Accordingly, as the standard account continues, the relevant questions to ask in view of the emergence of an entity are: Is there a territory? Is there a people? And is there effective control over both of them?[2]

But is this account correct? And if it is correct, how can we explain, to give a recent example, that the Islamic State of Iraq and the Levant/Syria (ISIS) was not considered a State by anyone even in the heyday of its extension? Perhaps the seeming straightforwardness and simplicity of the standard account is tempting, but

[1] See in particular Jellinek (1900), p. 245: "Das Völkerrecht knüpft daher an das Faktum der staatlichen Existenz an, vermag dieses Faktum aber nicht zu schaffen." ("Thus, international law ties in to the fact of existence of States, but cannot create this fact."; translation ATM).

[2] As regard the so-called "three-elements doctrine" see Jellinek (1900), p. 355 ff and the following chapter.

A. T. Müller (✉)
Department of European Law and Public International Law, University of Innsbruck, Innsbruck, Austria
e-mail: andreas.mueller@uibk.ac.at

N. Bersier Ladavac et al. (eds.), *The Normative Force of the Factual*, Law and Philosophy Library 130, https://doi.org/10.1007/978-3-030-18929-7_6

misleading, as it casually elides elements of legitimacy that are nonetheless relevant for the question of whether a State comes into being and joins the community of States as a new member.

Far from being a new question, it rather represents one of the age-old problems challenging the discipline of international law at all times. This does not make it a futile endeavor, but calls for the efforts of every generation of international law scholars to find adequate answers to it. Against this background, the present contribution argues that while the formation or creation of States is indeed a predominately fact-based phenomenon, it is not limited to a mere test of effectiveness. In fact, the formation of States has always incorporated elements of legitimacy and even more so over the last decades, notably by virtue of the development of international law in the wake of World War II. Issues of legitimacy become relevant particularly in extreme situations, i.e. in the event that the foundational principles of the contemporary international legal order are at stake.

To make these points, the contribution starts with analyzing the afore-mentioned standard or orthodox account of the purely factual character of State formation (Sect. 1). This account is then to be challenged in the light of the emergence of ISIS (Sect. 2). This example will help us to affirm that, and to locate where in the international legal order, we can find elements of legitimacy that co-govern the phenomenon of formation of States, notably in case of violation of the foundational principles of international law (Sect. 3). While legitimacy concerns have a rather limited scope of application with respect to State formation, they play a more important role in the design of the recognition policies of existing States. These two phenomena, although interrelated, should be conceptually distinguished. Recognition policies go beyond the scope of this contribution since these legitimacy concerns do not prevent a new State from coming into existence (Sect. 4).

1 The Orthodox Account: Formation of States as a Mere Fact

The law is permanently confronted with the task of managing and balancing the tension of effectiveness and legitimacy concerns. International law does not form an exception in this regard,[3] notably in regard to the phenomenon of State formation.[4] Nonetheless, the orthodox account of the phenomenon of State formation conceives of it as a pure question of fact, and not a question of law.

As mentioned, Georg Jellinek has famously embraced this view.[5] Thus, a new State comes into existence if all its essential elements—according to the "doctrine

---

[3] See only recently Tomuschat (2017), p. 309 ff.

[4] See e.g. von Arnauld (2016), p. 27, expressly referring to "the tension between effectiveness and legitimacy" (translation ATM) in this regard; see in a similar vein Shaw (2008), p. 198.

[5] See *supra* note 1; see also Jellinek (1900), p. 246: "Der Zeugungsakt selbst aber liegt gänzlich ausserhalb des Rechts." ("The act of procreation [of States] completely lies outside the law." translation ATM).

of three elements" ("Drei-Elementen-Lehre"), i.e. territory ("Staatsgebiet"), people ("Staatsvolk") and government ("Staatsgewalt")[6]—are realized and the entity in question can therefore actually operate as a State. This is the case as soon as the State's organs factually exercise control and as soon as they are factually obeyed.[7]

Jellinek's *Allgemeine Staatslehre*, inasmuch as it dismisses the attempt to conceive of the question of State formation as a legal problem as typical of natural law approaches,[8] both reflects nineteenth century positivist thinking[9] and has on its part influenced the then and subsequent constitutional and international law discourse. Also, its famous contemporary, Lassa Oppenheim's *International Law*, unequivocally states: "The formation of a new State is [...] a matter of fact, and not of law."[10] Propositions of this or a similar kind abound in the textbook literature of the twentieth century.[11]

It is important to note, however, that the proponents of such *ex factis jus oritur* approach do usually not intend to prostrate before the formation of the State as a *brutum factum* that is by its very essence beyond the reach of international law. While some may take pleasure in the idea of worshipping the act of State formation as an *arcanum* of international law and of thus leaving the very roots of the discipline in the obscure, a more sober approach acknowledges that the law, here as in other contexts, opts to attach legal consequences to a certain set of facts and thus makes it legally relevant.[12] It is in this and only in this sense that State formation should be conceived of as a non- or pre-legal phenomenon.

That being said, such a strongly fact-oriented approach embodies the wisdom that the law, as a normative order which aims at actually influencing the behavior of its addressees,[13] is well advised to keep an eye on relevant developments on the ground. It thus makes sense for international law to take note of the factual emergence of new players in the international arena. It is obvious that various legal institutions existing both at the level of domestic and international law (e.g. acquisitive

---

[6] Jellinek (1900), p. 354 ff; see also Oppenheim (1955), p. 118; Verdross and Simma (1984), pp. 223–225. See also Arbitration Committee attached to the Conference for Peace in Yugoslavia, Opinion No. 1, 29 November 1991, 3 *European Journal of International Law* (1992) 182; Report of the Independent International Fact-Finding Mission on the Conflict in Georgia, September 2009, Vol. II, 127.

[7] Jellinek (1900), p. 250.

[8] Jellinek (1900), pp. 243–244.

[9] See the useful account in Crawford (2007), p. 13 ff.

[10] Oppenheim (1955), p. 544.

[11] See the useful references in Crawford (2007), p. 4; Taki (2013), para. 6. See, for instance, also the statement of the then Israeli Foreign Minister Eban, Security Council Official Records, 340th meeting, 27 July 1948, 29–30: "[T]he existence of a State is a question of fact and not of law. The criterion of statehood is not legitimacy but effectiveness [...]." See also more recently Arbitration Committee attached to the Conference for Peace in Yugoslavia, Opinion No. 1, 29 November 1991, 3 *European Journal of International Law* (1992) 182: "the existence or disappearance of the state is a question of fact".

[12] See in this regard Crawford (2007), p. 5, 97.

[13] See notably Jellinek (1900), p. 304.

or extinctive prescription) serve the very purpose of (re-)aligning the legal to the factual state of affairs and thus pay homage, to draw on Georg Jellinek one more time, albeit in a somewhat decontextualized manner, to the "normative force of the factual".[14]

The sensitivity of international law when it comes to States as its principal legal subjects and actors may well also manifest itself in the reluctance to adopt any authoritative definition of the State or statehood.[15] To be sure, Article I of the 1933 Montevideo Convention states: "The State as a person of international law should possess the following qualifications: (a) a permanent population; (b) a defined territory; (c) government; and (d) capacity to enter into relations with other States."[16] While broadly relied upon,[17] this is a too ephemeral and geographically limited instance of international law-making as to be able to claim relevance on the level of general international law.[18] Moreover, it is well worth mentioning that the International Law Commission decided very early "that no useful purpose would be served by an effort to define the term 'State'".[19] Georges Scelle, one of the Commission's foremost members, was reported to have said that he "had been active in international law for more than fifty years and still did not know what a State was and he felt sure that he would not find out before he died".[20]

2 ISIS: Challenging the Dogma of the Purely Factual Character of State Formation

The theory of State formation has always been challenged by the diversity and intricacy of political realities and the ensuing meandering and often inconsistent State practice. Why, for instance, is Taiwan not considered a State even though it seems to easily and since long meet the 3-elements-test? The standard answer is that the government in Taipeh, while still insisting to be the government of China, is (at least for the moment) not itself making a claim of separate statehood of Taiwan.[21] And how come, to provide another example, that Somalia has at no moment been denied statehood even though, offering the textbook example of a failed state, its "government" only exercises effective control over a minor part of the Somali territory?[22]

[14] Jellinek (1900), p. 307.

[15] Grant (1999), p. 408; Crawford (2007), p. 37, 40.

[16] Montevideo Convention on the Rights and Duties of States, 26 December 1933, 165 LNTS 19.

[17] According to Grant (1999), pp. 413, 315 it is "[t]he source most often cited", with further references; see also Crawford (2007), p. 45: "best known formulation of the basic criteria for statehood".

[18] Grant (1999), p. 456.

[19] Yearbook of the International Law Commission, 1949, Report to the General Assembly, 289.

[20] Yearbook of the International Law Commission, 1950, Vol. 1, 2nd session, 22 June 1950, 84.

[21] Verdross and Simma (1984), p. 229.

[22] See in particular *infra* Sect. 4 regarding the case of Somaliland.

This takes us to an even more current phenomenon. After the Islamic State of Iraq had been proclaimed in 2006 and Abu Bakr al-Baghdadi had been appointed as its new emir in 2010, it was merged with the Syrian al-Nusra Front in 2013 to establish the Islamic State of Iraq and the Levant/Syria (ISIS). The following years brought the self-proclaimed worldwide caliphate considerable military successes. At its peak, ISIS controlled a landlocked territory in western Iraq and eastern Syria of more than 100,000 km^2 with a population up to 10 million persons. Since 2015, ISIS' military power was in decline and it lost all of its territory. In 2017, various leaders announced the military defeat of ISIS both in Iraq and in Syria.

However, although ISIS, in contrast to Taiwan, claimed to be an independent state (at least by name[23]) and although it used to rule over a territory and population outmatching that of many European countries, no one considered ISIS to be a State for the purposes of international law.[24] If and insofar as sticking to the orthodoxy of State formation, statehood can solely be denied to ISIS on the basis of the three traditional elements. One may argue, for instance, that ISIS might well have commanded over a vast territory, but that it was at no point (sufficiently) stable and pacified as to qualify as territory for the purposes of the 3-elements-test. In a similar vein, one may contend that while several millions of persons were under ISIS rule, they do not qualify as people, either because this group lacks homogeneity in terms of ethnicity, religion, language etc. or because the individuals in question did not voluntarily constitute themselves as a people, but were coerced into it by force, or once again because the community was too ephemeral and instable to qualify as a real people. Finally, it may be submitted that, while the control exercised by ISIS was extensive, it might not have amounted to the type of control required for a "government", either because it was too much focused on military rule or because it failed to meet basic standards of governance (e.g. democracy, human rights, rule of law).

All these arguments are not really convincing, however. The nuancing and qualification of the three criteria undermine the purely factual nature of the test and entail legal insecurity: What degree of stability of territory is needed, taking into account that controversial borders have generally not been considered an obstacle to the emergence of a State? Similarly, what degree of homogeneity is necessary to constitute a people, given that it is otherwise commonly accepted that State peoples may be highly heterogeneous in terms of ethnicity, religion and language (e.g. Canada, China, Ethiopia, India, Russia, Switzerland)? Furthermore, the very essence, and strength, of the 3-elements-test is that the criterion of government is subject to a purely factual assessment of whether there is effective control by the government over territory and people. Under this effectiveness assessment, the nature or quality of the control exercised is not relevant with the effect that a

23 The Arabic word *dawlah* which is used by ISIL as self-denomination can be translated as State although it carries various connotations beyond the modern "Western" concept of State.

24 See notably Security Resolution 2368 (2017), referring to ISIS as "a splinter group of Al-Qaida" and, more generally, as a terrorist group; as regards the latter see already Security Council Resolution 2249 (2015).

dictatorial regime is no less considered to constitute a government and thus to give rise to a State than a democratic one.

When discussing the (lacking) State quality of ISIS, some might find it useful to rely on the fourth criterion which the afore-mentioned Montevideo Convention adds to the doctrine of three elements, i.e. the capacity to enter into relations with other States.[25] After all, the community of States categorically refused to conclude agreements with ISIS, thus questioning its ability to enter into relations with States. At the same time, this criterion is mostly understood to take the perspective of the would-be State, i.e. whether the entity in question is factually able to fulfill treaty obligations it undertakes vis-à-vis other subjects of international law.[26] In addition, the prevailing opinion is that the fourth Montevideo criterion is rather a consequence than a prerequisite of statehood.[27]

Yet another strategy of dealing with the tension between the valid claims ISIS can make based on the three traditional elements of statehood and the international consensus regarding its non-State character, is to draw on the observation that if the formation of a State occurs to the detriment of an existing State and without its consent, i.e. in a situation of secession, the criteria are applied more strictly.[28] This holds true with respect to ISIS (the admission of whose existence would diminish the territory of Iraq and Syria), but is also a reasoning familiar in regard to the great many separatist movements all over the world (e.g. South Ossetia, Abkhazia, Transnistria) and may help to explain the persisting aversion of some (also European) States to qualify Kosovo as a State.[29] *Vice versa*, when it comes to the extinction of States, the elements are applied benevolently, i.e. in favor of existing States such as in the afore-mentioned case of Somalia, the prime example of a so-called "failed", but nonetheless not extinguished State.[30]

This clearly manifests the stability concerns of international law, its normative *status quo*-bias, as it were. This "law of inertia" within international law has a retarding effect both on the formation of new States and the extinction of existing ones. What is important for the present contribution, however, is that international law's bias for stability, comprehensible as it may be, transcends the realm of the purely factual. It induces elements of legitimacy into the concept of the State in the sense of a normative choice privileging the continued existence of States over the emergence of new ones. While this aspect would require an analysis in its own right, it points to a much more ambitious legitimacy-based argument regarding the formation, or rather the frustration of formation, of States inasmuch as the aspiring State's creation collides with the foundations of the international legal order.

---

[25] See *supra* note 16.

[26] Crawford (2007), pp. 45–46.

[27] Grant (1999), p. 435; Crawford (2007), pp. 61–62.

[28] Crawford (2007), p. 58; see in a similar vein Grant (1999), p. 440.

[29] For instance Cyprus or Spain, arguably particularly due to the separatist tendencies faced by these States.

[30] Grant (1999), p. 435.

3 The Advent of *Jus Cogens*: Frustrating State Formation Due to Fundamental Flaws of Legitimacy

3.1 The Contribution of the Kosovo *Advisory Opinion*

In the *Kosovo* Advisory Opinion,[31] the International Court of Justice (ICJ) took the view that unilateral declarations of independence (or, for that purpose, secessions) do not violate the principle of territorial integrity, as enshrined in Article 2(4) of the Charter of the United Nations,[32] since the scope of this principle is confined to the sphere of relations between States.[33] In this context, the ICJ also addressed the question of the impact of Security Council resolutions condemning certain instances of declarations of independence, such as in the cases of Southern Rhodesia,[34] Northern Cyprus[35] or the Republika Srpska.[36]

It is against this background that the ICJ stated in an *obiter dictum*[37] that "the illegality attached to the declarations of independence [...] stemmed [...] from the fact that they were, or would have been, connected with the unlawful use of force or other egregious violations of norms of general international law, in particular those of a peremptory character (*jus cogens*)".[38] Thus, the ICJ expressly refers to the concept of peremptory norms of general international law or *jus cogens*, as embodied in Article 53 of the Vienna Convention on the Law of Treaties (VCLT). More particularly, the Court links the *jus cogens* concept to the question of when a declaration of independence becomes unlawful under international law.

This brings a further question to the fore that is of particular interest for the purposes of this contribution: whether in case of a violation of *jus cogens* the very formation of a State is affected by illegality and the State therefore does not come into existence. The ICJ did not touch upon this problem specifically, as it did not need to do so in order to render its Opinion. According to the Court's reasoning, however, the illegality of an act of formation would arguably also infect the formation of the State itself. In particular, to the extent that *jus cogens* is considered to embody the overarching principles of the international law in opposition to which

[31] *Accordance with International Law of the Unilateral Declaration of Independence in Respect of Kosovo*, Advisory Opinion, ICJ Reports 2010, 403 (hereinafter: *Kosovo* Advisory Opinion).

[32] "All Members shall refrain in their international relations from the threat or use of force against the territorial integrity or political independence of any State, or in any other manner inconsistent with the Purposes of the United Nations."

[33] *Kosovo* Advisory Opinion, para. 80.

[34] Security Council Resolution 216 (1965), 217 (1965).

[35] Security Council Resolution 541 (1983).

[36] Security Council Resolution 787 (1992).

[37] According to the ICJ, Security Council Resolution 1244 (1999) did not have the effect of making the Kosovar declaration of independence illegal; see *Kosovo* Advisory Opinion, para. 81: "In the context of Kosovo, the Security Council has never taken this position."

[38] *Kosovo* Advisory Opinion, para. 81.

no legal act should be realized,[39] one might even argue that the existence of a State created in opposition to the precepts of *jus cogens* should be deemed unlawful *a fortiori* since it harms the foundations of the international legal order even more seriously. This kind of circular reasoning might look odd to some, and circular reasoning it is indeed. But what is reprehensible about a legal order seeking to preserve itself as well as the very values it seeks to protect and promote?

Let us assume therefore that we can count on the authority of the ICJ and more particularly the *Kosovo* Advisory Opinion for the proposition that, under international law, at least[40] the violation of *jus cogens* norms may prevent a State from coming into existence although all factual requirements to satisfy the three elements are otherwise met. This obviously contrasts with Jellinek's statement that international law can well determine the criteria under which third States may recognize other entities as a State *vel non*, but that it cannot determine the formation of States itself.[41] Yet, as already pointed out, it is up to the legal order to determine whether and to what extent to attach legal consequences to a certain set of facts and to make it legally relevant.[42] Hence, there is nothing problematic or inconsistent about conceiving of an international legal regime that limits the predominant factual approach with respect to State formation in favor of certain instances where issues of legitimacy modify or even trump the result usually to be expected in the light of the fact-focused 3-elements-test.[43] The decisive question is therefore whether international law, as it currently stands, is committed to such an *ex injuria jus non oritur* rule in the extreme case of *jus cogens* violations, thus complementing, and restricting, the *ex factis jus oritur* approach routinely governing State formation.

3.2 Jus Cogens *Violations as an Obstacle to State Formation*

There can be no doubt that the concept of peremptory norms of international law or *jus cogens* is today solidly grounded in international law. While being rooted in a provision of treaty law, i.e. Article 53 VCLT, its customary law character is not subject to controversy.[44] Furthermore, while the VCLT provides for treaties conflicting with a *jus cogens* norm to be void at the time of their conclusion (Article 53) or after the emergence of a new peremptory norm (*jus cogens superveniens*; Article 64), peremptory norms have also a derogatory effect vis-à-vis norms of customary law.[45]

---

[39] See *infra* Sect. 3.2.

[40] See *Kosovo* Advisory Opinion, para. 81: "egregious violations of norms of general international law, *in particular* those of a peremptory character" (emphasis added).

[41] Jellinek (1900), p. 245.

[42] See text preceding note 12.

[43] See Grant (1999), pp. 441–442.

[44] Schmalenbach (2018), p. 966.

[45] Schmalenbach (2018), p. 996.

This makes sense since peremptory norms are the very norms which, in a formal perspective, are accepted and recognized by the international community of States as a whole as a norm from which no derogation is permitted (Article 53 VCLT) and which, in a substantive perspective, embody the fundamental principles that govern the international legal order. They thus imply a normative hierarchy within international law, with *jus cogens* at its apex. As the "constitution" of international law, at least in a functional sense, it encompasses norms exercising public policy functions within international law, thus entailing that acts which are incompatible with international law's *ordre public* should not validly enter, or remain, within the realm of international legality.

That being said, it would be too simple to assume that every entity whose existence is linked to a violation of *jus cogens* is to be automatically considered null and void. According to Article 71(2)(b) VCLT, at least in the case of *jus cogens superveniens*, the voidness of a treaty is not fully retroactive, as it "does not affect any right, obligation or legal situation of the parties created through the execution of the treaty prior to its termination; provided that those rights, obligations or situations may thereafter be maintained only to the extent that their maintenance is not in itself in conflict with the new peremptory norm of general international law". Hence, also and even in case of *jus cogens*, international law's readiness to maintain the *status quo* to avoid legal insecurity and protect legitimate expectations becomes manifest. Yet, if and to the extent that there is a straightforward contradiction between an acquired right or legal situation and a new *jus cogens* norm, the latter will trump the former.

The differentiated balancing approach embodied in this provision of treaty law is also reflected in the international law of responsibility that governs the legal consequences of breaches of international law, so-called internationally wrongful acts. According to Article 41 of the Articles on State Responsibility (ASR),[46] States shall cooperate to bring to an end through lawful means any serious breach of a peremptory norm of general international law, and no State shall recognize as lawful a situation created by a serious breach nor render aid or assistance in maintaining that situation. Yet, these special legal consequences only arise in case of a "serious" breach of a *jus cogens* norm, i.e. pursuant to Article 40(2) ASR "if it involves a gross or systematic failure by the responsible State to fulfill the obligation", and therefore not in case of normal or simple breaches of *jus cogens* norms.

When putting these elements together, the existing international law on State formation can arguably be restated, as follows: State formation is essentially still governed by the effectiveness principle as manifested in the three-elements doctrine, i.e. the test whether the elements of territory, people and government are factually present to a sufficient degree for an entity to qualify as a State. However, on an exceptional basis and as a limited, but significant concession of contemporary international law to legitimacy concerns, if the coming into existence of a would-be State itself is directly tainted by, and not only indirectly linked to, a serious breach

[46] Articles on Responsibility of States for Internationally Wrongful Acts, as annexed to General Assembly Resolution 56/83 of 12 December 2001.

of a *jus cogens* norm, the ensuing entity is not to be considered a State even though the three elements of territory, people and government may otherwise have sufficiently materialized to qualify the entity as a State.[47]

3.3 *Relevant* Jus Cogens *Norms*

If this restatement of the law is accepted, it still remains to be clarified which *jus cogens* norms actually entail the voidness of a would-be State, i.e. its non-coming into existence despite meeting the effectiveness test. The afore-mentioned Security Council resolutions[48] provide important indications in this regard.

When qualifying the declaration of independence of the Turkish Republic of Northern Cyprus as legally invalid, the Security Council referred to the 1960 Treaty concerning the establishment of the Republic of Cyprus and the 1960 Treaty of Guarantee.[49] However, going beyond that, the Security Council's call on all States to respect the sovereignty, independence, territorial integrity and non-alignment of the Republic of Cyprus already hints at the relevance of the prohibition of the use of force in the context of the Northern Cyprus case.[50] Otherwise, the further call on all States not to recognize any Cypriot State other than the Republic of Cyprus[51] would be difficult to understand. After all, recognition of an unlawful situation is not *per se* forbidden by international law,[52] notably if the illegality arises from violation of a treaty to which the recognizing State is not a party.

In fact, it was the Turkish act of aggression vis-à-vis Cyprus and its creation, and maintenance, of a puppet regime in the island's northern part that guided the Security Council in its decision-making. This course of action stands in the tradition of the so-called Stimson doctrine which was developed by the then US Secretary of State Henry L. Stimson in view of the Manchurian crisis of the early 1930ies: the US and the League of Nations' answer to Japan's creation of the puppet state of Manchukuo in eastern China was the refusal to recognize territorial changes resulting from aggression.[53] Subsequently, in the wake of World War II, the prohibition of the use

---

[47] See in a similar vein Grant (1999), pp. 411, 441, 450; Crawford (2007), pp. 46, 98, 102, 105, 107; Taki (2013), para. 10, with further references; see also Report of the Independent International Fact-Finding Mission on the Conflict in Georgia, September 2009, Vol. II, 128, qualifying certain "criteria of legitimacy" as an "additional standard for the qualification of an entity as a state". See in general regarding the rise of legitimacy reasoning after World War II Franck (1990).

[48] See *supra* notes 34–36.

[49] Security Council Resolution 541 (1983), preamb. para. 3.

[50] Ibid., op. para. 2.

[51] Ibid., op. para. 7. Subsequently, Security Council Resolution 550 (1984) condemned the recognition of the Turkish Republic of Northern Cyprus by Turkey (which is still the only State to have done so).

[52] Crawford (2007), p. 158.

[53] Grant (2014), paras. 8 ff.

of force and the corollary prohibition of the acquisition of territory by force or annexation was solemnly enshrined in Article 2(4) of the UN Charter.[54]

Against this background, Northern Cyprus may serve as the textbook example of a purported act of State formation which has, however, not succeeded since it is the direct result of a major violation of the prohibition of the use of force and therefore of *jus cogens*.[55] In a similar vein, in reaction to the declaration of independence of the Republika Srpska, i.e. of the Serbian population within Bosnia and Herzegovina, the Security Council affirmed its call to respect strictly the territorial integrity of the latter State and that "any entities unilaterally declared or arrangements imposed in contravention thereof will not be accepted".[56]

The link becomes even clearer in view of Iraq's attempted annexation of Kuwait in 1990, where the Security Council decided that "the annexation of Kuwait by Iraq under any form and whatever pretext has no legal validity, and is considered null and void" and called upon all States "not to recognize that annexation, and to refrain from any action or dealing that might be interpreted as an indirect recognition of the annexation".[57] If due to the use of force not only the amputation of an existing State, but its very extinction is at stake,[58] international law strongly, and persistently, resists this arguably most momentous violation of *jus cogens*, despite prolonged lack of effectiveness.[59]

In view of the considerations above,[60] it must be conceded, however, that, fundamental as the prohibition of the use of force might be, not every single isolated instance of violation of that principle can be held to preclude the statehood of an entity otherwise qualifying under the traditional criteria. Correspondingly, if the violation of a peremptory norm such as the prohibition of the use of force is crucial to the existence of the entity in question, international law does justifiably not treat an effective entity as a State.

---

[54] "All Members shall refrain in their international relations from the threat or use of force against the territorial integrity or political independence of any state, or in any other manner inconsistent with the Purposes of the United Nations." See further, elaborating upon this basis, General Assembly Resolution 2625 (1970), the so-called Friendly Relations Declaration ("No territorial acquisition resulting from the threat or use of force shall be recognized as legal.") as well as General Assembly Resolution 3314 (1974): "No territorial acquisition or special advantage resulting from aggression is or shall be recognized as lawful."

[55] Even though it may also be explained in the traditional sense by referring to the lack of genuine governmental power of the Northern Cypriot authorities as they widely act under the orders of the government in Ankara, notably in the light of the significant military presence of Turkey in Northern Cyprus; see in this regard ECtHR, *Cyprus v. Turkey*, Appl. No. 25781/94, Judgment, 10 May 2001, para. 77.

[56] Security Council Resolution 787 (1992), op. para. 2.

[57] Security Council Resolution 662 (1990), op. paras. 1 and 2.

[58] See *supra* text following note 30 regarding the "law of inertia" in international law.

[59] See also the example of the Baltic States which were conquered by the Soviet Union in 1940, but were considered to continue to exist as sovereign States until they could regain their independence half a century later.

[60] See *supra* Sect. 3.2.

While this reasoning can explain Northern Cyprus' lack of statehood and also that of entities such as South Ossetia, Abkhazia or Transnistria which owe their current existence to violations of the prohibition of the use of force on the part of Russia, the non-acceptance of the statehood of ISIS cannot be explained in this manner. To be sure, the establishment of ISIS was evidently secured by massive use of force. However, the authors of this force are generally not considered to have acted on behalf of a State. As non-state actors they are not bound by the prohibition of the use of force which is addressed to States (and, for that matter, *de facto* regimes).[61]

The Southern Rhodesia case may bring further insights in this respect. In 1965, the Security Council condemned the unilateral declaration of independence made by the "illegal racist minority regime in Southern Rhodesia" and called upon all States not to recognize it.[62] As in the ISIS case, no violation of the prohibition of the use of force principle was involved. Alas, the project of the Ian Smith government to set up an apartheid state under the control of the white settler minority deeply affected, and violated, peremptory norms,[63] notably the principle of self-determination of peoples,[64] but arguably also constituted a systematic violation of fundamental human rights[65] such as the prohibition of apartheid. In a contemporary perspective, one would also include the prohibition of genocide and crimes against humanity in the list of relevant *jus cogens* norms. It is particularly with a view of the massive amounts of crimes of humanity and arguably even genocide committed for the sake of creating ISIS that, beyond the arguments on the factual level,[66] one can reasonably challenge the legitimacy foundations of ISIS since its very establishment has been intrinsically linked to violations of peremptory norms of general international law.

At the current stage of development of international law, however, while outright denial of self-determination and persecution amounting to genocide and crimes against humanity qualify as *jus cogens* norms whose violation may constitute a bar to State formation, it is doubtful whether the respect of democracy or the protection of minorities may qualify as peremptory norms for the afore-mentioned purposes.[67] This is not to say that they do not play any role at all in the context of State formation, notably in context of the design of recognition practices by States. Thus, it is

---

[61] See *Kosovo* Advisory Opinion, para. 80. Also Security Council Resolution 1244 (1999) did not contain any obligations for individuals even though the ICJ accepted that the Security Council could have created such obligations; see further Schroeder and Müller (2011), pp. 374–376.

[62] Security Council Resolution 216 (1965); Security Council Resolution 217 (1965), op. paras. 3 and 6.

[63] Grant (1999), p. 411.

[64] Crawford (2007), pp. 98, 148.

[65] See for the opposite view, Crawford (2007), p. 148: "there is so far in modern practice no suggestion that as regards statehood itself, there exists any criterion requiring regard for fundamental human rights"; see ibid., 155: "this has not matured into a peremptory norm disqualifying an entity from statehood even in the cases of widespread violations of human rights".

[66] See *supra* Sect. 2.

[67] Grant (1999), pp. 442–445; see further Orakhelashvili (2006), pp. 50–66.

important to conceptually distinguish between the prerequisites of State formation and the recognition of a State by its peers.

4 Legitimacy Concerns and Policies of Recognition

Recognition of States has so far only ephemerally been referred to, and chiefly in a negative manner. Indeed, there is consensus that in case of serious violations of peremptory norms of general international law, all States are under an obligation of non-recognition of the situation created by such serious breach (Article 41 ASR).[68] This rule has been confirmed in international jurisprudence, notably in cases of (attempts of) annexation[69] and is consistent with the Security Council practice discussed above.[70]

That this duty of non-recognition must be conceptually distinguished from the general practice of recognition of States, which rather reflects political choice than legal obligation, was aptly expressed by Judge Skubiszewski in the *East Timor* case: "While recognition of States or Governments is still a 'free act', it is not so with regard to the irregular acquisition of territory: here the discretionary nature of the act has been changed by the rule on the prohibition on the threat or use of force. [...] [T]he rule of non-recognition operates in a self-executory way. To be operative, it does not need to be repeated by the UN or other international organizations. Consequently, the absence of such a direction on the part of an international organization does not relieve any state from the duty of non-recognition."[71]

Furthermore, inasmuch as "premature" recognition, i.e. recognition of an entity as a State before it meets the 3-elements-test, is considered a violation of the obligation of non-interference,[72] also this aspect of recognition is governed by international law and not simply subject to State discretion.

Apart from that, however, States seek to retain for themselves as much freedom of action with regard to new States as possible.[73] This opens a space of maneuvering for the existing States in which they can develop their policies of recognition according to their political, economic, etc. preferences, their strategic and tactical choices. No State is under a legal obligation to extend recognition to a newly formed State even though it may clearly meet all requirements of the 3-elements test. (It may be

---

68 See *supra* Sect. 3.2; see in general also Lauterpacht (1947), and Talmon (2006).

69 See in this context notably *Legal Consequences of the Continued Presence of South Africa in Namibia (South West Africa)*, Advisory Opinion, ICJ Reports 1971, 16, para. 119; *Legal Consequences of the Construction of a Wall in the Occupied Palestinian Territory*, Advisory Opinion, ICJ Reports 2004, 136, para. 159.

70 See *supra* notes 34–36 as well as 57.

71 *East Timor (Portugal* v. *Australia)*, Judgment, ICJ Reports 1995, 90, Dissenting Opinion of Judge Skubiszewski, paras. 129–130.

72 See, for instance, Oppenheim (1955), p. 128.

73 Crawford (2007), p. 45.

added only in parenthesis that our discussion has now eventually arrived at the perpetual doctrinal dispute whether recognition is constitutive or only declaratory for the formation of new States, and it is obvious that the present discussion only makes sense when following that majority approach that recognition is not a condition for statehood in international law.[74] Beyond this clarification, there is no need to delve into the intricacies of this doctrinal dispute.)

It is rather of interest to direct the attention to the fact that, apart from all kinds of motives that may become relevant in shaping a State's recognition policy, also legitimacy concerns may play a role in this context. In particular, there have been attempts notably in the post-Cold War period to make recognition dependent on the respect of international law standards such as democracy, human rights, protection of minorities or the rule of law. The best known example are the 1991 Guidelines on the Recognition of New States in Eastern Europe and in the Soviet Union of the then European Community (today: European Union),[75] affirming the EU States' "readiness to recognize [...] those new States which [...] have constituted themselves on a democratic basis", including respect for the UN Charter and the Final Act of Helsinki and the Charter of Paris, "especially with regard to the rule of law, democracy and human rights" as well as "guarantees for the rights of ethnic and national groups and minorities".

In some ways, admission to membership in international organizations has become a functional complement of State recognition. In particular, admission to UN membership is today a very strong indicator, if not irrefutable proof of fulfillment of all necessary elements to constitute a State.[76] The requirement that only "peace-loving" states "which accept the obligations contained in the present Charter and, in the judgment of the Organization, are able and willing to carry out these obligations" (Article 4(1) UN Charter) would even permit the UN to pursue a more ambitious "recognition" policy on the model of the afore-mentioned European guidelines. However, in the practice of the Organization, this aspect of the provision has hardly become relevant.[77]

More generally, while legitimacy considerations may result in deferral or even refusal of recognition, the impact of such additional "conditions" to recognition of statehood should not be overestimated, notably given the host of competing interests

---

[74] See, for instance, Crawford (2007), p. 19 ff.

[75] Adopted at an Extraordinary EPC Ministerial Meeting on 16 December 1991, available in 4 *European Journal of International Law* (1993) 72; see also reflection of this in work of Arbitration Committee attached to the Conference for Peace in Yugoslavia (the so-called Bacinter Commission).

[76] After all, according to Article 4(1) of the UN Charter, UN membership is exclusively open to States. In practice, what counts even more is the requirement under Article 4(2) of the UN Charter that admission will be effected by majority decision of the General Assembly "upon the recommendation of the Security Council", which guarantees that the State quality of the candidate to membership must have the blessing of at least the five permanent members of the Security Council which could otherwise veto the recommendation resolution; see *Competence of the General Assembly for the Admission of a State to the United Nations*, Advisory Opinion, ICJ Reports 1950, 4, 10; see further Hillgruber (1998).

[77] Fastenrath (2012), p. 348.

that also inform the recognition policies of State.[78] The high volatility existing with respect to recognition practices also becomes manifest, for instance, in the example of Somaliland: The Republic of Somaliland declared its independence from Somalia already in 1991 and in fact claims that it thereby re-established the short independence it had already enjoyed in 1960. While Somaliland arguably meets all aspects of the 3-elements-test, and in a quite stable fashion, it is still not considered a sovereign State by any State. The reluctance to recognized Somaliland are obviously strongly linked to the afore-mentioned "law of inertia"[79] and the fear that giving recognition to such act of secession may give rise to an unwanted domino effect, taking into account that many States, in particular in Africa, face secessionist movements.

5 Conclusion

Thus, the effectiveness-legitimacy conundrum regarding State formation is far from being solved. According to the heterogeneous State practice, entities that meet the criteria of the effectiveness-based 3-elements-test are not recognized as States, and other entities that fail to fulfill its requirements may be still (prematurely) recognized as States, even for the price of engaging one's responsibility for unlawfully interfering with another State's affairs.

However, what can be said in the light of the previous discussion is that State formation remains to be chiefly governed by the effectiveness principle as manifested in the three-elements doctrine. At the same time, given the development of international law in the post-World War II period and notably in the light of the emergence of the *jus cogens* concept, on an exceptional basis, if the coming into existence of a would-be State itself is directly tainted by a serious breach of a peremptory norm of general international law, the international law of State formation has meanwhile incorporated legitimacy concerns in the sense that the ensuing entity is not to be considered a State although the three factual elements of territory, people and government may otherwise have sufficiently materialized to qualify the entity as a State. Against this background, it can be explained why an entity such as ISIS does not qualify as a State, without a need to re-interpret the factual elements of State formation.

Conversely, the increasing importance of legitimacy considerations vis-à-vis pure effectiveness reasoning also becomes manifest in the opposite direction. If *jus cogens*-related grounds militate in favor of the emergence of a new State, the effectiveness-based criteria might be handled more benevolently, thus working against the afore-described law of inertia regarding State formation.[80] The case in point would be post-World War II international law's strong option for

[78] See, for instance, the well-balanced discussion in Grant (1999), pp. 440–445.

[79] See *supra* text following note 30.

[80] See Taki (2013), para. 13.

self-determination of colonized peoples, with the consequence that early recognition of an entity with, for instance, only weak governmental power as a State may nonetheless not be qualified as a premature recognition and therefore in compliance with the principle of non-interference.

To be sure, one must be prepared for the criticism, already present in Jellinek's oeuvre,[81] that such opening of the regime of State formation to legitimacy considerations instead of exclusively relying on the factual situation, carries the risk of alienating international law from reality—the very situation the principle of effectiveness has traditionally sought to avoid. At the same time, international law might run the risk of becoming ineffective as a normative system precisely if it is not prepared to challenge effective but unlawful situations. To take the position that an entity that, while effectively existing, was created in the course of serious violations of the most fundamental principles of contemporary international law, should not only be denied recognition as a State, but considered not existent in the eyes of the international legal order, is not an irrational or irresponsible choice to make for international law.

Instead of simply giving in to power, such course of action can help to keep controversial issues on the agenda, for years and even decades to come (e.g. Northern Cyprus),[82] until the situation might change and render a settlement possible which is compatible with the normative foundations of international law. Acting in such a manner will obviously not always prevent the formation of political entities in contravention to peremptory norms. It may, however, nonetheless create significant disincentives for States and other actors on the international plane in the sense that they will be made aware of how long it may take and how much it will cost them, if they manage at all, to force the law into rubber-stamping the reality they seek to bring about.

References

Crawford J (2007) The creation of states, 2nd edn. Clarendon Press, Oxford

Fastenrath U (2012) Article 4. In: Simma B et al (eds) The Charter of the United Nations. A commentary, 3rd edn. Oxford University Press, Oxford, pp 341–361

Franck TM (1990) The power of legitimacy among nations. Oxford University Press, Oxford

Grant TD (1999) Defining statehood: the Montevideo Convention and its discontens. Columbia J Transnl Law 37:403–457

Grant TD (2014) Doctrines. In: Wolfrum R (ed) Max Planck Encyclopedia of Public International Law. http://opil.ouplaw.com/home/epil

Hillgruber C (1998) Die Aufnahme neuer Staaten in die Völkerrechtsgemeinschaft. Peter Lang, Frankfurt a.M

Jellinek G (1900) Allgemeine Staatslehre. Häring, Berlin

[81] Jellinek (1900), p. 244; but see also the continuing criticism and doubt whether conformity with international legal rules should be considered a prerequisite to statehood; Grant (1999), p. 442, with further references.

[82] See also Crawford (2007), pp. 98–99.

Lauterpacht H (1947) Recognition in international law. Cambridge University Press, Cambridge
Oppenheim L (1955) International law, vol 1, 8th edn. Longmans, Green & Co, London
Orakhelashvili A (2006) Peremptory norms in international law. Oxford University Press, Oxford
Schmalenbach K (2018) Article 53. In: Dörr O, Schmalenbach K (eds) Vienna Convention on the law of treaties. A commentary, 2nd edn. Springer, Berlin, pp 965–1012
Schroeder W, Müller AT (2011) Elements of supranationality in the law of international organizations. In: Fastenrath U et al (eds) From bilateralism to community interest. Oxford University Press, Oxford, pp 358–378
Shaw MN (2008) International law, 6th edn. Cambridge University Press, Cambridge
Taki H (2013) Effectiveness. In: Wolfrum R (ed) Max Planck Encyclopedia of Public International Law. http://opil.ouplaw.com/home/epil
Talmon S (2006) Kollektive Nichtanerkennung illegaler Staaten. Mohr Siebeck, Tübingen
Tomuschat C (2017) Effectiveness and legitimacy in international law. Heidelberg J Int Law 77:309–320
Verdross A, Simma B (1984) Universelles Völkerrecht. Theorie und Praxis, 3rd edn. Duncker & Humblot, Berlin
von Arnauld A (2016) Völkerrecht, 3rd edn. C.F. Müller, Heidelberg

How the Facts Enter Into the Law

Clemens Jabloner

Abstract This article addresses the role of "facts" in the application of the law; distinguishing "facts of reality"—things as they are—and the "state of facts" as established by a court when rendering a judgment. The law being a normative order, an order of "ought", can only process "facts of reality" by transforming them into "states of fact". This process designates their entry into the legal system. Hence the author construes the finding of fact as being a separate, procedural act of law, its formula being: "The court deems it established". Of course, the "state of fact" itself is often layered and contains normative elements, which are transformed into factual ones. This repeated transformation is prone to errors and conceals accountability in the relationship between the court and expert witnesses. This is a particularly topical issue which even increased cooperation may not change for the better; instead, the separation between expert knowledge and decision making should be made transparent.

1 Introduction: Legal Mind and Expert Mind

"Anyone who copies or falsifies currency with the intent that it be brought into circulation as real and genuine shall be punished with imprisonment of one to ten years," as stated in Section 232 para. 1 of the Austrian Criminal Code: The elements of the offence and the legal consequences.

Someone copies euro notes to pay for his opera tickets. This behaviour fits the elements of the offence, which should in turn trigger a legal consequence. The elements of the offence are therefore fulfilled when they correspond to something concrete. But since only a statement about facts—and not the facts themselves—is subsumable, only this constitutes the "state of facts", that is, the facts stated in the judgment. Hereinafter, "state of facts" shall therefore mean a linguistic *assertion* of facts, whereas the facts themselves are empirically knowable events or situations.

C. Jabloner (✉)
University of Vienna, Vienna, Austria
e-mail: clemens.jabloner@univie.ac.at

N. Bersier Ladavac et al. (eds.), *The Normative Force of the Factual*, Law and Philosophy Library 130, https://doi.org/10.1007/978-3-030-18929-7_7

The so-called "legal subsumption", i.e. bringing into correspondence the elements of the offence and the state of facts, is the most important tool for the application of law: when the legal facts of the offence are met, a person authorized to do so should impose the prescribed legal consequences.

Before the authority appointed to enforce the law—be it a court or an administrative authority—imposes the legal consequences, it must therefore resolve a twofold task: on the one hand, it has to determine the legal framework for the elements of the offence and the legal consequences; on the other hand, it has to determine the facts as provided in the elements of the offence and bring them into the form of "state of facts".[1] The former is a normative-doctrinal task, the latter a logical-empirical one.[2] Both are knowledge, i.e. "knowledge functions", for which the authority needs a specialized "legal mind" and an expert mind. Moreover, both functions lead to a decision, that is to say a "function of the will". The expression of the "function of the will" is a legal act, a well-founded judgment—or even an act of coercion.

The court must have its own legal mind: *iura novit curia*. The required expertise, on the other hand, can be so demanding that it needs support. For the provision of expertise there are different legal and technical models, including (but not limited to) an officially appointed expert, a collegiate body of experts, an official representative of an administrative authority, an expert advisory board, and finally the use of private expertise.[3]

When the same person exercises legal and expert knowledge, the distinctions discussed in this contribution are psychologically less noticeable as when the two functions are divided among different people. That does not alter the fundamental problem, however. Only when the expert witness comes into play does it become very clear. The sole task of the expert witness is to identify certain facts and to clarify them by means of his particular expert knowledge. The division of responsibilities between law and expertise—where it is personalized—can even be considered a special element of the separation of powers.[4]

At the first glance one is tempted to equate the distinction between matters of law and matters of fact with the separation of competence between the judge and the jury, as it is the case in American civil procedure.[5] However, generally speaking, this

[1] Cf., for example, Engisch (1996), p. 57.

[2] Here, concrete, individualized facts, general empirical propositions and logical inferences are linked together—cf. Wolff (1947), p. 165, and, more in-depth, Petschek and Stagel (1963) p. 215. On "empirical judgments", cf. Rechberger (1974), p. 113; on the problem of judicial everyday theories, see also Pawlowski (1999), para 266.

[3] Cf. for more details Merli (2013), pp. 173–188.

[4] According to Klecatsky (1961), p. 311. On the other hand, the Austrian Administrative Court does not consider it problematic that an administrative body draws on its own expert knowledge when deciding a case (cf. VwSlg 8303 A/1972; VwGH 31 January 1995, 92/05/0230).

[5] Cf. Weiner (1966).

is only one possible way. In many jurisdictions, and especially in criminal procedure, the jurors also decide upon questions of law.[6]

The relationship between the legal mind and outsourced expertise has always been delicate and has often been addressed in the literature.[7] Today, the problems have only become clearer; they first appear as issues of bias: at the request of the Austrian Supreme Court, the Constitutional Court rejected the unrestricted dual role of the expert witness in criminal proceedings, who works first as an in-house expert for the prosecution, then as an expert witness for the court.[8] In administrative procedure, the role of the agency's in-house experts is questionable with regard to the fair trial requirement of Article 6 of the European Convention on Human Rights.[9] The issue is only more pressing in continental jurisdictions, where the court typically has to appoint an expert witness on its own if it lacks the necessary expertise, without the parties being involved, and without them being able to present their own expert witnesses.

Even deeper than these issues lies the question of demarcation: on the one hand, it is about the practical incompetence of the legal mind in the face of expertise—a situation that is sometimes criticized on an abstract level, but is oftentimes accepted not unwillingly. Across the entire legal system, we perceive that the substantive content of the law, whether it is statutory or case law, is dispensed with when a tired jurist becomes too familiar with expertise. It is certainly clear that, in an increasingly complex world, more and more expertise is required. As a result, this may, of course, lead to a "privatization of the law", in the specific sense that the standards and norms drafted by expert circles are blindly incorporated into the law. In this way, certain interests can be enforced by means of the democratic process.[10] Nevertheless, if genuine political decisions are masked as neutral expertise, this certainly is a problem for democratic legitimacy.[11]

On the other hand, there is also the opposite tendency, where issues become regulated by law or by the courts that one might think are the sole responsibility of experts. This problem only intensifies when dealing with a knowledgeable defendant, such as a physician who does not want his medical assessment to be measured by criminal law, a frequent problem in medical malpractice trials. Both tendencies collide when there is a governmental regulatory impulse, which is then immediately delegated to expert circles.

The following is an attempt to shed some light on the problems outlined above. The main aim is to determine the status of the legal facts, which oscillates so

[6] For example, Article 91 of the Austrian Federal Constitutional Act empowers the jury (Geschworene) to decide upon the "guilt" (Schuld) of the accused, which is understood to encompass both the facts and the law.

[7] Cf. Kaufmann (1985), p. 1065.

[8] Cf. VfGH 10 March 2015, G 180/14, among others.

[9] Cf. Merli (2015), p. 29.

[10] For a basic explanation, cf. Eisenberger (2016), pp. 118, 128.

[11] Cf. Eisenberger (2016), p. 150.

peculiarly between the normative and the factual spheres. If this succeeds, we could gain a clearer—and more ideologically critical—view of the problems mentioned.

2 The State of Facts as a Component of Legal Procedure

2.1 Is and Ought

If we understand law as a normative order and, accordingly, see the task of jurisprudence in describing, but not creating or evaluating the law, then everything stands or falls by the consequent distinction between what is and what ought to be, between norms and facts, between knowing and willing.[12] However, the law does not exist for its own sake; it is intended to control human conduct, so it needs to be applied. In doing so, the law naturally runs into the facts and must incorporate them without losing its normative character.

The linkage between these two spheres is what operates as the "state of facts", or *Sachverhalt* in German, which must be distinguished from mere "facts", or *Tatsachen*.[13] With its help, the law—here in its judicial concretization—processes the facts. This coupling is also necessary because a social system can only communicate with its environment through specific interfaces.[14] The carefully guarded border between norms and facts thus becomes permeable at certain crossings. At these points, however, the facts (*Tatsachen*) are not simply rubber-stamped but are transformed, translated or imported as needed. That is the function of the "state of facts" (*Sachverhalt*).

2.2 The Truth of the Facts

The court determines the facts with which it applies its legal provisions, applying rules of evidence. Today, these rules require the court to determine the true facts by proceeding logically and empirically in order to reach appropriate conclusions. Historically this is by no means a self-evident as examples as the trial by ordeal or a confession extracted through torture amply demonstrate.

Of course, the procedural rules can still prescribe more or less specifically which sources may be used and which may not (inadmissible evidence) and, if necessary, even in which hierarchy. Both the receiving of evidence as well as its appraisal can be regulated in a constitutional framework (Article 6 ECHR). In addition, there is

12 Cf. Kelsen (1967), pp. 70 ff.

13 The modern German terminology is very keen to distinguish correctly between the elements of the offence (*Tatbestand*) and the state of facts (*Sachverhalt*). For the historical development of this wording, see the original German version of this article: Jabloner (2016), p. 203.

14 Cf. Luhmann (2004), p. 381.

the principle of "free evaluation of evidence," (*freie Beweiswürdigung*) which is a subset of judicial discretion.[15] The court is, in principle, free to appraise the evidence in any way it sees fit. This does not amount to arbitrariness, since the court remains obliged make its conclusions in a transparent way. Finally, the court must, in principle, be certain of at least the "superior probability" of the facts; their mere possibility is not enough. However, procedural law may provide for further mitigation, for example if "prima facie evidence" already suffices. Only when the court is no longer able to balance alternative versions of the "state of facts" does it reach for the "*in dubio pro reo* rule" in criminal law.[16]

The free evaluation of evidence is of central importance in several respects: on the one hand, it is the expression of a paradigm shift away from the medieval Inquisition process, which equated truth with absolute certainty—and, out of longing for the same, resorted to torture—until insight into the inefficiency of this method prevailed.[17] More rational, and, incidentally, more humane, are empirically obtained findings and confidence in the court's power of judgement. On the other hand, this modern legal understanding is thoroughly compatible with a modern understanding of science, according to which science cannot provide absolute truths, but (only) falsifiable theses.

It must be admitted that, in the course of a trial, ultimately everything is negotiated, including the truth.[18] However, from an internal point of view, the court is thoroughly committed to a correspondence theory of truth: that the state of facts is understood as a mirror of the real conditions or circumstances.[19] The evaluation of evidence thus only compensates for the uncertainty that is gradually deconstructed—or rather, that is continuously reconstructed—in the scientific falsification process; a process which has no end. In a trial, which must legally come to an end, this is done by the court.

That even the truth is negotiated before the court is strikingly exemplified by the principle of "formal truth", as it is known to some continental traditions. In civil procedure, the parties can "agree on the facts", which means that the court has to take for granted what the parties assert unanimously, even if that is untrue; it has to confine itself to the law and has to take the facts as given: *da mihi facta, dabo tibi ius*. The parties' assertions are not understood as statements of knowledge but are put forward as manifestations of intent; as Georg Petschek has elegantly phrased it, the party wants "*to accept the relevant facts as binding regardless of their truth*".[20]

[15] Ringhofer (1966), p. 25.

[16] Cf. Engisch (1996), p. 69.

[17] It is a feature of a more modern worldview that certainty has been dispensed with. Such a view can permit only one religion. If God is no longer properly believed in, then certainty must be defined differently. So here it is precisely the beginning of the Enlightenment that gives birth to monsters.

[18] On why a seemingly pragmatic model of scientific truth finding—consensus theory—approaches a legal proceeding, cf., pointedly, Möllers (2010), p. 127.

[19] Cf. Schweizer (2015), p. 79.

[20] Petschek and Stagel (1963), p. 227.

However, beyond this disposition, in criminal and administrative procedure, the principle of "substantive truth" applies; meaning that the court has to investigate the facts itself regardless of the will of the parties.

2.3 The "Ought" of the Facts

To which world does the state of facts belong? Kelsen addresses this question in the second edition of his *Pure Theory*, in a discussion on the constitutive nature of case law: "*Even the ascertainment of the facts that a delict has been committed represents an entirely constitutive function of the court*", and further: "*It is only by this ascertainment that the fact reaches the realm of law, only then does a natural fact become a legal fact – it is created as a legal fact*."[21]

Kelsen calls "legal fact" what in this essay has been called "state of facts". What is relevant is that the mere facts of reality need to be transformed into the facts of the case by an act of the court: Apparently, Kelsen does not refer to the triviality that the court can only determine what it knows, but that the court generates the facts in their normative meaning in the first place by "ascertaining" them. Thus, even with regard to the facts, the court has to impose an act of volition according to its cognitive function. This may not always be self-evident. Nevertheless, even where there is no room for free evaluation of evidence, because the facts are so clear, the court must seek to establish *this* fact rather than *another*.

The normativity of the state of facts does not therefore result from the court's compliance with legal rules, as those also exist for factual activities such as driving a car. Nor is the sole determining factor that the court makes a decision. To be sure, every decision contains a normative element insofar as "making a decision" means, at a minimum, setting a norm for oneself, binding oneself to a certain behaviour. However, by no means is every decision aimed at producing an act of law. It is also necessary for the subjective "ought" to be an objective "ought". Moreover, for that, it is decisive for the court to be in a procedure that leads to an act of law—the judgment.

Having thus obtained the facts logically and empirically, the law-applying body must transform this knowledge into a statement that becomes part of the verdict's reasons. Through this act of volition, the facts mutate from the realm of the "is" into that of the "ought": *so shall it be*; or: *so shall it have been*; or: *the court takes it for granted.*[22] *The court deems it established*—that is the positively magical incantation for it.

---

[21] Kelsen (1967), p. 239.

[22] *Prima vista*, one could understand the facts as fiction. The concept of fiction, however, is dubious. In a legal sense, it can only be used where something is established as counterfactual, not merely if it is established. In contrast to Vaihinger, Kelsen argued that, although the law can be seen as fiction, this view is not helpful within the law. Of course, the court's acceptance of the facts does not preclude that things have actually happened; on the contrary. Seen in this way, the facts are normalized by the court, but not fabricated. For more detail, cf. Kletzer (2015).

2.4 The Function of the State of Facts

In the context of the judgment, the state of facts has a specific relationship to the verdict: the state of facts has no meaning on its own, but exists only because it underpins a judgment, whereas the judgment does not make sense without the specific state of facts. A judgment is an individual legal norm. As such, it applies only within a certain scope. It regulates human behaviour, so it must be determined who has to behave in what way, when and where. In its specificity as an individual and concrete norm, a judgment cannot be thought of without this provision.[23]

That the determination of the state of facts in the judgment occurs in due course with other elements does not affect its logical precedence. It can therefore be understood as a "constituent component of legal procedure".[24] That means that a legal act can be a constituent part of another legal act, just as a statute is composed at least of three component acts: the adoption of the bill in the two chambers of Congress and the signing into law by the President.

Ultimately, the independent existence of the state of facts is also shown in how they can be more or less "taken for granted" in the appeals process if the appellate court is not allowed to rehear the facts.[25] Strictly speaking, the appeals court cannot "review" the evidence procedure[26]: either the evidence is examined anew or the court only looks for procedural errors. At most, evidence can be produced in this context in order to verify the relevance of procedural errors.[27]

As soon as a judgment finally enters into legal force—that is, when it is no longer appealable—it creates an "ought-fact", which includes not only the legal evaluation, but also the state of facts. Fundamentally, the "dogmatization" of an event or other facts that has been achieved in this way is immutable; that any dispute must end corresponds to one of the most fundamental functions of the law, keeping and restoring the peace. In modern, constitutional procedural rules, this is of course limited once again. Very serious errors in fact-finding can lead to the case being reopened, even after a long period. This may be restricted, however, to such instances as when sources have been forged or new sources emerge, not merely if the existing sources are reappraised. Here, of course, we have a decisive difference to—ever revisionist—science.[28]

[23] Alternatively, state of facts could also be interpreted as a resolute condition of validity.

[24] The other founder of the "Pure Theory", Adolf Merkl, remarked that in a dynamic perspective, a legal act of a certain force is composed of various partial acts like the many frames of a film. Cf Merkl (1927), pp. 91 ff.

[25] The binding effect of the facts resulting from the force of law (in the broader sense) is discussed in doctrine and case law in two contexts, first with regard to which factual changes terminate the scope of the decision and how to react to this in procedural terms—cf. Ringhofer (1953), pp. 87, 120.

[26] Cf. Pawlowski (1999), para 267.

[27] Cf. VwSlg 6714/A and 9723A/1978 as well as *Ringhofer* (n. 14) 366. This case law, however, has rarely gained practical relevance.

[28] The discipline of historiography, as any science (*Wissenschaft*), is involved in a constant process of falsification. Here it should be noted that, in exceptional cases, the law "dogmatizes" certain

3 The Janus-Faced Facts

3.1 The State of Facts as a Re-Entry of the Facts

In this transformation of the facts from "is" to "ought", one may well observe a triviality, an exercise of thought and will, which is envisaged by the law all the same. It has not yet been clarified, however, how this transformation takes place. A closer look shows that the "law"[29] has to perform a special mental operation: it can only admit those facts that have previously been carefully isolated from it by transforming them in components of the legal act; an operation of "re-entry".

We have to thank Niklas Luhmann for the use of this conceptual figure for the purposes of legal theory.[30] George Spencer-Brown's "laws of distinction" provide the theoretical basis for this.[31] The area of law is distinguished from its environment, the realm of facts. In order to make statements about facts within law, an operation of re-entry is required: The law somehow needs to identify and process the facts within its own system. But we also find re-entry in other places within the law: for example, if one wants to talk about natural law within positive law, then positive law must mention it somehow, must explicitly or implicitly adopt it, e.g. via a reference in the constitution. When we speak of declaratory judgments, we mean "authoritative clarifications" within the legal system, that is, legal acts, and not—as the word "declare" suggests—claims about the truth.

We now propose to also use this conceptual figure for the processing of the facts, for the ascertainment of the state of facts. This can also be connected to an important concept introduced by the late Kelsen, the *modally indifferent substrate*. According to this, the same content, "X exists", could be *dressed* either in the modus of the "is" or in that of the "ought".[32]

Admittedly, re-entry borrows a conceptual figure from mathematics for purposes of legal theory, while ignoring its specific context. Ultimately, Kelsen, too, borrowed the—explanatory—basic norm, avowedly quasi *per analogiam*, from the transcendental philosophy of Kant.[33]

historical truths positively or negatively. This is the case when Holocaust denial is a criminal offence or, vice versa, when it is not allowed to accuse someone of an offence that has already been struck from his criminal record. The motive behind such prohibitive norms is not the suppression of lies or truths, but to contain the danger emanating from certain assertions.

[29] Which is to say, the people who apply the law.

[30] Cf. Luhmann (2004), p. 226 and Luhmann (2000), p. 130.

[31] Spencer-Brown (1972). On the reception of this idea, see Luhmann (2013), pp. 46 ff.

[32] Kelsen (1991), p. 60, and Mayer (1990), p. 144. Cf. also Röhl (1995), p. 80.

[33] Kelsen (1967), p. 205 and Walter (1999), p. 11.

3.2 *The Stratification of the Facts*

The efficacy of "re-entry" as a conceptual figure, however, becomes clear only when we dissect the state of facts more closely. This analysis is necessary because such facts are—in the words of Karl Engisch—"*the result of circuitous cognitive findings and conclusions*."[34] The "circuitousness" arises mainly because the facts of a case are by no means "brute facts", but are often social facts, which are themselves the result of an interpretation according to pragmatic rules, like a communicated self-commitment that we interpret as promise. We create social facts with linguistic means. John Searle vividly describes how our reality, from money to football matches, is shaped by such facts.[35] A subset important for us are those facts that are not only the result of a linguistic convention but also, when interpreted in the schema of a legal norm, are supposed to be objective with the addition of an "outside convention", in Searle's terminology. If, for example, the money received on the basis of a reward is to be taxed, then the reward, itself the product of interpretation, re-enters the proceedings as a fact—and, in a next step, is transformed into a fact of the case in a component of the legal act.[36]

But even at the level of the "natural" facts remaining after this distinction, the game goes on: for the expert witness does not merely determine "brute facts", as if by measurement; rather, she may also be required to qualify them as "reasonable", "probable", "dangerous", and so on, and often only this statement is subsumable.

A well-known example is mental illness: if properly seen as scientific fact—not deconstructed as purely social phenomenon—then it is impossible to overlook the extent to which normative interpretations are involved. This applies in particular to forensic psychiatry, which deals with such concepts as "dangerousness" and the like.[37] Since the law uses corresponding terms, the expert witness is often able to obtain her facts only on the basis of norms, whether they are predetermined standards or even values set by herself. These rules come in many forms: as diagnoses or prognoses, technical standards, accounting rules, professional customs, or occupational ethics. All these normative elements may overshadow the court's role, which should—at least *prima vista*—be responsible for the normative assessment in the first place.

At this point, it should become clear that facts in more complex cases could be the result of a multiple layering process, precisely in the form of "re-entries" in both directions: normative interpretations become facts and facts become norms. Obviously, such an iterative process is susceptible to factual errors as well as to the concealment of responsibility.

---

[34] Engisch (1996), p. 61.

[35] Cf. Searle (2010), p. 90.

[36] This also applies to foreign law, in the sense of private international law. The court hears an expert witness on foreign law, thus treating the law as a fact.

[37] Cf. fundamentally Foucault (1977), p. 21. Cf. also Kopetzki (1991), p. 2. Expert opinions in forensic psychiatry often lack in quality.

4 On the Possibility of a Distribution of Roles

4.1 A Question of Law or of Fact as a Criterion?

It is basic legal knowledge that the determination of the facts takes place from the perspective of possible statements of facts, and that these in turn determine the applicable legal norms, in Engisch's famous formulation of the *focus wandering back and forth*.[38] Heinz Mayer made it clear that this can only be achieved methodologically safely by the court developing a theory regarding a relevant fact—that is to say, something like a blueprint—which is then procedurally examined to determine whether the established facts confirm or reject this theory.[39] This is also precisely the crux of the matter, as the quality of the proceedings depends greatly on whether the judge is able to express the theory to be proven, the questions to the expert witness, as precisely as possible. The expert witness then responds by stating the facts and draws conclusions from them based on her knowledge. These conclusions in turn lead to the elements to which the law ties a legal consequence. Based on this, the court establishes the state of facts. Before that—contrary to an often inaccurate legal or doctrinal way of speaking—it would be better not to speak of the "facts" at all.

One might think that this division of tasks alone would lead to a clear demarcation of the functions of factual and legal authority. Here, however, the notoriously difficult problem gets in the way of distinguishing questions of law and of fact.[40] This problem occurs in particular when the relevant facts require "informed evaluations" from an expert.[41] It is true that the demarcation can be very difficult, not least as a consequence of the phenomenon of "mixed legal and factual questions" in the handling of undefined legal terms, which is well known to the every court.[42] Ultimately, however, it is up to the lawmaker, who can clarify whether he is formulating actual facts or referring to legal findings of fact.

If the law remains unclear, the demarcation between questions of law and questions of fact falls within the discretion of the court, namely of the final appellate court with regard to its jurisdiction: as it typically does not rehear the facts, treating an issue as a question of law means a deeper appellate review.[43] One example here is whether industrial plants or factories pose a hazard according to regulations of public economic law, which today is considered to be a question of law, but initially

[38] Engisch (1996), p. 15. For a critique of this metaphor, cf. Müller (1994), p. 254. At this point of consideration, however, it is not a question of how the authority establishes the facts, but how the established facts become "state of facts", that is to say, how they find their way into the proceedings.

[39] Mayer (1990), p. 145.

[40] This is—so to say—the global problem of applying the law. Cf. Weiner (1966).

[41] "Sachkundige Wertungen", cf. Funk (1990), p. 9.

[42] For more detail, see the original German version.

[43] Cf. Pawlowski (1999), para 268.

was a question of fact.[44] If an issue qualifies as a question of fact, the court is more closely bound by the findings of experts than if it is established as a question of law. The demarcation is therefore the reflection of the judge's bond to the facts; the more vague legal terms that are used, the more judgments that are required, the sooner the court makes it a question of law.

4.2 *Knowing and Willing*

It is by no means a concern that expert witnesses have normative resources. Of course, it should be noted that the lawmaker—or, if necessary, the court—has the authority to decide on the scope of these resources. To how great an extent is a question of policy. Accepting all of the assessments of the experts would lead to overly casuistic and inflexible regulations and would arguably be nonsensical. We must therefore acknowledge that normative standards also apply to factual issues. However, this also makes clear what really is going on: the issue is not the demarcation of questions of law and fact, but the separation of the functions of knowledge and volition, of cognition and decision.[45]

Courts and expert witnesses have in common that they are reluctant to admit that their product is not only the result of a process of thought, but also one of decision. This has to do with the nature of mere "decision-making" as entirely democratic: anyone can do it, whereas the application of expertise conveys prestige. Naturally, one will argue here that it is about "well-balanced decisions", and so forth, but that does not change the fact that courts are "*apparatuses for the permanent transformation of decision-making functions into cognitive functions*"[46] and that every court makes their recent (even if unprecedented) case law look like interpretations of well-established law.

Therefore, what really matters is transparency and the renunciation of ideology on both sides. As far as the court is concerned, I would like to emphasize the case law of the Austrian Administrative Court, which requires the administrative authority to determine *"the facts underlying the decision ... concretely"*.[47] This obliges the court to expresses that it has critically noted the findings of the expert witness and has adopted his view as its own. It would really be too limited to see this requirement only an admonition for the smartest and appeal-proof wording in the reasoning. Of course, as always with the law, this can only be done by means of an imputation; whether the judge actually has these thoughts remains concealed and is a question of judicial ethics.

---

[44] For more, cf. Pürgy (2013), pp. 27 ff.

[45] Cf. Grunsky (1974), p. 412.

[46] Franßen (1998), p. 417.

[47] The Administrative Court has now restated this classic case law—cf. most recently Erk Ro 2014/03/0076; Ro 2014/04/0068; Ra 2014/03/0038; 2014/18/0097; Ra 2014/19/0171 and Ra 2015/10/0024.

Expert witnesses must not pretend to always base their findings on pure expertise. Even the argument that certain norms are inherent to a field—such as medical research requiring a specific ethics that doctors can only handle it, and that it is fundamentally inaccessible to the law—is ideology. It is important to emphasize here that this does not mean, for example, that certain decisions should not be left to doctors, but rather that they act in an open space into which the law is more or less "inserted". The borders of this space can be quite fussy. What is essential is that the expert witness discloses normative spaces, that is to say evaluations, in order to open them up to judicial control. In no case, however, may the expert anticipate the judicial evaluation of evidence.

4.3 Coexistence

In the application of law, legal knowledge and expert knowledge must work together; the court and the expert witness are dependent upon one another. It is sometimes assumed that ongoing and deepened cooperation can lead to a kind of "osmosis", in the sense that, over time, a court becomes better acquainted with a material issue and an expert witness becomes increasingly familiar with the legal circumstances.[48] As always in situations of ambiguity, we also hear claims for an increased "dialogue".[49]

These are certainly welcome approaches and considerations. Nevertheless, it is also possible to view the matter critically: precisely because the expert witness has expertise, which is subsequently cast as a norm by the judge, and is therefore immunized, it is possible that there can be too close a relationship in which the two "work for one another" in a negative sense. In order to legitimize its decision, the court relies on the knowledge of the expert witness, who in turn relies on a subsequent immunization by the norm-setting judge. As a result, this means not only a loss of quality, but above all of responsibility: the court thinks it is the expert, and the expert witness thinks she is the court. It seems to me that this danger exists especially where there is regular interaction of a particular court with very specific expert witnesses. The problems certainly do not arise from corruption, but rather from overload or convenience. In a thoroughly counterintuitive way, it just may be a matter of breaking old routines. Of course, this would have to be verified empirically and is therefore already beyond the expertise of the author.

Acknowledgments This essay is a modified English version of my inaugural lecture at University of Vienna on 3 December 2015. Hence, it is still clearly embedded in the German—better to say: Austrian—language of academic legal discourse (Rechtswissenschaft). An earlier version was published under the title "Der Sachverhalt im Recht" in the Journal of Public Law (Zeitschrift für

[48] Similarly, cf. Klecatsky (1961), p. 316.

[49] From Bergthaler (2012), p. 59, who has in mind a situation in which a court has to decide a dispute over the correct scientific method.

Öffentliches Recht), Vol. 71 (2016), at pp. 199–214. For extended acknowledgements and thanks, see there. Here I have to thank Christoph Bezemek and Ulrich Wagrandl for helping me with the English version. It remains for the author to express his hope that the present attempt offers an abstract academic perspective that allows the essay's core claims to be reflected on a general level.

References

Bergthaler W (2012) Ingenieure versus Juristen. RdU 20:55–60
Eisenberger I (2016) Innovation im Recht. Verlag Österreich, Wien
Engisch K (1996) Einführung in das juristische Denken, 9th edn. Kohlhammer, Stuttgart
Foucault M (1977) Discipline and punish. The birth of the prison. Vintage Books, New York
Franßen E (1998) 50 Jahre Verwaltungsgerichtsbarkeit in der Bundesrepublik Deutschland. DVBl 103:413–421
Funk B (1990) Aufgaben des Sachverständigen im Rahmen rechtlicher Entscheidungen. In: Aicher J, Funk B (eds) Der Sachverständige im Wirtschaftsleben. Manz, Wien pp 1–24
Grunsky W (1974) Grundlagen des Verfahrensrechts, 2nd edn. E u W Gieseking, Bielefeld
Jabloner C (2016) Der Sachverhalt im Recht. ZÖR 71:199–214
Kaufmann A (1985) Das Problem der Abhängigkeit des Strafrichters vom medizinischen Sachverständigen. JZ 40:1065–1072
Kelsen H (1967) Pure theory of law, 2nd edn. University of California Press, Berkeley
Kelsen H (1991) General theory of norms. Clarendon Press, Oxford
Klecatsky H (1961) Der Sachverständigenbeweis im Verwaltungsverfahren. ÖJZ 16:309–316
Kletzer C (2015) Kelsen on Vaihinger. In: Del Mar M, Twining W (eds) Legal fictions in theory and practice. Springer, Cham, pp 23–29
Kopetzki C (1991) Unterbringungsrecht, vol I. Springer, New York
Luhmann N (2000) Organisation und Entscheidung. Westdeutscher Verlag, Opladen
Luhmann N (2004) Law as a social system. Oxford University Press, Oxford
Luhmann N (2013) Introduction to systems theory. Polity, Cambridge
Mayer H (1990) Der Sachverständige im Verwaltungsverfahren. In: Aicher J, Funk B (eds) Der Sachverständige im Wirtschaftsleben. Manz, Wien, pp 131–150
Merkl A (1927) Allgemeines Verwaltungsrecht. Springer, Berlin
Merli F (2013) Instrumente der Integration von Sachverstand. In: WiR – Studiengesellschaft für Wirtschaft und Recht (eds) Sachverstand im Wirtschaftsrecht. Manz, Wien, pp 173–188
Merli F (2015) Unabhängiges Gericht und abhängiger Sachverstand. ZfV 40:28–35
Möllers C (2010) Kognitive Gewaltengliederung. In: Röhl HC (ed) Wissen – Zur kognitiven Funktion des Rechts (Die Verwaltung, Beiheft 9). Duncker und Humblot, Berlin, pp 113–134
Müller F (1994) Strukturierende Rechtslehre, 2nd edn. Duncker und Humblot, Berlin
Pawlowski HM (1999) Methodenlehre für Juristen: Theorie der Norm und des Gesetzes, 3rd edn. Müller, Heidelberg
Petschek G, Stagel F (1963) Der österreichische Zivilprozess. Manz, Wien
Pürgy E (2013) Rechts- und Sachfragen. In: WiR – Studiengesellschaft für Wirtschaft und Recht (eds) Sachverstand im Wirtschaftsrecht. Manz, Wien, pp 17–34
Rechberger W (1974) Die Überprüfung von Erfahrungssätzen in der Revisionsinstanz. ÖJZ 28:113–118
Ringhofer K (1953) Von der Bedeutung des Sachverhaltes für die Rechtskraft verwaltungsbehördlicher Bescheide. ÖJZ 8:87–93, 120–124
Ringhofer K (1966) Strukturprobleme des Rechtes. Dargestellt am Staatsbürgerschaftsgesetz 1965. Manz, Wien
Röhl K (1995) Allgemeine Rechtslehre. Heymanns, Köln

Schweizer M (2015) Beweiswürdigung und Beweismaß. Rationalität und Intuition. Mohr Siebeck, Tübingen
Searle J (2010) Making the social world. The structure of human civilization. Oxford University Press, Oxford
Spencer-Brown G (1972) Laws of form. The Julian Press, New York
Walter R (1999) Hans Kelsens Rechtslehre. Nomos, Baden-Baden
Weiner S (1966) The civil jury trial and the law-fact-distinction. Calif Law Rev 54:1867–1938
Wolff K (1947) Grundriss des österreichischen Zivilprozessrechts, 2nd edn. Springer, Wien

The Fact of Norms

Michael Potacs

Abstract Notwithstanding the distinction between "is" and "ought" each norm is expressible in language. This article argues that to that effect all norms can be regarded as an "is", empirically equivalent to other facts.

1 The Problem

As Hans Kelsen points out, the word "norm" means that "something ought to be or ought to happen, especially that a human being ought to behave in a specific way".[1] In most cases, norms in that sense are created by human beings. Insofar, norms are the expression of a will of human beings directed to a certain behavior of others. But this is not necessarily so. Religious norms might have their cause in the metaphysical order of god and moral norms may be based on the commands of one's conscience. All these different kind of norms may be accepted or not by particular persons, whole societies or even the whole mankind. There is no doubt that this kind of acceptance of norms is a social fact and therefore part of the realm of "is". Statements about such an acceptance and effectiveness of norms might be true or false which is characteristic of an "is". This perspective has to be distinguished from discussions about the *content* of norms, which is an "ought". The justification of such an "ought" is basically independent of its factual acceptance and effectiveness. The correctness of the sentence "you should not steal" is independent from the fact whether it is accepted and effective in a particular society or not. This points to a fundamental difference between facts and norms or between "is" and "ought". It seems that facts ("is") require a different epistemological approach than norms ("ought") and neither can norms be derived from facts nor can facts be derived from norms. The following contribution considers how far-reaching this difference is.

[1] Kelsen (2009), p. 4.

M. Potacs (✉)
University of Vienna, Vienna, Austria
e-mail: michael.potacs@univie.ac.at

N. Bersier Ladavac et al. (eds.), *The Normative Force of the Factual*, Law and Philosophy Library 130, https://doi.org/10.1007/978-3-030-18929-7_8

2 Is and Ought

It was David Hume's accomplishment to draw attention to the difference between "is" and "ought". He realized that authors of moral disputes suddenly shift from the propositions "is, and is not" to propositions "connected with an ought, or an ought not" and put an emphasis on the importance of this shift from "is" to "ought" as it "expresses some new relation or affirmation".[2] Ever since David Hume, the "unbridgeable gap"[3] between norms and facts has been intensively discussed. There have, of course, been several attempts to attack the idea of a fundamental difference between facts and norms and to develop a deduction of an "ought" from an "is".[4] However, these positions were eventually discarded[5]; leaving the fundamental distinction between facts and norms widely acknowledged.

The reason for this "unbridgeable gap" between norms and facts is hard to find. Even Hans Kelsen, who based his Pure Theory of Law on the "dualism of is and ought", has to confess: "The difference between *is* and *ought* cannot be explained further. We are immediately aware of the difference. Nobody can deny that the statement: 'something is' – that is, the statement by which an existent fact is described – is fundamentally different from the statement: 'something ought to be' – which is the statement by which a norm is described. Nobody can assert that from the statement that something is, follows a statement that something ought to be, or vice versa."[6] A closer look at this quotation shows, however, that Kelsen equates a "statement by which a norm is described" with a "statement that ought to be" and treats both statements in the same way as an "ought".

But is this equal treatment acceptable? There is no doubt "that from the statement that something is" no statement follows "that something ought to be". Insofar, it is evident that an "ought" cannot derive from an "is". But does this also mean that there is an equal difference between a "statement by which a norm is described" and a "statement by which an existent fact is described"?

A similar question appears also in further conclusions Hans Kelsen draws from the "dualism of is and ought". Due to this dualism, for Kelsen norms do not exist in the same way as facts. In contrast to the (factual) existence of facts, norms are "valid". For Kelsen, the validity of a norm is the "specific existence of a norm".[7] The choice of the word "validity" shall express "the special manner in which the norm in contradistinction to a natural fact – is existent".[8] Validity means for Kelsen that the norm "is binding – that an individual ought to behave in the manner determined

[2] Hume (2017), p. 278.

[3] Von Wright (1985), p. 264.

[4] See for instance Searle (1964), pp. 43–58.

[5] See Von Wright (1985), pp. 265 f.

[6] Kelsen (2009), pp. 5 f (emphases in original).

[7] Kelsen (2009), p. 10.

[8] Kelsen (2009), p. 10.

by the norm".[9] Because of the "dualism of is and ought", the reason for this binding force cannot be a fact. Therefore, Kelsen argues: "The reason for the validity of a norm can only be the validity of another norm. A norm which represents the reason for the validity of another norm is figuratively spoken of as a higher norm in relation to a lower norm."[10] In this sense a norm "exists" in a normative order (like a legal order) if its binding force is derived from a "higher" (authorizing) norm of this particular normative order. Insofar Kelsen's argumentation is convincing. Obviously, it follows from the "dualism of is and ought" that norms can only be derived from other norms. In that sense, it seems reasonable to see the "specific existence of a norm" in its validity due to another (higher) norm. However, the question remains if this view of a "specific existence" of norms excludes a perspective in which norms also have a "factual existence".

3 Perception

Any considerations of this question must take into account that norms may have different manifestations. Legal norms often find their expression in written texts and sometimes in oral announcements. Customary law as well as different social norms become manifest in social behavior. Norms of morality sometimes might appear as a certain movement of conscience. Still, it is an essential feature of all kinds of norms that they are expressible in language.[11] Sometimes norms are expressed in an artificial language as the example of road signs demonstrates. Apart from that, however, all norms may be expressed in natural language. In this respect, norms can be defined as the meaning of a linguistic utterance, expressed in terms of a natural language. On this aspect, I will focus my following considerations.

The forms of linguistic expression of norms as texts or oral communications may be perceived by our senses. These perceptions (black ink on white paper or sounds) have, of course, to be interpreted in order to express their meaning as a norm. Such an interpretation requires the knowledge of the rules governing the language in which the norm is presented. The rules for the use of natural languages may be divided into semantic and pragmatic rules.[12] While semantics takes the ordinary meaning of words (literal interpretation) and phrases in the use of language into account, pragmatics concerns additional rules of communication, most notably such as the context of a statement in its different forms.[13] Semantic and pragmatic criteria are also reflected in the traditional methods of legal interpretation. These methods include not only semantic rules of interpretation of the wording, but also know pragmatic criteria as the systematic, teleological or historic interpretation. The criteria of legal interpretation are,

---

[9] Kelsen (2009), p. 193.

[10] Kelsen (2009), p. 193.

[11] Von Wright (1985), p. 267.

[12] See Potacs (2015), pp. 134 ff.

[13] See to this "context principle" also Endicott (2011), pp. 946 ff.

therefore, in principle not different from the methods of interpretation in everyday communication. This makes sense, since legislators use natural language to convey their commands and thus want to have them understood according to the rules of common use of language. In the same way as legal norms all other norms can be conveyed by semantic and pragmatic modes of expression. Their utterance has to be interpreted in accordance with semantic and pragmatic rules of communication.

However, what is the character of these semantic and pragmatic criteria of interpretation? They represent regularities of the usage of a natural language. The rules of interpretation contain propositions about communication which enable an understanding of linguistic utterances. General statements about observable regularities are referred to as "theories".[14] It was Karl Popper, in particular, who emphasized that "theories" in general play an important role to understand the world. In his words, theories "are nets to catch what we call 'the world': to rationalize, to explain, and to master it".[15] By expressing general statements about regularities in the use of natural languages, the rules of interpretations can be understood as theories about linguistic usage. Linguistic utterances (spoken or written) are, therefore, the result of an interpretation based on theories about the use of a language. This applies also to norms as an expression of a linguistic utterance: norms are the meaning of a linguistic utterance in the light of theories (called "rules of interpretation") about the use of language. Therefore, the perception of a norm presented in a natural language is never a perception of pure facts but a perception, pre-interpreted by "theories". The result of such an interpretation is of course an "ought".

Does therein lie the essential difference between "is" and "ought"? Do we perceive facts (linguistic utterances) which we interpret as an "ought" in a different way than facts perceivable by our senses concerning an "is" (like physical or economic phenomena)? Is a perception of pure facts in relation to an "is" possible? The answer to this question has to be no. In this there is no difference between "is" and "ought". It was again Karl Popper who demonstrated that every perception is "theory-impregnated" and "that there is no observation which is not related to a set of typical situations – regularities – between which it tries to find a decision".[16] That is true for scientific observations as well as for our daily perceptions like the observation of a glass of water: Popper shows that by "the word 'glass' we denote physical bodies which exhibit a certain *law-like behavior*, and the same holds for the word 'water'".[17] This leads to the consequence "that there are no uninterpreted visual sense data"[18] and "*'direct' or 'immediate' observational experiences*"[19] do not exist: "whatever is 'given' to us is already interpreted, decoded".[20] Therefore, the

[14] Popper (1972), p. 72; Popper (2002), p. 37.

[15] Popper (2002), pp. 37 f.

[16] Popper (1972), p. 72.

[17] Popper (2002), p. 76 (emphases in original).

[18] Popper (1980), p. 139.

[19] Popper (1972), p. 72 (emphases in original).

[20] Popper (1980), p. 139.

perception of an "is" does not differ from the perception of a linguistically formulated "ought". In both cases empirical data are interpreted in light of theories: the result is in one case an "is" and in the other case an "ought". The perception of an "ought" is as well theoretically constructed as the perception of an "is" which is why in this respect there seems to be an "empirical equivalence"[21] between "is" and "ought".

4 Existences

This "empirical equivalence" however refers only to the *perception* of "is" and "ought". Can we conclude from this that norms have the same form of existence as facts which we understand as an "is"? The answer is yes and no.

On the one hand, it is a feature of norms that they may be characterized as the meaning of a linguistic expression. As such, norms have an empirical existence as the meaning of perceivable facts. Insofar, they exist in the same way as the meaning of any other linguistic expression or empirical observation. In this respect, norms are facts which have the meaning of an "ought". Therefore, norms can be described as an "is" whose specific sense is an "ought". On the other hand, we must not disregard the special character of this meaning. This character has to consider the dualism between "is" and "ought". Because of this dualism norms have not only a factual but also a normative dimension. And the normative dimension means that norms have to be justified by other norms and not by facts in order to be valid. Beside the *factual* existence ("is") as the meaning of a linguistic utterance, norms might therefore also have a *normative* existence ("ought") which is described by Kelsen as "validity". As already mentioned, norms can "exist" in that sense as part of a particular normative order *if* they are valid within this system. However, we should accept that this is only one form of existence of norms as they also have a factual existence as the meaning of a linguistic utterance.

Quite remarkably, the normative existence of a norm does not always coincide with its factual existence. As each norm is expressible in language, all norms have a factual existence as a meaning of a linguistic utterance. Nevertheless, of course, only some of these norms have validity and in that sense "existence" in a particular normative order. Above all, the factual existence and the normative existence serve different functions. The importance of the normative existence lies in the *justification* of the content of a norm and the unbridgeable dualism between "is" and "ought" refers only to this function. In contrast, the main significance of the factual existence of norms lies in the recognition of the content of norms and only this function is necessary for its *description*. Therefore, it is at least misleading when Kelsen, while explaining the dualism between "is" and "ought", states that nobody "can deny that the statement: 'something is' – that is, the statement by which an existent fact is described – is fundamentally different from the statement: 'something ought

[21] See Potacs (1994), p. 198.

to be'-which is the statement by which a norm is *described*".[22] The factual existence of norms can be described in the same way as the meaning of other facts. Still, the *justification* of norms cannot be based on facts. Therefore, it would be in contradiction to the dualism between "is" and "ought" if we were to derive the normative existence of a norm merely from its factual existence (a norm is valid just because it is introduced). However, this dualism does not prohibit the acceptance of a factual existence of norms as the meaning of a linguistic utterance and, thus, as an "is".

5 Objectivity

By accepting a factual existence of norms not all questions concerning the fact of norms are answered. The question remains as to whether norms might have an objective existence in the sense of an existence independent from the mind of their particular observer or group of observers. The existence of an objective world in that sense is of course subject of heated discussions among philosophers. However, even if we basically acknowledge an objective existence of facts, the question remains open as to whether facts with the meaning of an "ought" objectively exist in the same way as other facts. Especially the dualism of "is" and "ought" raises the question if the recognition of an objective existence of norms ("oughts") requires a different approach to the awareness of the objectivity of other entities.

Hans Kelsen's theory of the "basic norm" rests on the requirement of such a different approach. He argues that because of the dualism of "is" and "ought" the norm which is the reason for the validity of another norm can only be a "higher" norm. "But the search for the reason of a norm's validity", Kelsen continues to argue, "cannot go indefinitely like the search for an effect. It must end with a norm which, as the last and highest, is presupposed. It must be *presupposed*, because it cannot be 'posited', that is to say: created, by an authority whose competence would have to rest on a still higher norm. This final norm's validity cannot be derived from a higher norm, the reason for its validity cannot be questioned. Such a presupposed highest norm is referred to in this look as basic norm".[23]

The function of this basic norm is to allow for an "objective validity"[24] of a norm. "Objective validity" means that "the behavior at which the act is directed is regarded as something that ought to be not only from the point of view of the individual who has performed the act, but also from the point of view of the individual at whose behavior the act is directed, and of a third individual not involved in the relation between the two".[25] The "basic norm", therefore, is the presupposition that the norm is "objectively valid" in the sense that its content is accepted by everybody and one

[22] Kelsen (2009), pp. 5 f (emphases not in original).

[23] Kelsen (2009), p. 194 f (emphases in original).

[24] Kelsen (2009), p. 202.

[25] Kelsen (2009), p. 6 (emphases in original).

ought to obey it.[26] As Kelsen wants to develop a theory whose "exclusive purpose is to know and to describe its object",[27] the presupposition of the "basic norm" is, in Kelsen's view, the requirement of the objective knowledge and description of norms.

However, is this theory of the basic norm really convincing? Do we need such a normative presupposition for the objective knowledge and description of norms? It has to be conceded that the presupposition of a basic norm has to be made if we want to describe a norm as "objectively valid" in the sense that it has to be "objectively" obeyed, which means it is valid for everybody. Therefore, the basic norm is a convincing presupposition for the "objective existence" of a norm within the meaning of its "objective validity". Nevertheless, as demonstrated above, the validity of a norm is only one form of existence of a norm. Beside its validity, norms also have a factual existence as the meaning of a linguistic utterance and insofar can also be regarded as an "is". It is not necessary to make the assumption of a basic norm if we only want to recognize and describe this linguistic meaning. Obviously it is possible to discover and describe norms which we think should *not* be obeyed. Moreover, we must be aware of the content of norms which we reject in order to assess whether we should follow them or not.

One could object to this position that the dualism of "is" and "ought" requires the presupposition of a basic norm in order to interpret a linguistic utterance as a norm. As this dualism is fundamental, it might be argued that an utterance can only be interpreted as a norm under the condition of an assumption that one should obey it. This argument would be a strong one if the dualism of "is" and "ought" would necessitate such a consequence. But this is not the case. This dualism merely asserts that a norm can only be justified by another "higher" norm. It does not tell us that the knowledge and description of the factual existence of a norm is only possible under the presupposition that this norm is "objectively valid". Moreover, the dualism between "is" and "ought" does not indicate any statement about the knowledge and description of a norm as the meaning of a linguistic utterance.

However, do norms have an objective factual existence in the sense that they exist independently from the mind of their observers? And is it possible to recognize and describe this objective existence of norms? An answer to these questions has to take into account that any objective reality is neither demonstrable nor refutable.[28] This has to be accepted even if common sense anticipates such an objective reality. Nevertheless, this objective reality on which we rely in our everyday experiences could be an exclusive product of our mind. As all perception is "theory-impregnated", this cannot be discarded.[29] And we finally cannot prove whether this "theory-driven" observations are in accordance with a mind-independent reality or not. With good reason, the idea of an objectivity, which exists independently of the human mind, is signified as an idea of "metaphysical objectivity".[30] However, this metaphysical

[26] Raz (1974), p. 105.

[27] Kelsen (2009), p. 1.

[28] Popper (1972), p. 38.

[29] See Sect. 3.

[30] Leiter (2011), p. 969.

character of an objective reality does not exclude that objective knowledge is pursued. Certain assumptions, which are referred to as "metaphysical hypotheses",[31] are inseparably connected with this objective. Such "metaphysical hypotheses" are the assumptions that an objective reality exists ("metaphysical objectivity"[32]), that this objective reality is recognizable for human minds ("epistemological objectivity"[33]) and that this objective reality can be described in human language ("linguistic objectivity"[34]).

What follows from these considerations for the answer to the question about the objective existence of norms? As the factual existence of norms is "empirically equivalent" to the existence of other facts, these "metaphysical hypotheses" must also be applicable to norms. Equal *assumptions* are inseparably connected with the aim of knowing and describing the objective meaning of norms. First, this is the assumption that norms have an objective existence as the meaning of a linguistic utterance. Based on this assumption, norms are "metaphysically independent" in the sense that they have an objective meaning which is independent from the mind of their interpreters. Second, also the assumptions of an "epistemological objectivity" and "linguistic objectivity" are inseparably linked with the purpose to know and describe norms as objects. That means the assumptions that the objective content of norms is recognizable and can be described in linguistic terms. All these assumptions are based on the "correspondence theory of truth" which says that a statement is true if it corresponds to the facts.[35] Concerning the factual existence of norms as the objective sense of linguistic utterances, this means: a statement about the sense of a norm is true if it corresponds with the objective meaning of that norm.

It could be objected to this conception that norms as the meaning of linguistic utterances are always the product of the human mind. Therefore, they could not have an objective existence which is completely independent from the mind of their observers. Based on this argument, it is assumed that legal norms can just have a "weak mind-independent" form of objectivity: Their "objective" existence is not dependent on the mental activity of any particular individual but also not independent of the functioning of any members of any group individually or collectively.[36] However, such an objection is not really convincing because we should remember again that every perception is "theory-impregnated". That is the case for the observation of an "is" like a glass of water as well as for an "ought" as the meaning of a linguistic utterance. Insofar, the observation of an "is" is as well a product of the human mind as the knowledge of a norm. The objective meaning of a norm is expressed by the rules of communication of a particular natural language. And it

---

[31] Albert (1987), p. 44.

[32] Leiter (2011), pp. 970 ff.

[33] Leiter (2011), pp. 973 f.

[34] Leiter (2011), pp. 975 f, calls this form of objectivity "semantic objectivity". As the rules for the use of natural languages consist not only of semantic but also of pragmatic rules the designation "linguistic objectivity" seems more reasonable.

[35] Popper (1972), p. 46.

[36] See to this opinion Kramer (2007), pp. 3 ff, referring to Marmor (2001), p. 138.

may be well assumed that this meaning has an objective existence which is independent from its knowledge and description by anybody. This does not even change by the fact that norms in general (as well as water glasses) are the products of human minds. What Karl Popper asserts about books also holds for norms: "It is its possibility or potentiality of being understood, its dispositional character of being understood or interpreted, or misunderstood or misinterpreted, which makes a thing a book. And this potentiality or disposition may exist without ever being actualized or realized".[37]

Finally, the objective existence of norms could be questioned with the argument that linguistic expressions are often vague and ambiguous. Insofar, the content of a norm is to a large extent indeterminate and not "objective" because its interpretation requires subjective valuations. In response to this objection, it should first of all be noted that usually the meaning of linguistic utterances like legal orders is sufficiently clear and precise in the particular context.[38] Otherwise communication based on natural language would not work in general, which is obviously not true. However, even the "hard cases"[39] where the content of a normative order is vague or ambiguous do not call the assumption of an objective existence of a norm (as the objective meaning of a normative utterance) seriously into question. This is because in these cases the objective existence of a norm consists in the fact that they have an unclear meaning and entitle "objectively" to a certain discretion when obeying or executing them.

6 Conclusion

Norms have a "double existence". On the one hand, a specific existence of norms can be seen in their validity. This form of existence can be described as the "normative existence" of norms. Because of the fundamental distinction between "is" and "ought", the validity of a norm can only be derived from another "higher" norm. Insofar, norms might have an existence as a valid part of a hierarchical system of norms (like a legal order). On the other hand, each norm is expressible in language. As such, norms have a "factual existence" as the meaning of a linguistic utterance and they can be seen as an "is" which is why to that extent norms are "empirically equivalent" to any other fact. Because of their factual existence, norms can objectively be known and described like other facts. The dualism between "is" and "ought" is not in contrast to this view as it bars from justifying norms with facts but allows to acknowledge norms as facts.

[37] Popper (1972), p. 116.

[38] To this aspect especially Greenawalt (1992), pp. 11, 73 ff.

[39] Dworkin (1977), p. 81.

References

Albert H (1987) Kritik der reinen Erkenntnislehre. Mohr Siebeck, Tübingen
Dworkin R (1977) Taking rights seriously. Harvard University Press, Cambridge
Endicott T (2011) Law as language. In: Coleman J, Shapiro S (eds) The Oxford handbook of jurisprudence and philosophy of law. OUP, New York, pp 935–968
Greenawalt K (1992) Law and objectivity. OUP, New York
Hume D (2017) A treatise of human nature. 1739, reprinted by Amazon Fulfillment, Breslau
Kelsen H (2009) Pure theory of law. The Lawbook Exchange, Clark
Kramer MH (2007) Objectivity and the rule of law. Cambridge University Press, Cambridge
Leiter B (2011) Law and objectivity. In: Coleman J, Shapiro S (eds) The Oxford handbook of jurisprudence and philosophy of law. OUP, New York, pp 969–989
Marmor A (2001) Positive law and objective values. OUP, Oxford
Popper KR (1972) Objective knowledge. Clarendon Press, Oxford
Popper KR (1980) Unended quest. Fontana/Collins, Glasgow
Popper KR (2002) The logic of scientific discovery. Routledge, London
Potacs M (1994) Rechtsdogmatik als empirische Wissenschaft. Rechtstheorie 25:191–211
Potacs M (2015) Rechtstheorie. Facultas, Vienna
Raz J (1974) Kelsen's theory of the basic norm. Am J Jurisprud 19:94–111
Searle J (1964) How to derive "ought" from "is". Philos Rev 73:43–58
Von Wright GH (1985) Is and ought. In: Bulygin E, Gardies J-L, Niiniluoto I (eds) Man, law and modern forms of life. D. Reidel Publishing, Dordrecht, pp 263–281

Ex facto jus oritur

Alexander Somek

Abstract The legal relation is the mode in which we allow action to go forward, that is based on reasons that do not appeal to us or may even strike as wrong. The reasons remain foreign to us. We treat, therefore, the having of reasons as a social fact. Someone wants something. At the same time, the law also reconciles ourselves with the traces of foreign reason that we encounter in the sources of law. Indeed, the true story that is to be told about sources of law is that they help us to bridge difference. This reconciliation is, however, never complete and eventually mediated by the serene irony that is the benchmark of genuine hermeneutic suspense.

1 The Historicity of Reason

Hermeneutics is based on a remarkable dual premise. Above all, it suggests that there is something matter-of-factual about how other people reason or used to reason in the past. Put differently, encountering difficulties in making sense of others indicates for hermeneutics that those whom one has trouble understanding inhabit slightly different intellectual worlds or belong to contexts where matters are taken for granted that are not considered to be commonplace among us.[1] The experience of inexplicability is that which lends their reasoning an element of the factual (Peirce: "secondness"[2]), for it resists absorption into principles that we all share. In a rather perplexing manner their thinking seems to be just in place. "This" is how "they" account for the world and what "they" take to be reason. In the final analysis, as Wittgenstein memorably remarked, the indexical "this" refers to something factual.[3] The foreign is encountered in the form of a datum. Certain conservatives

[1] See Marquard (1981), pp. 117–146.

[2] See Pierce (1998), pp. 160–178.

[3] See Wittgenstein (1988) § 28, S. 125.

A. Somek (✉)
University of Vienna, Vienna, Austria
e-mail: alexander.somek@univie.ac.at

N. Bersier Ladavac et al. (eds.), *The Normative Force of the Factual*, Law and Philosophy Library 130, https://doi.org/10.1007/978-3-030-18929-7_9

believe *de facto* that access to abortions is tantamount to extending the holocaust into an indefinite future. Perplexing as the claim must appear, it is, nonetheless, undeniably what they hold to be true.

Arguably, while such a view is difficult to understand, it may not be impossible to adhere to it. In addition to being reconciled to seeing reason disintegrate into scattered islands of sense-making that do not sum up to something universal, philosophical hermeneutics suggest that efforts at understanding involve fusing our horizon with the seemingly inscrutable outlook of others.[4] Indeed, hermeneutics suggests that insight and intellectual growth require an effort to understand those whose texts or utterances may at first glance appear entirely foreign to us.[5] Reason is not a given. It is susceptible to growth and possesses, in this sense, *perfectibilité*.[6] All true knowledge and insight is, thus, the effect of *Bildung* ("edification" is how Rorty used to translate this term).[7]

In what follows I would like to take up these two themes and to show how they are relevant to our understanding of law. I would like to remind us of the fact, in particular, that dealing with the reasoning *of others* that is experienced as *another* form of reasoning results in the attribution of something that is not rational but factual. The legal relation is the mode in which we allow action to go forward in spite of being based on reasons that appear foreign or even somewhat repugnant to us, such as the production of guns, the observance of rigid dietary restrictions or the distribution of religious pamphlets. Viewed against the background of hermeneutics, the legal relation stands for the unfolding of difference, namely, the proliferation of scattered islands of sense-making concerning either oneself or the world. But the law is also *Bildung* in the sense that it helps us to reconcile ourselves with the traces of foreign reason that we encounter in the sources of law. Indeed, the true story that is to be told about sources of law is that they allow us to bridge difference. This reconciliation is, however, never complete and eventually mediated by the serene irony that is the benchmark of genuine hermeneutic suspense.[8]

2 The Legal Relation

Approaching the law by examining the relation or relationships that we call "legal" is surprisingly uncommon. The only English author I am aware of who ventured into this field was Michael Oakeshott.

[4] See Gadamer (1976), p. 278; Lafont (1999), pp. 92–108.

[5] See, from that angle, on "edifying philosophy", Rorty (1979), pp. 357–365.

[6] See Rousseau (2012), pp. 89–90.

[7] See above note 5.

[8] These themes are further elaborated in German in Somek (2018b) *Wissen des Rechts* (Tübingen: Mohr Siebeck, 2018).

In an article of the rule of law,[9] Oakeshott sketched a type of relationship in which we are cast as abstract personae that are ultimately only interested in mutually pursuing their own interests and in no manner involved in advancing shared objectives. His sketch of a legal philosophy is thus—and students of Oakshott's work must be aware of this—a specification of his theory of civil association.[10] This explains why Oakeshott's approach is both rather specific and, indeed, much too closely tied to an old-fashioned liberal perspective on the social world in order to pass as a truly elementary exposition of the concept of law. What he gets right, however, is the distance inherent in the legal relation, which reflects the mutual abstention from judging the other's objectives. What he does not explore is that the law is a response to a predicament of morality.

The question that needs to be asked, in the first place, is why it is that we would not get along if moral judgments were our only guide. This is indeed not a live possibility. Social theorists often point out that coordinating and organizing conduct by moral means alone would never work because we could not be assured of the compliance of others. The possibility of their potential defection or, worse perhaps, of their playing by the rules would give us reason to breach the rules ourselves. Since the same is true of them, we could never count on others honoring their moral obligations if it were not for the coercive power of the state.[11] But with that conclusion we are already leaving the domain where people are governed by moral insight and commitment alone. We are then replacing the moral foundation of social cooperation with the harsh realities of law.

While this commonplace cannot be disputed, it does not get to the heart of the matter. The truly vexing problem is that we would still need law if men (and women) were angels.[12] The reason is that we universalize differently (and this is not merely a consequence of the "burdens of judgment").[13]

3 Universalization

Universalization is the form with which we justify our conduct towards—or make moral demands on—others. If you universalize you say that anyone who is in a like situation should do the same.[14] The justification for this claim may consist of putting yourself into the shoes of others and to suggest that it would be reasonable to see them agree.

A moral justification is not likely to be met with contestation so long as merely our interests *in general* are at stake. Everyone wants to be safe and everyone wants

[9] See Oakeshott (1999), pp. 129–178.

[10] See Oakeshott (1975), pp. 127–128.

[11] See Hobbes (2010), p. 104; Ullmann-Margalit (1977), p. 65.

[12] See The Federalist (2009), p. 341.

[13] On the latter, see Rawls (1991), pp. 54–58.

[14] See, for example, Mackie (1977), p. 90.

to enjoy the liberty to be left alone. Undoubtedly, we want that for all. Problems arise, however, whenever we need to decide whether the interest in safety is to be accorded priority over the interest in privacy. As Madison once observed, when people reason about matters coolly and freely, they inevitably fall into different opinions on some of them.[15] Some say that absent an imminent threat, searches of private possessions are an abomination. Others retort that occasional invasions of privacy are a prize worth paying for greater safety. Both universalize. They are putting themselves in the positions of whoever may be affected by a rule, thereby giving one or the other principle precedence. What they do, however, is to evaluate the consequences of searches differently owing to the different evaluative outlooks with which they arrive at the issue. And both may at a certain point and after some discussion conclude that they "do not get it" why their opponents do not perceive matters in the manner they do. How the others think does not speak to them. The others appear to be unmoved by reason. Somehow and strangely, their way of thinking is written into stone.

4 From Judgment to Choice

Remarkably, such a recognition marks the point at which moral judgment can distinguish within itself a substantive and a moral dimension—and if it does not draw this distinction something goes wrong.[16] Along the substantive dimension disagreement persists and could be eliminated only by "taking care" of the relentless dissenters, for example, by locking them up. Why should moral falsehood be tolerated? The matter looks different, however, along the social dimension, for it brings the diversity of moral opinion into focus. The experience of disagreement can be *morally* accounted for by universalizing the conflict-ridden relation between and among substantive universalizations and by viewing yourself as being on an equal footing with others. One is merely one judging person among others. On a reflective level, one can become another to oneself. This is the step toward recognizing the judgment of others.

Such recognition of judgment has to be mutual, not least because it is a matter of good judgment along the social dimension that others recognize your own judgment as a judgment that could be theirs were they different persons.

In mutually recognizing our judgment we can then say to one another[17]:

> I yield to your view if you yield to mine.

---

[15] See The Federalist (2009), No. 50, p. 338.

[16] For slightly different elaborations of this idea, see Somek (2017), pp. 118–121 and Somek (2018a), pp. 26–29.

[17] On "double contingency", see Luhmann (1984), pp. 148–150.

Such yielding is only possible, however, if the substantive disagreement drops out of the picture, for if it did not the conflict could never be resolved. Rather, we would have to clinch stubbornly to our moral insights. Only if we regard one another as "having beliefs" or "having views" can we discover the common ground on which we recognize that what we share is wanting something to have or to happen, regardless of what it might be:

I want what you want if you want what I want.

What we both want, regardless of our specific wants, is volition itself. We both want to want,[18] with no strings attached. This recognition is the origin of the legal relation. We end up saying to one another:

I want you to want if you want me to want.

That there would not be law unless we made mutually room for volition, thus understood, explains why the law, in order to avail of *substance*, has to embrace the existence of wants as *a matter of fact*.[19] It has to give way to actual determinations, such as routines or choices. The factual is rendered, then, within the form of law. What others may find to have reason to do is cast as a choice. Legal subjects possess and exercise freedom of choice. Such freedom is the hieroglyph that denotes and takes the place of the reasons of others. "Choice" is the mysterious token for the enigma encapsulated in taking actual or potential reasons of others as mere facts for us. The manifestation of such "taking" is the legal relation.

This means that in the law we encounter the work of foreign reason, which is not unreason, but merely reason that we may not have yet grasped as such, let alone fully understood.

5 Limits of the Reasonable

Before examining why the law has to have sources, three supplementary comments are in order. One is short, the others are somewhat more extensive.

First, as Savigny put it, the legal relation is based upon a legal rule.[20] From the perspective introduced here, legal rules are essentially nothing but the presuppositions necessary to make the recognition of that foreign reason mutual which is represented within the legal relation as a choice.

Second, the recognition of choices is, indeed, premised on the idea that the recognition of the judgment of others gives rise to what Rawls called *reasonable* disagreements.[21] The idea entails, however, that there is a limit beyond which disagreements must appear to be unreasonable. It is only within the compass of

[18] See Hegel (1991) § 26, pp. 55–56.

[19] This is a major theme of Menke's most recent work. See Menke (2016).

[20] See von Savigny (1840), p. 7.

[21] See Rawls (1991), p. 55. See also Waldron (1999).

reasonableness that we make room for a variety of pockets of disagreements and of choices. Interestingly, answering the question of where the line needs to be drawn—that is, where the limits to choices have to be drawn—is itself subject to disagreement, in particular where line-drawing is notoriously contested. It follows, hence, that that which is limiting—our reasons for setting a limit to reasonable disagreements—may itself be located within that which it limits. What is limited only by itself is, using Hegelian parlance, infinite.[22] The law is infinite, for it determines its limit itself, and such determinations are a matter of historical fact.

Third, this infinity indicates a normative priority of the factual. There would be no legal authority if it were not for *de facto* determinations of the limits set for the reasonable within which legal relations may legitimately abound. Another name for the same phenomenon is "politics". The authority of law is political.[23] Rule-making is the attempt to arrive at common action and successful coordination of conduct in the face of the diversity of views and judgments. Setting up such authority is a historical achievement.

Establishing and sustaining legal relations by yielding to the volitions of others is superior to any morality that remains entirely substantive and denies the judgments of others their requisite place. The relation between law and morality is that of substantive moral self-restrain resulting in legal rights that take precedence over substantive moral concerns.

It would be entirely misconceived, therefore, to regard the law as a particular field or application of our practical reason. It is not the case that the law is, as it were, some social mechanism to which practical reason can address high-minded demands. On the contrary, any system of positive law is an *embodiment* of our practical reason. Any substantive demands on the legal system coming out of an applied ethic must pay heed to the moral self-restraint from which the law originates.

6 The Subjectivity of Law

With these observations we arrive at the claim that the law necessarily has to have sources.

Any recognition of another person's reasons that do not speak to oneself transmutes these reasons into social facts, *i.e.*, into something that might possibly trigger that other person's conduct. The person believes to have these reasons and might likely act on them regardless of their soundness. Leaving the potential causal connection aside, the having of reasons is the *seed* of what legal positivists understand by a source of law, namely, a social fact that is amenable to being described in "value-neutral terms".[24]

---

[22] See Hegel (1991) at § 22, p. 53. For an illuminating analysis, see Houlgate (2006), pp. 397–400.

[23] See Loughlin (2017), p. 6.

[24] On the "sources theses", see Raz (1979), p. 47.

Nevertheless, legal positivists—in virtue of who they are—have consistently and persistently ignored, that sources are also forms of knowing the law. They have, that is, neglected that law is an embodiment of practical reason. Correctly understood, however, the law not only belongs, as an intelligible object, to the sphere of objectivity, but rather to the sphere of the subjective. The law is composed of modes of knowing what the law is.

At first glance, this claim must appear to be quite confusing and possibly nothing short of preposterous. But it becomes immediately plausible once we take the most elementary source, customary law, into account.

Ordinarily, this source is presented as though it were a composite of a behavioral and an intentional element.[25] There is steady practice, on the one hand, and that practice is accompanied by the conviction that the practice is mandatory, on the other. This ordinary account gives rise to a rather facile picture, for it does not reveal how one and the other come together and why the behavioral and the intentional element appear in juxtaposition.

By contrast, the alternative to the ordinary account suggests that customary law originates from common or overlapping intuitions of what is lawful.[26] Their normative force is manifest—and cannot be denied—in driving people to create and to sustain common practices. Once the internal composition of customary law is construed from this angle, it becomes immediately clear that the form of custom ("We know that this is wrong and our conviction is shown in how we have acted in the past") is derivative of the form of knowing (viz., asserting, claiming) what the law is in this or that case ("We don't allow this here, we have never seen something like that happen before"). This does not rule out that customary law can develop unconsciously, as people may be unaware of their intuitions.[27] They may develop certain habits and only later realize that they also share the conviction that they are right about doing what they habitually do. The belief that practices have to continue in a certain way can also be reinforced by the sheer fear of the social ostracism awaiting a dissenter. The intuitions about what is right merely need to overlap, but they do not have to reflect the same reasons. Even if the normative relevance of custom is recognized only on the ground of the mere desire to fit in it is, understood from the perspective of a participant, that things *have* to be done in a certain way.

Thus understood, customary law is a form of knowing what to do and how to react to the conduct of others. Something factual is a condition of the authority of that knowledge, namely, some amazingly mute social practice. The reference to "settled practice" serves as an exclusionary reason[28] that makes us yield to intuitions that represent either the beliefs of others ("There is no way to dissuade them") or convictions that overwhelm us as though they were stubborn facts about us. In the latter instance, you view yourself as someone who happens to have a belief as

[25] See, choosing a random example, Crawford (2012), p. 23.

[26] See Puchta (1828), pp. 143–147.

[27] See Gardner (2012), p. 72.

[28] See Raz (1990), p. 41. Exclusionary reasons exclude the relevance of certain reasons as reasons for action and may imply that one must not act on the balance of reasons.

though it were a preference or, worse still, an affliction, and you defend it as though you were entitled to it. You are free to take something as a reason even if the ground for having the reason may remain inscrutable to you.

In the case of sources, then, the legal standard—the norm—is presented as originating from a fact ("It is the law that … because we happen to belief and practice that …"). Moreover, the recognition of this origin from facts is a fact as well. Both types of fact bring the law into existence. Not only is it a fact that something is a law because someone believes or practices something else, it is also a fact that this fact is deemed to be legally relevant.

This dual relevance of the factual is often rendered obscure. Legal scholars refer to legal rules as though they were abstract entities belonging to the "third world" of ideas (and neither to the "first world" of brute facts nor the "second world" of inner experiences).[29] The law is thus presented in the form of an object and lent the appearance of abstract entity.[30] What disappears from view, however, are *both* its subjectivity and the relevance of the factual. If one retrieves either, the other is brought back into the picture as well.

7 Sources Speaking Themselves

Sources operate quite straightforwardly. They say that from the existence of X follows the normative relevance of Y, which can be prescription or proscription, permission or power. For example, if the legislature is in session (fact) it can adopt legislation (power). This conditional is established in the constitution *qua* source of law.

Ordinarily, legal thinking focuses on the resulting Y and refers to it as "law". Y is taken to be an abstract object of "description" by legal scholars.[31] It is the law that has been laid down by someone. Choosing another example, for the existence of a vote in parliament follows, very roughly speaking, the validity of a piece of legislation. Its ground is the observance of secondary rules governing the legislative process (X). The resulting piece of legislation (Y) is then called "a law". It is subsequently applied to a set of facts. X gives rise to Y, and juxtaposing Y with facts warrants the conclusion that Z ought to follow.

$$X \wedge Y \wedge \text{facts} \Rightarrow Z$$

What is being eclipsed, thereby, is that sources embody subjectivity. The latter can be retrieved, however, by focusing on the very point of sources. Any source is supposed to say or to establish what the law is. That's its inherent teleology. Therefore, it is not at all bizarre to assume that sources would, if they could, apply

[29] See Frege (1976), p. 50.

[30] See Künne (1980), and Somek (1996).

[31] See Potacs (2015), pp. 55–62. See also Potacs' contribution in this volume.

themselves to facts by declaring what the law is in this or that case. A piece of legislation lays down what ought to be done in certain situations. It legislates as though it had a view of what things should be like in each and every single case. For if it did not raise this claim it would not truly legislate. Hence, it is necessary to attribute to legislation the intent to dispel all doubts and, hence, to apply the law itself. After all, it is supposed to clarify what the law is.

If the source took care of the application of its own product (Y) it would simply say from case to case that Z ought to follow because of X. For example, the legislature would point out to criminal defendants that they are deserving of punishment because it has said so before.

$$\mathrm{X}\left[\wedge \mathrm{Y}\right] \wedge \text{facts} \Rightarrow \mathrm{Z}$$

Mind that the law rendered in object form disappears once the subjectivity of sources is brought into focus. This reflects the fact that if sources spoke themselves and controlled the application of their product, the problem of application would be entirely submerged. Actually, it would cease to exist.

$$\mathrm{Y} : \mathrm{X} \wedge \text{facts} \Rightarrow \mathrm{Z}$$

A hostile takeover of this kind would be wholly consistent with the ambition of sources to clarify what the law is.

8 Different Outlooks

The above analysis demonstrates that just like focusing on the law *qua* object of description eclipses the subjectivity of law, retrieving this subjectivity is liable to submerge the problem of application. What is also lost, as a result, is the normativity that links X and Y and inheres in Y as a legal rule.[32] It becomes absorbed by the autonomous operation of the source. The gain to be had from submerging normativity is, however, that it brings the law-creating facts into perspective.

Quite remarkably, the facts that matter for the purpose of creating law are rendered quite differently depending on the subjective outlook of legal knowledge that is manifest within the source. Legislation, for example, in virtue of resting on a decision, recognizes what the law is with an eye to what has been decided. Knowing the law from the perspective of legislation, therefore, requires adhering faithfully to the text of a statute or to its original meaning. The pertinent maxims of interpretation mark what it takes to know the law "legislatively". By contrast, the law is known in a manner congenial to customary law if claims are made that "this" or "that" is not what we are ready to condone here. If the law is known "customarily"

[32] The normativity that links X and Y is manifest in a rule saying that Y ought to follow from X. Y can be a proscription, prescription, immunity or legal power. Y would lack any normative force if it were not for the rule linking it with X.

this knowledge is replete with appeals to common understandings. Finally, law that is known "scholarly" comes about in appeals to a different form of fact, actually to argumentatively established differences in situations that are supposed to warrant the application of the appropriate legal rule. The law emerges, ideally, from a better argument.

The forms of legal knowledge that are inherent in sources express varieties of subjectivity. They, in turn, make a legal consequence conditional upon something factual. The sources say "you ought to" because "we see it that way", "we have decided it that way" or "the stronger argument requires that you follow this rule". The law flows from common understandings or decisions or, finally, from better views concerning what is to be considered the applicable rule.

9 From Subjectivity to Intersubjectivity

Obviously, sources *cannot* speak for themselves. This is a well-known truth that was already stated by Rousseau and Kant.[33] If the legislature decided every single case by its own, even by claiming to authoritatively apply its own general rules, no one would be in a position to tell whether the legislature applied the rules correctly or incorrectly. Rather, any authentic interpretation of its own rules casts the legislature in its proper role. Interpretation by the legislature is, using Derridian parlance, "iteration that alters".[34] The distinction between rule-making and rule-application collapses into a continuum that admits of no intelligible differentiation. Any general rule is dissolved into discrete acts of application that no longer add up to applications of general rules. Wittgenstein made a similar point when he recognized the impossibility of rule-following by one person considered in isolation.[35] If a rule does not serve as a public standard and one person on its own determines whether or not he or she is observing a rule, that person is unable to tell whether he or she is right about this. Indeed, in such a situation, just like in the situation of a legislature applying the law itself, the normative force of the rule evaporates (as Marx and Engels might have put it).[36] This reconfirms the point that emphasizing the subjectivity of sources submerges the normative character of the links between X and Y and Y and Z. That is so because the source, if it speaks only to itself, ends up connecting X and Z in a manner that is just as spontaneous as it is inscrutable.

It follows that sources can play their *normative* role only if one is apprehended by another. Custom remains obscure unless some body, then acting in a legislative capacity, articulates it explicitly as a rule. Legislation cannot apply itself to the facts. It depends for its full articulation on legal scholarship.

---

[33] See Rousseau (2012), p. 205 (*On Social Contract* III 1); Kant (1986), pp. 133–134.

[34] See Derrida (1988), p. 53. See also Menke (1988), pp. 220–222.

[35] See Wittgenstein (1971) § 258, p. 145. See also Kripke (1982), pp. 68–69.

[36] See Marx and Engels (1966), p. 215.

The apprehension of one source by another entails, however, a relationship of mutual recognition. The application of legislation through the lens of scholarly analysis presupposes that scholars commit themselves to letting the legislature speak. Scholarship must lend its *own* voice to legislation. The recognition needs to be, however, mutual. The legislature has to concede to scholarship the right to elaborate its meaning from a perspective that accords priority to the appropriateness of rule application. Of course, the relationship is rife with tension and conflict, for the later source in the sequence is always inclined to impose its own point of view on the former. Nevertheless, a claim concerning "it is our common understanding" requires a decisive "it is settled law that…" in order to become clear. Likewise, whatever "we have decided" needs to be supplemented with the "force of the better legal argument" so that it can be determined which decision is relevant for which case. Finally, the identification of the force of the better argument presupposes common understandings or may require even a decision. The law-applying official creates new law in the sense that, simply, a norm comes to this world as the progeny of another; and yet, this simple process involves the intervention of something factual: an interpretation of the relevant facts or a reading of the norm that has not been anticipated. In order to fulfill their function, sources require recognition by other sources. This means that law-creating facts are recognized only in virtue of other law-creating facts.

As the sources interact, they are engaged in some struggle of recognition.[37] From the perspective of common understandings, legislation appears wooden and detached from real life; from the same angle, legal arguments are perceived as sophistry. From the perspective of legislation, legal scholarship is always prone to commit some act of usurpation and custom is a perversion of legality that is supposed to flow from the top down to those located below. And from the perspective of legal scholarship, custom is the domain of obscurity and legislation some unfinished project that requires for its completion the benefit of legal expertise. All sources mutually reject *and* depend on one another. This is the *Komödie der Sittlichkeit*.

The sources of law do not only embody subjectivity. This subjectivity is part of intersubjective relations. The relations account for the fact that the normativity that is built into the sources can be made explicit and sustained. Knowledge of the law is something factual. It is essential for the efficacy of the legal system. The law would not come into existence were it not authoritatively known.

10 Reconciliation

Legal scholarship, traditionally understood, is about construing the relevant legal materials in a manner that suggests why it is appropriate to apply one or the other rule in one or the other case. To that end scholarship has to establish coherence, that

[37] See Somek (1996), pp. 35–38.

is, to arrive at an arrangement of the legal materials that demonstrates how the relevant pieces "fit together".

Scholarship could never accomplish this task if it did not attempt to make sense of the *substance* of the legal materials. If, choosing a random example, the law distinguishes between "murder" and "manslaughter" any defensible construction of the legal materials has to arrive at some sensible conception of how and why the line needs to be drawn between one and the other.

Therefore, in the course of preparing the ground for rational adjudication, legal scholarship runs the risk of becoming strangely complicit with this substance. The considerations that scholarship needs to adduce in order to determine the appropriately applicable norm indirectly invest a whole set of norms with an aura of reasonableness. While the validity of these norms cannot be disputed, a rational determination of their scope of application will have to suppose that they are an expression of practical reason. Assuming that a law-applying official is confronted with the question of having to choose among different "interrogation methods" in the context of the implementation of anti-terrorism policies, this official will have to draw out the relative merits of, say, either water boarding or electroshocks. In the course of a determination of the types of case where the former ought to be used rather than the latter the practice of torture is likely to look normal and, even worse, based on principles of rational conduct.

The substantive engagement with the substance of source-based law explains why hermeneutics is not only relevant to legal scholarship but essential to our practical reason as such. The legal relation is based on yielding to a determination of other persons without evaluating, or engaging with, the substantive reasons underpinning their choice. Indeed, in speaking of a "choice" we resort to a hieroglyphic referent in order to leave possible reasons for action unexamined. In virtue of recognizing that reasons may remain hidden, the law holds out a promise of reconciliation. We either do what other persons make us do (for example, by paying our dues) or tolerate what they have a right to do (for example, acquire and even read silly books). Our recognition of their choices reconciles us with what they *may* have reason to do, even if the reconciliation is only indirect, for we are reconciled with their reasons only by rendering them obscure. Cast in the terms of hermeneutics, our understanding is, if at all, *de dicto*, that is, we take note that it is this or that that they want.[38] Nevertheless, however idiosyncratic or unexamined an individual's reasoning may be, it is given entry to the domain of the practical reasons that we share inasmuch as we accord normative relevance to a choice. More importantly perhaps, in that others recognize what we want because we want it we are liberated from the rigor of moral self-examination and free to develop a legal relation with ourselves. We are free to enjoy our own inconsistency and whimsicality.

[38] More precisely, a *de dicto* interpretation attempts to reconstruct the historical horizon from within which a speaker has spoken or is speaking. See Brandom (2002), pp. 99–102.

11 Irony

The legal relation reconciles us with those whom we perceive to be wired differently. This reconciliation is merely held out as a promise. The legal relation depends on rules the validity of which is based on the mute reality of custom or on decisions, that is, on the existence of law-creating facts. The factual element of the sources is a replica of the hieroglyphic "choice". Again, the reconciliation remains indirect, in particular if legal scholarship makes it a point to let the sources speak for themselves.

We would be fully reconciled with these forms of indirect reconciliation, if the rules providing the basis for legal relations were substantively correct. Engaging with these rules in a substantive manner is—as was pointed out above—what legal scholarship is invariably about. This means, however, that the reconciliation inherent in the legal relation is deferred until legal scholarship goes about its hermeneutic business *de re* and engages in various attempts to make sense of the foreign reason, that it encounters in the legal materials.[39] Interestingly, the work of practical reason, which is at bottom a work of reconciliation, is unfinished until legal scholarship puts it all together and attempts to straddle the gap, dividing the materials and the horizon of contemporary scholarship. Any residual "merely factual" disappears within the medium of a theory (Dworkinian style) that underpins the existence of formal powers with good practical reason. This explains why the practical reason of law would not be finished if it were not for systematic legal reasoning.

Legal scholarship, therefore, is capable of overcoming the decisionism inherent in sources. The danger that emerges, in turn, is that it becomes far too reconciliatory and loses its respect for the authority of the factual. That which is distinctively legal would disappear if that respect vanished.

This explains why any great legal scholarship must partake of the irony inherent in the interpretation of the works of great masters such as Kant, Hegel or Wittgenstein. The interpreter seeks to make the best possible sense of the legal materials, by retaining, however, the reservation that, at the end of the day, it can all turn out to be utter nonsense.[40]

References

Brandom RB (2002) Tales of the mighty dead. Historical essays in the metaphysics of intentionality. Harvard University Press, Cambridge, pp 99–102

Crawford J (2012) Brownlie's principles of public international law, 8th edn. Oxford University Press, Oxford

Derrida J (1988) In: Weber S (ed) Limited Inc. Northwestern University Press, Evanston, p 53

Frege G (1976) In: Patzig G (ed) Logische Untersuchungen, 2nd edn. Vandenhoek & Ruprecht, Göttingen

[39] See ibid.

[40] See Williams (2004), p. 98.

Gadamer H-G (1976) Wahrheit und Methode: Grundzüge einer philosophischen Hermeneutik, 4th edn. Mohr, Tübingen
Gardner J (2012) Law as a leap of faith: essays on law in general. Oxford University Press, Oxford
Hegel GWF (1991) Elements of the philosophy of right (trans: Nisbet HB). Cambridge University Press, Cambridge
Hobbes T (2010) In: Shapiro I (ed) Leviathan. Yale University Press, New Haven
Houlgate S (2006) The opening of Hegel's logic. Indiana University Press, West Lafayette
Kant I (1986) In: Ludwig B (ed) Metaphysische Anfangsgründe der Rechtslehre. Meiner, Hamburg
Kripke SA (1982) Wittgenstein on rules and private language: an elementary exposition. Harvard University Press, Cambridge
Künne W (1980) Abstrakte Gegenstände: Semantik und Ontologie. Suhrkamp, Frankfurt aM
Lafont C (1999) The linguistic turn in hermeneutic philosophy (trans: Medina J). MIT Press, Cambridge, pp 92–108
Loughlin M (2017) Political jurisprudence. Oxford University Press, Oxford
Luhmann N (1984) Soziale Systeme: Grundriss einer allgemeinen Theorie. Suhrkamp, Frankfurt aM
Mackie JL (1977) Ethics: inventing right and wrong. Penguin Books, Harmondsworth
Marquard O (1981) Frage nach der Frage, auf die die Hermeneutik die Antwort ist. In: Abschied vom Prinzipiellen: Philosophische Studien. Reclam, Stuttgart
Marx K, Engels F (1966) Manifest der kommunistischen Partei. In: Reinoß H (ed) Karl Marx, Eine Auswahl aus seinem Werk. C.A. Koch Verlag Nachf, Berlin, pp 211–242
Menke C (1988) Die Souveränität der Kunst: Ästhetische Erfahrung nach Adorno und Derrida. Suhrkamp, Frankfurt aM
Menke C (2016) Kritik der Rechte. Suhrkamp, Berlin
Oakeshott M (1975) On human conduct. Oxford University Press, Oxford
Oakeshott M (1999) The rule of law. In: On history and other essays. Liberty Fund, Indianapolis, pp 129–178
Pierce CS (1998) 'The categories defended' (1903). In: The Peirce Edition Project (ed) The essential Peirce, vol 2. Indiana University Press, Bloomington, pp 160–178
Potacs M (2015) Rechtstheorie. Facultas, Vienna
Puchta GF (1828) Das Gewohnheitsrecht, vol 1. Palmsche Verlagsbuchhandlung, Erlangen
Rawls J (1991) Political liberalism. Columbia University Press, New York
Raz J (1979) The authority of law: essays on law and morality. Clarendon Press, Oxford
Raz J (1990) Practical reasons and norms, 2nd edn. Princeton University Press, Princeton
Rorty R (1979) Philosophy and the mirror of nature. Princeton University Press, Princeton
Rousseau J-J (2012) The major political writings (trans: Scott JT). University of Chicago Press, Chicago
Somek A (1996) Der Gegenstand der Rechtserkenntnis: Epitaph eines juristischen Problems. Nomos, Baden-Baden
Somek A (2017) The legal relation: legal theory after legal positivism. Cambridge University Press, Cambridge
Somek A (2018a) Rechtsphilosophie zur Einführung. Junius Verlag, Hamburg
Somek A (2018b) Wissen des Rechts. Mohr und Siebeck, Tübingen
The Federalist (2009) In: Sunstein C (ed) The Federalist. Harvard University Press, Cambridge
Ullmann-Margalit E (1977) The emergence of norms. Clarendon Press, Oxford
von Savigny FC (1840) System des heutigen römischen Rechts, vol 1. Veit & Co, Berlin
Waldron J (1999) Law and disagreement. Oxford University Press, Oxford
Williams B (2004) Truth and truthfulness. Princeton University Press, Princeton
Wittgenstein L (1971) Philosophische Untersuchungen. Suhrkamp, Frankfurt aM
Wittgenstein L (1988) Über Gewißheit = Werkausgabe in acht Bänden, vol 8. Suhrkamp, Frankfurt aM

The Many Forces in Law: Rational, Physical and Psychological Coercion

Jorge Emilio Núñez

Abstract There is a gap between the Kelsenian and Hartian traditions in legal theory, legal philosophy and jurisprudence. This gap is more evident in central concepts such as sanction and coercion. The paper examines how Kelsen understands different variants of *coercion*, that is rational, physical and psychological; and why the Hartian tradition misunderstands the Kelsenian approach. The paper has five main sections. The first section presents the reception theory in hermeneutics as a frame of reference. The second section reintroduces the idea that law is generally coercive but occasionally may be not. The third part examines the Kelsenian views on coercion and how Hart misunderstands these views. The fourth section focuses the attention on how Kelsen differentiates variants of coercion. The last section explores familiar examples of coercion culled from international law.

1 Reception Theory: Kelsen and Hart

Words create worlds (Gadamer 1976). The worlds created by words are at least three, that of the text itself, the one that the authors aimed to create (that may not be necessarily the one he actually created),[1] and the one each reader creates. If we add time and space to these worlds, the result will be an exponential growth *ad infinitum*. For example, what Machiavelli and Locke wished to tell their audiences at the time of writing and how their works are received may be very different (Skinner 1969, p. 15). Last but not least, when interpreting any text, it is important to add

Previous papers on the relationship between law and force by the author are Núñez (2012, 2016a, b, 2017).

[1] For an insightful distinction between motives and intentions on interpretation of texts, see Skinner (1972).

J. E. Núñez (✉)
Manchester Metropolitan University, Manchester, UK
e-mail: j.nunez@mmu.ac.uk

N. Bersier Ladavac et al. (eds.), *The Normative Force of the Factual*, Law and Philosophy Library 130, https://doi.org/10.1007/978-3-030-18929-7_10

another factor that is external to the text, the author, and the audience: its translation.[2]

From the above, the main—but not only—three factors that can be considered are the text, the author, and the reader. It is evident that texts are written by a certain author at a given time and arguably intended for certain readers or audience. Two main theories can be distinguished at this point: substantialist text theory and pragmatic text theory.[3] In brief, the substantialist theory centres the interpretation on the text as written by the author, what he intended the text to mean. The pragmatic theory has to do with the text as interpreted by the reader. It is clear that this distinction has to do with focusing either on the production of the text or its reception.

These theories, although clear at the time of putting together classifications, fail to recognise other elements important to any interpretation such as cultural, stylistical, and disciplinary differences. Moreover, what a text means and both the process of writing by the author and that of the assessment by the reader will differ depending on many circumstances amongst the most obvious which are time and space.

The following pages will centre the attention on the reader and how certain concepts particular to law—more specifically legal theory, legal philosophy, and jurisprudence—have been received. Reception theory (Jauss 1982) has to do with interpreting the texts according to how that text has been received by the reader. Linked to this, there is a case for a variety of interpretations or "unlimited semiosis" (Bullo 2014).

In principle, what appears to be the same very basic concepts in legal theory, legal philosophy, and jurisprudence are still discussed globally. I maintain that although these discussions seem to be centred on and disagree about the same concepts, in actual terms they are centred on conceptions of these concepts and therein the disagreement in their hermeneutics. It is not that these concepts are different but because the way in which these concepts are received by the reader we may identify different conceptions. That has to do, I believe, with the still existing gap between the Kelsenian and Hartian traditions in legal theory, legal philosophy, and jurisprudence.[4] More specifically, I maintain the debate is really one between a certain strand of post-Hartian legal theory on the one side and several other approaches, pragmatists and Kelsenians, on the other.

Examples of these different conceptions—i.e. Kelsenian and Hartian—of the same concepts that have to do with what I believe reception theory are *sanction* and *coercion*. Therein, what in principle may seem to be a disagreement about the concepts, I argue, it is a disagreement about different conceptions of these concepts. In order to show more clearly how the differences between styles have affected our current understanding of sanction and coercion Kelsen and Hart, respectively, will be questioned.

---

[2] For an example of how the word "sovereignty" and its meaning has evolved. See for example, Núñez (2011, 2014, 2015).

[3] See Thompson (1993), p. 251 citing Jauss and Grimm.

[4] Few have attempted to bridge the gap between these traditions. A good example of these attempts comes with Navarro and Rodriguez (2014). See Núñez (2016a, b).

In previous papers I discussed the nature of law and whether law is essentially coercive, and if so, in what sense.[5] This paper will revise some of the previous arguments, the reason coercion is *generally* part of the concept of law (and of its nature), and, *occasionally* absent from such concept (and its nature). The focus this time will be to examine how Kelsen understands different variants of *coercion*, that is rational, physical and psychological; and why the Hartian attacks on Kelsen's view about *coercion* are unjustified. In short, the Hartian tradition misunderstands the Kelsenian approach. It is intended to introduce familiar yet controversial examples that have been used to illuminate not only the concept of law (and its nature) but also—particularly—the theory of coercion. Such examples will be culled from international law.

2 Coercion Is *Generally* Part of the Law But *Occasionally* May Be Not

Coercion is *generally* part of the law—i.e. part of the law *by default*. To be more precise, we may distinguish coercion as: (a) a sanction—i.e. a broad interpretation of coercion or coercion arising *by default*; and (b) a view *sensu stricto*—i.e. a narrow account of coercion.

Law may be defined as a set of legal norms or rules. These legal norms are statements characterised as being hypothetical—i.e. in the hypothetical case a certain antecedent ought to have a respective consequence (Kelsen 1992, p. 23). That consequence may be either positive or negative. In the case of law as a social order, whether the consequence is positive or negative, is, in all cases, independent of the subject's will.

Coercion means—broad account or coercion *by default*—that somehow the choice of an antecedent conduct is limited to the subject as only such antecedent will bring about the consequence prescribed by the legal norm and the consequence that ought to happen. The circumstance that the consequence that follows the antecedent is positive or negative does not alter the fact that the given human conduct is limited and ought to happen even against the subject's will. Therefore, in relation to a coercive sanction that is negative in nature, if the antecedent happens, the consequence ought to follow independently of (even against) the process in the mind of the individual subject to the norm. On the contrary, in relation to a coercive sanction that is positive in nature, the consequence ought to follow independently of the process in the mind of the individual subject to the norm if, and only if, the subject complies with the antecedent prescribed by the legal norm. For instance, the subject either (a) follows the antecedent and therefore the prescribed consequence ought to follow—e.g. he murders and ought to be sentenced to a penalty or he signs a contract and ought to have consequent rights and obligations; or (b) he does not follow

[5] See n. 1.

the antecedent and the prescribed consequence does not follow—e.g. he does not murder hence he ought not to be sent to prison or he does not sign the contract and hence ought not to have consequent rights and obligations.

Coercion *sensu stricto* may be used in the event "resistance is encountered in applying the sanction" (Kelsen 2007/2009, p. 18). In that sense—and that sense only—coercion is an element that has to be considered in the quest to define what law is. Kelsen himself made it clear: "[i]f 'coercion' in the sense here defined is an essential element of law, the norms which form a legal order must be norms stipulating a coercive act, i.e. a sanction. In particular, the general norms must be norms in which a certain sanction is made upon certain conditions [...]" (Kelsen 2007/2009, p. 45). However, that does not mean that actual force—i.e. a broad account of coercion—will be used. Therefore, law may *occasionally* function without coercion *sensu stricto*.

The problem arises, it is argued, from a different understanding of the meaning of the term "sanction." In short, for Kelsen sanctions *may be legally coercive*. But, Hart's understanding of the Kelsenian account is rather different: for Hart a Kelsenian account of sanction inter-defines the term sanction with coercion. Thus, coercion is usually discarded, at least by the post-Hartian tradition, because it is inter-defined with terms such as "force" or "threat." That is to say, according to Hart, Kelsen defines law through sanctions; sanctions are coercive; coercion means force or threat; ergo, according to the Kelsenian account of law (i.e. what Hart thinks Kelsen tries to say) all legal norms are defined as threat, force. And, that is not plausible. The irony is that Kelsen did not define the law in such a way—or at least, not in such a loose way. This is how Hart understands Kelsen as a reader—i.e. reception theory—but not what Kelsen intends to say. Let us be more precise.

Once upon a time, there were many theories in legal philosophy, legal theory, or jurisprudence that included coercion when defining and describing the nature and characteristics of law—i.e. Bentham, Austin, Kelsen, to name a few classical examples. They all maintain—at least broadly—that law needs some form of coercion; such a view is, indeed, intuitively plausible. An obvious example is the criminal law. Although Hart does not include the notion of coercion directly, he concedes that legal rules circumscribe behaviours and therefore individuals are not free to do what they want (Hart 1997, p. 87).

But dissent came and Kelsenian and Hartian traditions followed different paths. Currently, it is a truism in post-Hartian legal philosophy that law cannot be defined as commands backed by force. Indeed, Bentham, Austin, Kelsen, and many others before them were intellectually blind to the reality that law included other norms too (e.g. power conferring norms); the views of such authors were so utterly misconceived that Hart had to enlighten us all. Therein, it is arguably a dogmatic view in post-Hartian legal philosophy that coercion is not integral to the nature and characteristics of law.

In order to disentangle these apparent differences we need to consider what questions we ask and what assumptions we raise when we characterise the law and when we discuss whether coercion is a precondition for law. More specifically, what assumptions the Hartian tradition has and whether these assumptions are shared by the Kelsenian tradition.

Some may maintain that coercion is conceptually necessary to define "what the law is" (classically, but not only, Austin, Bentham, Kelsen's view); some may maintain that coercion is not conceptually necessary to define "what the law is" (Hart and his followers).[6] It is argued that both sides of the jurisprudential divide disagree on the answer, not because of differences on the perceived conceptual necessities pertaining to "what the law is", but because of their different views about the term "coercion."[7] These different views stem from the different reception by the Kelsenian's and Hartian's style reader.

3 What Hart Thinks of Kelsen and What Kelsen Actually Intended to Say

On the one hand, since Hart, the prevailing view in legal theory is that "sanction" means privation, that is, a negative consequence. Even Yankah identifies sanctions with breach of norms and, therefore, with a negative consequence (2008: 21 ff). On the other hand, sanction may be seen as rewards—i.e. Schauer refers to carrots and sticks (2015: Chapter 8). Sanctions, however, may be more broadly defined as any type of consequence that follows an act within the law whether that consequence is positive or negative.[8]

Hart—and thereafter his followers (for example very recently Green 2016, p. 9)—starts from a presupposition based on an oversimplification when he says that for Kelsen[9] "[l]aw is the primary norm which stipulated the sanction" (Hart 1997, pp. 20–25, 35; Kelsen 2007/2009, p. 61). In this regard, Hart somehow assumes that Kelsen identifies sanction with threat; rules therefore, accorded to this distorted view, have the form of "[…] the antecedent or 'if clause' of conditional orders backed by threats or rules imposing duties" (Hart 1997, p. 37). Hart's understanding of Kelsen's theory, as manifested in this quotation is—to say the least—incomplete. His logic is flawed and his assessment plainly unfair.

Kelsen tells us that law, similar to any other normative system, is a social order that regulates human behaviour (Kelsen 2002/2009, p. 24). In order to distinguish these norms from any other normative system, Kelsen tells us that they are

[6] For a list of authors that argue coercion is not necessary see Schauer (2015), p. 2 and 171 n. 3.

[7] See my previous papers, n. 1. For a reference to the meaning of "coercion" from Austin to Schauer see Morrison (2016), p. 3 n. 6.

[8] Note that the author uses the term "positive consequence" and not reward since reward may be an example of "positive consequence" but not the only one.

[9] The author will refer only to Kelsen's view on sanction, coercion, and force. The bibliography that refers to Bentham and Austin in relation to this point, at least with what has to do with the Anglo-American jurisprudential tradition, is already very rich. See Austin (1832), p. 9 ff; Bentham (1970), p. 54; Hart (1997), pp. 82–84.

hypothetical statements (Kelsen 2007/2009, p. 38). These hypothetical statements—"ought statements" linking antecedent and consequence—prescribe a coercive act, i.e. a sanction (Kelsen 2007/2009, p. 45). Thus, from a Kelsenian perspective, sanction is the consequence that *ought to* follow a given antecedent (understanding antecedent as a given free human conduct). In simple terms, if there is no human conduct there cannot be a sanction (technically speaking). If there is human conduct and the law prescribes a consequence that ought to follow that human conduct, then a sanction arises regardless of the consequence being positive or negative. In simple terms:

- If *A* ought to be *S*
- If ~*A* ought not to be *S*

In the above two statements *A* means free human conduct and *S* means sanction. Where the antecedent of a given legal norm or rule states a set of conditions and in cases in which these conditions are fulfilled by free human conduct, it is only in these cases the sanction will happen—or better expressed, *ought to* happen. To be even more precise, the antecedent may be an action, a group of actions, and activity, a group of them or even an omission. The key is that in any case, the antecedent refers to free human conduct.

As with any other normative system—i.e. group of norms that regulate human social behaviour (Alchourrón and Bulygin 1971; Kelsen 2002/2009, p. 15, 24; Kelsen 2007/2009, p. 15)—law's function is to coordinate human conduct in intersubjective interference. (Cossio 1964) Depending on how these behaviours are dealt with, we may distinguish various normative systems, law being amongst them. Law, as any other normative system, utilises different means to motivate human conduct that may be broadly classified into direct and indirect[10] (conf. Kelsen 2007/2009, p. 15; Kelsen 2002/2009, p. 24). In any case, for the purpose of this paper, whether a norm of given human conduct brings about advantages or disadvantages, such are going to be seen as sanctions. In other words, sanction means the consequence prescribed by any norm as a result of a given human conduct regardless of that consequence being positive or negative.[11] The confusion starts when coercion and sanction are inter-defined.[12]

In a well-known move in legal philosophy, Hart argues that there is more to law than "orders backed by threat" (Hart 1997, p. 27). Indeed, this is a correct statement. However, in light of the above considerations, it can be seen that coercion does not mean only "threat"—at least according to a Kelsenian account of coercion. Therefore, Hart's criticism—at least with regard to Kelsen—is plainly unfair. The point may be developed further. Paraphrasing Hart the law may say "do X regardless of whether you wish or not to do it" but may also say "if you wish to do X, this is how you do it." The classical distinction between duty-imposing and

[10] The author will further clarify the point referred to as motivation and law in the next section of this paper.

[11] For a more detailed analysis on positive and negative consequences see my previous papers, n. 1.

[12] See Schauer (2015), Chapter 9, in particular p. 127 ff. See my previous paper, n. 1.

power-conferring norms applies here. Hart made clear that the former group may be characterised as coercive but the latter cannot. That is because—according to him—for all his predecessors (including Kelsen), coercion implies threat. This observation, the author submits, is an oversimplification. It is obvious that "legal rules defining the ways in which valid contracts or wills or marriages are made do not to require persons to act in certain ways whether they wish to or not" (Hart 1997, p. 27). Kelsen also acknowledges duty-imposing rules and power-conferring ones, even permissions (Kelsen 2007/2009, p. 75 ff). In all these cases, however, human conduct is subject to coercion. That is because, although law does not require persons to act in certain ways in all circumstances—e.g. with respect to contracts, wills, marriage—it does require persons to comply with a given antecedent if they wish a certain consequence to follow in law. In that sense, law limits human conduct—i.e. human conduct is being coerced—as, in order for a consequence to follow, the subject must comply with what the antecedent prescribes. The law is not simply suggesting or advising a subject that if he wishes to sell his house he may do so by signing a piece of paper called a contract. The law clearly states that if the subject aims to sell his house in such a manner that no third party may have any right whatsoever over the property, he ought to comply with certain conditions prescribed by the norms. In this way, the law is intervening in the subject's conduct by making clear what the antecedent is in order to achieve a given consequence binding in law. To that extent, the subject's conduct is also being coerced by power-conferring norms. The consequence ought to follow (the contract will be legally binding) independently of the process in the mind of the individual subject to the norm if, and only if, the subject complies with the antecedent prescribed by the legal norm.

4 Rational, Physical and Psychological Coercion

And now the crucial question, what is coercion?[13] Part of the confusion has to do with including non-legal elements when assessing this question. In this way, by adding extraneous elements we obscure the picture rather than offer a more pristine view of what the law is. When Hart points out that there is more to law than "orders backed by threat" (Hart 1997, p. 27) Hart is right. Hart is wrong, however, in assuming that for Kelsen "[l]aw is the primary norm which stipulated the sanction." (Hart 1997, pp. 20–25, 35; Kelsen 2007/2009, p. 61) and from there "[…] the antecedent or 'if clause' of conditional orders backed by threats or rules imposing duties" (Hart 1997, p. 37). The way in which Kelsen's views have been criticised is flawed and therefore, Hart's assessment is rather unfair.

Let us consider what Kelsen said in more detail. If we pay a closer look at Kelsen we will be able to distinguish three different forms of coercion: rational, physical

[13] For other views see Morrison (2016), p. 3, n. 6. For an extensive analysis see Edmundson (1995). However, Edmundson recognises, taking Wertheimer's two-prong analysis, a moralised account of coercion.

and psychological coercion. Kelsen defines legal norms or rules by means of rational coercion. Hart's criticism of Kelsen has to do with physical coercion only and hence it is incorrect.

4.1 Rational Coercion

With reference to coercion, Kelsen made clear the distinction between the inner and outer considerations. He also made clear that only the outer, objective side of coercion is relevant to the law—i.e. the rational side of coercion. In his words "[t]he element of coercion is relevant only as part of the contents of the legal norm, only as an act stipulated by this norm, not as a process in the mind of the individual subject to the norm" (Kelsen 2007/2009, p. 30).

In a norm of the form *If A ought to be S* both *A* and *S* are free human conducts that have been prescribed by a normative authority—e.g. the legislator. Therefore, there are independent of the volition of any subject who may (may not) do *A* and as a consequence, ought to be *S*—i.e. sanctioned. These have to do with outer considerations in the sense that the centre of *imputation* of any legal norm will always be free human conduct. Since *A* and *S* have been prescribed by subjects that are different from the ones that ultimately will have to comply (or not) with the legal norm, they are out of their volition.

The author follows this path too. For the purpose of this paper, coercion—or more specifically, coercive sanction—arises when the consequence that follows a given human conduct ought to be independent of (even against) the subject's will—i.e. the word "independent" is used rather than "against" as the subject may, as we will see, be willing to align his volition with the consequence.[14] In other words, the legal norm (in large, the legal system) provides specific acts as consequences that ought to follow specific antecedents in specific cases regardless of whether we want them or not (Kelsen 2007/2009, pp. 29–30).

Whether force is deployed or not is a different aspect in this enquiry. We will see in the next section of this paper that actual *force* may be applied but this does not necessarily have to be done. For a narrow account coercion may be identified with the potential use of force in particular cases. Nevertheless, force does not need to be present in order to have coercion as it is a factual question as to whether power is actually used (Green 2016, p. 8; Kelsen 2007/2009, p. 29 *in fine* and 30 *supra*). Therefore, it is misleading to use the classical examples of rules of contract or wills in order to show that because they do not prescribe coercive sanctions they are not included in, for example, Kelsen's theory of law (Green 2016, p. 9). It is correct to say that if we do not comply with the rules of contract, *force* will not be used—this is a narrow account of coercion or coercion *sensu stricto*. However, to state that not

[14] Indeed, as Kelsen rightly points out, the subject may act or omit to act because of motives other than the reward or punishment (Kelsen 2002/2009, p. 26).

complying with the rules for formation of contract will not have legal consequences is something different. That is because, even in cases such as the ones sub-examined, the subject has his conduct coerced, as if he does not comply with the rules of contract, there will be no contract and, therefore, no consequent rights and obligations. This is a broad account of coercion or coercion *by default*. In this regard, coercion is *generally* or *by default* part of the law.

4.2 Psychological Coercion

From the above we can infer that law is not the only social order that may use sanctions. Morality and religion as social orders exert a certain form of coercion too (Kelsen 2002/2009, p. 35). The difference between law and any other social order is *not* whether they prohibit, permit, or command a given act or omission. They are different *not* because of what they prohibit, permit, or command. The difference between law and any other social order relates to *how* they prohibit, permit, or command. In other words, law as a social order conditions certain antecedents to consequences that ought to follow even against our will—i.e. coercive sanctions (Kelsen 2002/2009, p. 62). Morality and religion may exert coercion too but of a different kind. We may argue that our behaviour is limited by morality and religion, and that for a given antecedent—e.g. murder—a consequence ought to follow—e.g. rejection, hell; in this sense, morality and religion may be characterised as coercive. However, this kind of coercion is only psychic or psychological coercion.

Law may bring about psychic coercion too, but this characteristic does not define law. The motivation may be triggered by psychic impulse but it is not necessary to law (Kelsen 2007/2009, p. 23). In other words, human conduct that complies with what the legal norm prescribes may happen by other motives, for instance moral and religious principles. However, this psychic coercion has nothing to do with the coercive act prescribed by the legal norm (Kelsen 2002/2009, p. 35). Examples of such coercion would be, say, where someone commits a criminal offence and regrets his action to the extent that he wishes to go to prison and does not further view that punishment as a threat, or someone who commits a criminal offence in order to go to prison only because he is interested in having his meal served daily (Kelsen 2002/2009, p. 33). Another example would be the case of a person getting married in order to be granted the same nationality as his spouse and therefore, to receive social benefits otherwise limited to nationals. All these sanctions are coercive from the perspective of the law because they ought to happen provided the respective antecedents also happen regardless of whether the subject wants them to happen or not. Whether the subjects in each situation choose to act or not to act in response to psychic coercion is a matter that goes beyond the law. Whether the subject considers the sanction a curse or a blessing has no relevance whatsoever to defining the legal norm. That the legal norm brings about coercive sanctions in the form of punishment or reward means that the legal order prescribes consequences that ought to follow certain antecedents independently of (even against) our will. Indeed, from a sociological and psychological point of view, we may argue whether psychic coercion is present—i.e. whether the subject acted or omitted to act due to moral, religious, or even practical reasons such as food and shelter—but that is irrelevant to the legal norm in the sense it does not define the law.

4.3 Physical Coercion

There are several ways in which human behaviour may be motivated and coercion is just one of them. There are situations in which our conduct may be somehow limited with regard to what we ought to do or not to do—antecedent—in order for something else to happen—consequence. It is in these situations that our behaviour is coerced. More specifically, coercion may refer to the use of force but need not necessarily do so. Indeed, it will be argued that there are other means to motivate subjects and the use of coercion will be rejected in certain cases. It is intended to show that *occasionally* law may do without coercion.

Social orders such as religion, morality, and law exist in order to let subjects and social aggregations (Nozick 1974: Part I, Chapter 2) have their conducts regulated within an interactive framework of society. As Kelsen says such orders make subjects "refrain from certain acts which, for some reason, are deemed detrimental to society, and to … perform others which, for some reason, are considered useful to society" (Kelsen 2007/2009, p. 15). In this way, law, as with any other social order, may motivate subjects to act or refrain from acting directly or indirectly (Kelsen 2007/2009, p. 15).

Law "may attach certain advantages to its observance and certain disadvantages to its non-observance" (Kelsen 2007/2009, p. 15). Even though the former "plays a far more important role" (Kelsen 2007/2009, p. 17) in social reality, sanctions do not only imply negative consequences but may also include positive ones. In tune with this, Schauer attempts to include both advantages and disadvantages in his account when maintaining that "there can be rewards as well as punishments, and law's coercive […] power often includes its ability to create positive as well as negatives incentives" (Schauer 2015, p. 7). Unfortunately, Schauer falls victim of oversimplification too as he defines advantages or positive consequences in terms of rewards only (Schauer 2015: Chapter 8). Kelsen goes further and asserts that social orders may even function without advantages or disadvantages and still "require conduct that appeals directly to the individuals" (Kelsen 2007/2009, p. 15). Therefore, legal rules may—according to a Kelsenian view—specify duties but also confer powers—therefore, all three fundamental deontic concepts, obligation, prohibition, and permission are included (Navarro and Rodriguez 2014, p. 18).

Evidently, coercion is an example of a direct means to motivate behaviour—i.e. you ought to act or not to act in such a way in order for this or that consequence to happen. However, coercion does not imply *per se* the use of force. This is another difference between the Hartian and Kelsenian accounts that is still present amongst us. Kelsen clearly states that "[t]his does not mean that in carrying out the sanction physical force must be applied" (Kelsen 2007/2009, p. 18). In tune with this, Schauer and Yankah's accounts of the inclusion of force as a way to characterise coercion is rather hasty. Schauer maintains, "law's brute force [...] is the principal identifying feature of legality has in the past been conventional wisdom. [...] But precisely the opposite—that force is not the characteristic or identifying feature of law—is now conventional wisdom [...]" (Schauer 2015, p. 10) In turn, Yankah tells us that "Kelsen [...] conceived of law as simply proscribed norms the violation of which give rise to a corresponding sanction" understanding "sanction is a penalty attached to the breach of a norm [...]" (Yankah 2008, pp. 21–22) These accounts are not true; or at least, they are not an accurate description of the Kelsenian view.

Sanctions are coercive measures in the sense that consequences happen *independently* of—not necessarily against—subject's will. Thus far, a broad account of coercion or coercion *by default* has been presented, as per the previous sections in this paper. Coercion—so defined—has two different facets: rational coercion, and, physical coercion (Yankah 2008, p. 31 ff). Legal norms, it is argued, are coercive in one sense but not necessarily in the other. More specifically, all legal norms apply rational pressure or bring about rational coercion but not all legal norms have the ability or need to deploy physical coercion.

On the one hand, because a legal norm brings about rational coercion a given consequence ought to follow an antecedent, not as a process in the mind of the individual subject to the norm—that is for other normative systems such as morality and religion—but as an objectively prescribed consequence. This is common to all legal norms and in this sense all norms are coercive. Physical coercion, on the other hand, may follow a given antecedent but does not necessarily have to do so. After all, some coercive sanctions may, *if and only if necessary*, be applied by the employment of physical force (Kelsen 2007/2009, p. 19). For clarity, this last account will be named coercion *sensu stricto*.

Thus far, all normative systems follow a similar structure in that they prescribe a consequence to a given antecedent in order to regulate human conduct. When the consequence ought to follow as objectively prescribed by the norm, independently of—even against—the process in the mind of the individual subject to that norm, we have sanctions that are coercive. More specifically, these coercive sanctions are *rationally* coercive—i.e. the consequence ought to follow the antecedent regardless of the process in the mind of the subject. In addition to this, some coercive sanctions may be *physically* coercive too—i.e. in the event that the subject does not follow the consequence. Law has the exclusive prerogative in comparison with all other normative systems to *force* the subject. Let us be even more precise here.

The use of *force*—i.e. physical coercion—is the exclusive prerogative of law as a social order (Kelsen 2002/2009, pp. 33–37). However, that does not mean that the use of force as exclusive to law defines it. In other words, force is instrumental to law as a form of coercion—i.e. physical coercion. However, that does not imply that coercion is defined only as force—i.e. force is but one of the modes coercion presents; or that force is the only form of coercion law has at its disposal. It only means that force, as a form of coercion, is exclusive to law. This is also an accurate reading of Kelsen's thesis[15] (Kelsen 2007/2009, pp. 18–21).

5 The Case of International Law… or Is It International Morals?

The theme of whether coercion is integral to the legal system has also arisen in the context of international law, taxing the minds of an assortment of legal scholars not accustomed to discussing jurisprudential questions.[16] "Is the international legal order law at all?" is still a focal point of debate (Hathaway and Shapiro 2011, pp. 252–255). Some still argue that because the international legal order does not offer the features of domestic legal systems such as a world government that can make law, a supranational system of sanctions, and authorities that can enforce these sanctions, it cannot be classified as law.[17] It follows from this that, because consequences prescribed by international law are largely unenforceable, they may not be legal but moral in nature. Ergo, the question necessarily arises, if international law may bring about consequences that are not enforceable, is the international legal system law at all? Hart too dealt with international law and its enforcement (Hart 1997: Chapter X). His arguments to discard coercion and at the same time consider the international legal system as law may be summarised as follows:

PREMISE ONE:	to argue that international law is not law because of the lack of sanctions is to accept that law is defined as orders backed by threats (Hart 1997, p. 217)
PREMISE TWO:	law cannot be defined as orders backed by threats (Hart 1997: Chapter III)
PREMISE THREE:	"aggression between States is very unlike that between individuals" (Hart 1997, p. 219)
PREMISE FOUR:	"for States, long years of peace have intervened between disastrous wars" (Hart 1997, p. 219)
CONCLUSION:	enforcement is not present in international law because is not needed.

What Hart argues, in the last chapter of *The Concept of Law*, is that international law bears a family resemblance to municipal law but fails to qualify as a genuine legal order; for the reason that there is no international rule of recognition and hence

[15] For an example of post-Hartian misinterpretation of Kelsen's view see Green (2016), p. 7. Green groups together Bentham, Austin, and Kelsen and tells us that "[t]hey meant that law not only necessarily has such powers, but also that it necessarily uses them."

[16] This paper will offer a brief account. A more detailed analysis of the role coercion plays in international law will be left for more detailed analysis. For an account see Raponi (2015).

[17] For an account of this model see Raponi (2015), p. 36, in particular n. 3.

no true international legal system. Whether there is or not international rule of recognition and whether, as a consequence, there is an international legal system at all is a question out of the scope of this paper. What is relevant to these pages is the fact that Hart discharges the use of force in the international arena with no further or deep considerations than the ones summarised above. Hart's view, at least on this point, is questionable. The question as to whether States have maintained peaceful relationships—thereby obviating the necessity for the establishment of enforcement mechanisms—fails to take cognisance of changing global realities. Furthermore, it does not answer the question "may international law be defined as law?" At least, it does not answer the question as to whether the international legal order is law at all based on understanding coercion as a conceptual necessity. It does, however, adjust the angle in *The Concept of Law* and, on this issue, Hart employs natural necessity to remove coercion from the picture. In this regard, Hart's shift implies the use of practical reasons to construct a set of arguments in order to discard conceptual implications. The shift has been viewed as deeply problematic by certain analysts (Morrison 2016, p. 18).

If we follow the approach proposed in this paper, and distinguish sanction from coercion, and recognise that the latter has different facets—in what is of interest here, rational coercion and physical coercion—the international legal order can undoubtedly be characterised as law. Kelsen was more sympathetic to international law that Hart. But part of the reason was that Kelsen did not think that international law lacked coerciveness. He argued, rather, that international law is an under-institutionalised system that permits the subjects of the law to execute sanctions by way of self-help. In principle, international law follows a similar path to that taken by national legal orders (Kelsen 2002/2009, p. 320 ff; Kelsen 2007/2009, p. 328 ff). In other words, international legal norms may be characterised as hypothetical statements in which a given consequence ought to follow a given antecedent. In that sense, and that sense only, the international legal order can be characterised as coercive. Sovereign States' conducts are regulated by the international legal order. However, this does not mean that in the event they do not comply with the strictures of international law, force will be deployed. By defining the law in light of the manner in which this paper characterises sanction, coercion, and force, the international legal order is undoubtedly law too. This way of reasoning has to do with accommodating what seem on the surface to be competing narratives. Having accepted that legal norms prescribe coercive sanctions—i.e. consequence ought to follow independently of (even against) the process in the mind of the individual subject to the norm—the international legal order can be characterised as law. Whether these international norms are actually enforced or not—i.e. whether the deployment of force follows or not—is irrelevant to defining the legal character of international law for, to do this, is to define the very essence of law. This is because, similar to what happens in national law, even in the extreme case of the use of force—i.e. coercion *sensu stricto*—this circumstance will be prescribed by the law. Hence, regardless of the fact that force is deployed, in all cases the law will prescribe when, how, and by whom that force ought to follow a given antecedent—e.g. war, reprisals, humanitarian intervention, fines. In all other cases, the use of force will simply be contrary to law—e.g. invasion, occupation, genocide, piracy.

6 Conclusion

There is a gap between the Kelsenian and Hartian traditions in legal theory, legal philosophy and jurisprudence. There are many examples that could be used to demonstrate the gap. The paper considered in depth how Kelsen understands different variants of *coercion*, that is rational, physical and psychological; and why the Hartian tradition misunderstands the Kelsenian approach. In order to do this, reception theory resulted helpful as a frame of reference. Indeed, hermeneutics help to show what Kelsen intends to say and how Hart, and thereafter his followers, misunderstands the role coercion plays in law for the Kelsenian view.

For simplicity, and in order to demonstrate the main claim, the paper reintroduced two different standpoints on coercion: (a) a narrow account of coercion or coercion *sensu stricto*; and (b) a broad account of coercion or coercion *by default*.

Following a Kelsenian approach, the rules that constitute law are hypothetical statements relating antecedent with consequent regardless of the process in the mind of the subject—i.e. rational coercion, not psychic or psychological coercion. Specifically, the consequent is a sanction that may—but is not necessarily required to—incorporate the use of force—i.e. physical coercion.

References

Alchourrón CE, Bulygin E (1971) Normative systems. Library of exact philosophy. Springer, Wien

Austin J (1832) The province of jurisprudence determined. John Murray, Albemarle St, London

Bentham J (1970) Of laws in general. Continuum International Publishing Group Ltd

Bullo S (2014) Evaluation in advertising reception: a socio-cognitive and linguistic perspective. Springer

Cossio C (1964) La Teoría Egológica del Derecho y el Concepto Jurídico de Libertad. Abeledo Perrot, Buenos Aires

Edmundson WA (1995) Is law coercive? Legal Theory 1:81–111

Gadamer H-G (1976) Philosophical hermeneutics. University of California Press, Berkeley

Green L (2016) The forces of law: duty, coercion, and power. Ratio Juris 29:164–181

Hart HLA (1997) The concept of law. Oxford University Press, Oxford

Hathaway O, Shapiro SJ (2011) Outcasting: enforcement in domestic and international law. Yale Law J 121:252–349

Jauss H (1982) Toward and aesthetic of reception. University of Minnesota Press

Kelsen H (1992) Introduction to the problems of legal theory. Oxford University Press, Oxford

Kelsen H (2002/2009) Pure theory of law. The Lawbook Exchange, Ltd

Kelsen H (2007/2009) General theory of law and state. The Lawbook Exchange, Ltd

Morrison AS (2016) Law is the command of the sovereign: H.L.A. reconsidered. Ratio Juris 29(3):364–384

Navarro P, Rodriguez J (2014) Deontic logic and legal systems. Cambridge University Press, Cambridge

Nozick R (1974) Anarchy, State and Utopia. Basic Books

Núñez JE (2011) The origins of sovereignty in the Hellenic World. In: Frenkel DA (ed) International law, conventions and justice. ATINER, Athens

Núñez JE (2012) Normative systems as law in synergy: validity and effectiveness. In: Philosophy of law and state responsibility. St. Petersburg State University, St. Petersburg

Núñez JE (2014) About the impossibility of Absolute State sovereignty: the early years. Int J Semiotics Law 27:645–664

Núñez JE (2015) About the impossibility of Absolute State sovereignty: the middle ages. Int J Semiotics Law 28:235–250

Núñez JE (2016a) The logical analysis of law as a bridge between legal philosophical traditions. Jurisprudence 7(3):627–635

Núñez JE (2016b) The force of law: law and coercion, validity and effectiveness, and synergy. In: Bezemek C, Ladavac N (eds) The force of law reaffirmed. Springer

Núñez JE (2017) The forces in law: sanctions and coercions. Aust J Legal Philos 42(1):145–164

Raponi S (2015) Is coercion necessary for law? The role of coercion in international and domestic law. Wash Univ Jurisprud Rev 8:35

Schauer F (2015) The force of law. Harvard University Press, Cambridge

Skinner Q (1969) Meaning and understanding in the history of ideas. Hist Theory 8:3–53

Skinner Q (1972) Motives, intentions and the interpretation of texts. New Lit Hist 3:393–408

Thompson MP (1993) Reception theory and the interpretation of historical meaning. Hist Theory 32:248–272

Yankah EN (2008) The force of law: the role of coercion in legal norms. Univ Rich Law Rev 42:1195–1256

Legal Facts and Reasons for Action: Between Deflationary and Robust Conceptions of Law's Reason-Giving Capacity

Noam Gur

Abstract This chapter considers whether legal requirements can constitute reasons for action independently of the merits of the requirement at hand. While jurisprudential opinion on this question is far from uniform, sceptical (or 'deflationary') views are becoming increasingly dominant. Such views typically contend that, while the law can be indicative of pre-existing reasons, or can trigger pre-existing reasons into operation, it cannot constitute new reasons. This chapter offers support to a somewhat less sceptical (but still qualified) position, according to which the fact that a legal requirement has been issued can be a reason for action, yet one that is underpinned by bedrock values which (under certain conditions and constraints) law is apt to serve. Notions discussed here include a value-based conception of reasons as facts (Sect. 1); a distinction between complete and incomplete reasons (Sect. 2); and David Enoch's idea of triggering reason-giving (Sect. 3). Following a discussion of criticism against the view adopted here (Sect. 4), the chapter concludes by considering some more 'robust' conceptions of law's reason-giving capacity (Sect. 5).

Can the fact that the law requires an action constitute a reason for its performance? That is, can the fact that a requirement has been issued by a law-making institution (or, at least, a law-making institution of a reasonably just and decent legal system)—independently of the merits or demerits of that specific requirement, and of the risk of suffering a sanction—be a reason for action? While jurisprudential opinion on this matter is far from uniform, sceptical views—sometimes referred to as "deflationary" approaches to legal normativity—seem to have become increasingly dominant in contemporary discourse.[1] One response comes in roughly the following

[1] See, e.g., the deflationary positions put forward in Regan (1989), pp. 1003–1033, 1086–1095; Regan (1990), Enoch (2011a). Cf. moderately deflationary elements featuring in Marmor (2018). Marmor's account differs from the deflationary position presented in the main body text and is, I

N. Gur (✉)
Queen Mary University of London, London, UK
e-mail: n.gur@qmul.ac.uk

N. Bersier Ladavac et al. (eds.), *The Normative Force of the Factual*, Law and Philosophy Library 130, https://doi.org/10.1007/978-3-030-18929-7_11

form. When the law requires an action, there will sometimes (perhaps even often) be reasons for its performance, and some of such reasons may be *related to* the fact that the action is legally required, but the latter fact itself is not a reason for action. Thus, for example, in situations where my failure to comply with the law would likely result in a sanction, I have a prudential reason to comply—the reason to avoid a sanction. Moreover, insofar as the requirement's content coincides with what is anyway (regardless of the law) right or desirable—as is the case, for example, when the law requires us to avoid *mala in se* conduct such as murder, theft, or physical assault—clearly I have a content-dependent reason to act in conformity with the requirement. With regard to such reasons, the law can at best play an indicative role. And, finally, there will sometimes be reasons to comply that are not sanction-based and are (at least relatively) independent of the specific content adopted by the legal requirement. If, for instance, compliance will help me coordinate with my fellows, and if doing so is desirable, I have pro tanto a coordination-based reason to comply—as is the case, for example, with the rule that requires me to drive on the left (and as would equally be the case if the rule required me to drive on the right). But the reason in this example is not the rule itself, or the fact of its issuance, but the background desideratum of coordinating with my fellow drivers, which is antecedent and external to the law. All that the law does in this instance is to change the relevant factual landscape by affecting the likely behaviour of my fellow drivers, thus making it possible for me to satisfy a reason that lies in the background of the rule, namely a coordination need.[2] The very fact of there being a rule does not, on this view, constitute the reason.

In this chapter I wish to highlight some aspects of the relevant conceptual terrain that can lend support to, or at least facilitate acceptance of,[3] a somewhat less sceptical (but still qualified) position, according to which the fact that a legal requirement has been issued can be a reason for action,[4] yet one that is underpinned by bedrock values that (under certain conditions and constraints) law is apt to serve. I will also briefly point at an attitudinal aspect of legal normativity (i.e., one that pertains to

think, closer to the views I will defend in Sects. 1–4. Similarly, some of Fred Schauer's remarks suggest a certain affinity with deflationism (see, e.g., Schauer 2016), but I am not sure if the extent of his deflationary affinity marks a discord with my claims in Sects. 1–4. I should also note that the label 'deflationary', in connection with legal normativity, can be used for a range of possible claims, including ones I do not discuss here. See, e.g., Bix (2018) and the symposium published in Revus (2019) 37 (https://journals.openedition.org/revus/5195) on Bix's essay.

[2] Regan (1989), pp. 1019–1033. See also Enoch (2011a), pp. 4–5, 26–33, who argues in a similar vein by reference to his notion of "triggering reason-giving". This notion will be discussed in Sect. 3.

[3] I am framing my objective in these rather modest terms ("facilitate acceptance") because a fair amount of what will be said here does not squarely establish the above view, but rather only draws attention to some notions against the background of which it becomes comparatively easy to accept that view.

[4] Occasionally, I will speak of a legal requirement as a reason for action. When doing so, I am merely using terminological shorthand that should be read as saying that *the fact of there being* a legal requirement is a reason for action.

reasons vis-à-vis attitudes, rather than reasons for action),[5] which I have explored elsewhere at greater length.[6] The set of concepts that will be discussed or highlighted here includes a value-based conception of reasons as facts (Sect. 1); a distinction between complete and incomplete reasons (Sect. 2); and David Enoch's notion of triggering reason-giving (Sect. 3). I will then consider and reject a possible objection—on behalf of a more deflationary approach than mine—according to which my position is guilty of a misattribution of reason-giving power (Sect. 4). Before concluding the chapter, I will consider whether, and in what sense, law can gain a more robust status as a source of practical reasons (Sect. 5).

1 A Value-Based Conception of Reasons as Facts

Reasons for action, in the sense pertinent to this discussion, are a *normative* beast, so to speak; they bear on what we *ought* to do or avoid doing.[7] And, since deriving a genuine normative inference[8] from purely and exclusively non-evaluative premises would seem to involve an unwarranted leap, it appears plausible to think that reasons for action are grounded (at least partly) in some values or goods. I should be quick to add, by way of qualification, that the foregoing is a contested view of practical reasons,[9] which finds its most notable rival in desire-based theories of practical reasons.[10] But my present focus will be confined to a value-based view of practical

---

[5] Sect. 5 herein.

[6] Gur (2018), Chaps. 7–9.

[7] I am not discussing herein reasons in the *motivational* sense, or what some writers have labelled "motivating reasons for action". On the distinction between the normative and motivational senses of reasons, see, e.g., Smith (1994), pp. 94–98; Dancy (2003), pp. 1–5, 20–25; Parfit (2001), p. 17. Other writers have used alternative terms in this connection, e.g., "justifying" or "grounding" instead of "normative" reasons, and "explanatory" instead of "motivating" reasons. See, e.g., Raz (2011), pp. 13–35, where Raz distinguishes between normative and explanatory reasons. Cf. Alvarez (2010), Chap. 2. For jurisprudential references to the normative/motivating-reasons distinction, see, e.g., Coleman (2001), pp. 71–72; Enoch (2011a), p. 15; Bix (2011), pp. 413–414; Ehrenberg (2016), pp. 150–152.

[8] That is, such that one judges it to be warranted from the viewpoint of the normative universe at large, rather than, say, merely identifying that it is supposed by some social practice, or that it features in the perception of some people.

[9] The body of philosophical writings on this matter (and more generally on the concept of reasons) is voluminous. For some relatively recent surveys, see Wiland (2012), Bongiovanni (2018), pp. 3–33.

[10] I should note incidentally that, in comparison to value-based views of reasons, desire-based views of reasons seem to me, prima pacie, to fit less smoothly into a discussion of law's normative force. For it is a salient and important feature of law that it seeks to address reasons for action even to those who have no desire or want that corresponds to what it requires. And though the law does not always have the reason-giving power it purports to have, we do not attribute such failures to the absence of this or that desire on the part of a given subject. But a question might be raised here: could desire-based/internalist conceptions fully account for law-given reasons by focusing on

reasons. Confining the discussion to this ambit is commensurate with my modestly framed objective here, which is merely to highlight some (tenable, even if not uncontested) aspects of the relevant conceptual landscape in view of which it becomes easier to accept that legal requirements can form reasons for action.

Another clarification should be made about value-based conceptions of reasons. To say that reasons for action are grounded in values is not to say that reasons for action *are* values. To be sure, we sometimes speak of values as reasons—as when one says, for example, that the value of human life is a reason for stricter arms control, or that equal respect for persons is a reason against arbitrary discrimination. And, when making statements of this form, we are not likely to prompt the objection that we have misunderstood the concept of reasons—on the contrary, such statements may well accord with our intuitions about the concept. Nonetheless, to conceptualize reasons as values would fall considerably short of capturing the full range of common discourse and thought in which reasons feature. When we say that Jane's being late for work is a reason for her to hurry up, that the light bulb in Ali's table lamp being burnt out is a reason for him to replace it, or that Rosie's waiting for Claudine at the station is a reason for Claudine to go there, what we are referring to as reasons are *facts*.[11] And, indeed, the idea that reasons are facts, albeit a contested idea, enjoys a fair amount of support among writers on the nature of reasons,[12] including proponents of a value-based theory of reasons.

A terminological clarification should be added at this point. I intend the term "fact" in a sense similar to that which is employed in Joseph Raz's seminal book *Practical Reason and Norms*. Raz stipulates that he uses this term "in an extended sense to designate that in virtue of which true or justified statements are true or justified"[13] and that by "fact" he means "simply that which can be designated by the use of the operator 'the fact that ...'."[14] "Facts" in this sense include, for example, "the occurrence of events, processes, performances and activities".[15] And using this sense of "fact" also accommodates what was identified above as the intuitive appeal in treating values as reasons—for X's being a value can also be designated by the operator "the fact that ..." (as in: "The fact that human life/equal respect for persons is a paramount value ...").[16]

more abstract and less immediate human desires whose fulfilment is helped or made possible by the law? Such an exercise, it seems to me, would require considerable strain, but I express no stronger view on whether it might succeed.

[11] Or, at least, this is what we are referring to in the explicit part of our statement.

[12] On reasons as facts see, e.g., Raz (1990), pp. 17–20. See also Gardner and Macklem (2002), pp. 442–447. Factualist views of reasons are often contrasted with the position that reasons are some mental states (e.g., beliefs, pro-attitudes such as desires, or both)—a position sometimes referred to as a "psychologistic" approach to reasons.

[13] Raz (1990), p. 17.

[14] Ibid., 18.

[15] Ibid.

[16] In this connection, see also Gardner and Macklem (2002), pp. 449–450, where the authors point out "the error of thinking that while there may be mixtures of facts and values there are no true

Thus far I have briefly indicated some of the arguable merits of conceiving of reasons as facts and of thinking that they are grounded in values. These two views can be combined into something like the following understanding of reasons for action: (1) Reasons for action are facts that count in favour of a certain action; (2) Facts that constitute reasons for action are facts in virtue of which the action has some value (or its consequences do)[17]; they are facts in virtue of which the action is, in some way, good or desirable.[18] By way of illustration, the fact that it is raining today is a reason for me to carry an umbrella. For that fact is part of what makes carrying an umbrella an act that will effectively contribute to a desirable condition, that is, my not being drenched (and there are further explanations of why it is a desirable condition: otherwise I would be likelier to develop a cold, feel uncomfortable, have to waste time on changing clothes, etc.). A person may, directly or indirectly, refer to such a reason without fully stating why it is a reason, as when one says simply: "It's going to rain today. I'd better take an umbrella." But part of what one implies when making such a statement is that being soaked by the rain would be a bad thing.[19]

As indicated earlier, it falls outside the scope and aim of this paper to make a case for the above conception of reasons for action. The point I wish to make instead is that under one notable conception of reasons—which holds a fair degree of intuitive appeal and congruence with the way reasons feature in ordinary discourse—it becomes relatively easy to see how the fact of there being a legal rule in place can be a reason for action. Under this conception, the fact that the law requires an action (φ) need not inhere any moral metaphysical qualities for it to be a reason for action. If it is the case that, due to the introduction of a legal requirement, my φ-ing would serve certain values (whose status and importance as values do not derive from the law itself) which it would not otherwise serve—say, values associated with the desirability of social coordination, social order and stability, or 'fair play' consider-

compounds of the two", and give examples of "value-laden facts", such as "the fact that the Lake District is beautiful, or the fact that the Thames is dangerous" (ibid., 450).

[17] In defence of a value-based theory of reasons, see, e.g., Bond (1983), Parfit (2001), Gardner and Macklem (2002), pp. 450–457. Raz, too, seems generally to support a value-based theory of practical reasons (see, e.g., Raz 1999, pp. 22, 29–31, 63–64; Raz 2011, pp. 70, 75–79), albeit with certain qualifications (see, e.g., Raz 1999, p. 62; Raz 2016, pp. 141–156). See other relevant references cited in Maguire (2016), p. 234, n. 2. Cf. Chang (2004), pp. 56–90, who advocates a "hybrid" view, according to which "[s]ome practical reasons are provided by the fact that the agent wants something, while others are provided by the fact that what she wants is of value" (ibid., 57).

[18] A notable alternative is Scanlon's "buck-passing view" of value, according to which reasons have an explanatory priority over value (Scanlon 1998, pp. 95–100). But on this view, too, reasons are grounded in properties, or features of the world, external to the agent, and not in the agent's subjective states, such as her desires. In this light, it has been suggested by Parfit that the buck-passing view is reconcilable with a value-based theory of reasons, so long as the latter makes no reference to "value", "good", or "bad" save as abbreviations of reason-giving properties, such as safe, effective, painful, etc. (Parfit 2001, p. 20).

[19] See related comments in Raz (1990), pp. 22–25; Raz (2011), pp. 14–15.

ations that apply in mutually beneficial cooperative schemes[20]—then, on the conception described above, that fact that the requirements has been issued is (at least pro tanto) a reason for action.[21] I should be quick to clarify that the claim just made is not that the fact of there being a legal requirement in place is always a reason for action, but rather that it is a fact that *can* be a reason when and insofar as certain conditions hold—namely, when and insofar as the law serves values such as those mentioned above through the compliance rendered by its addressees.

2 Legal Directives as Incomplete Reasons

A further conceptual feature that can supplement, and moderately alter, the above picture is a distinction between complete reasons and different components thereof (which I will refer to as incomplete reasons). The distinction, as I characterize it below, draws on Raz's analysis in *Practical Reason and Norms*,[22] though the way I apply it to the question at hand is not strictly committed to, or intended to mirror, his views. An illustration may help explain the intuitive idea encapsulated by this distinction. Suppose Jenny buys a bunch of flowers for her grandmother on the way to visit her. Another person asks Jenny why she has bought the flowers. There is more than one way in which Jenny could conceivably respond (and her choice between alternative responses will depend on factors such as who asks the question, what their prior knowledge of the circumstances is, the specific way in which the question is intended, etc.). Thus, for example, she might say that (a) the flowers are for her grandmother, who she is about to visit; or that (b) her grandmother would be happy to get the flowers; or that (c) making one's grandparent happy is a good thing. Although each of these possible responses would logically and structurally feature

[20] I have considered the 'fair play' argument (though not specifically in the context of reasons discourse) in Gur (2013), pp. 333–337.

[21] I am not addressing here the question of whether—when certain prerequisites of legitimate authority are met—law can generate not merely reasons for action, but what Raz calls pre-emptive or protected reasons (which include second-order exclusionary reasons). I confine myself at this point to a more modest claim focused on what Raz calls first-order reasons for action. I have examined the pre-emption thesis elsewhere (Gur 2018, Chaps. 2–4) and will briefly refer to it in Sect. 5 below.

[22] Raz (1990), pp. 22–25. See also the discussion in Gardner and Macklem (2002), pp. 447–450. According to Raz, a complete reason comprises either an "operative reason" (such as the fact that X is a value: e.g., if respect for persons is a value, that fact is an operative reason, because my belief in that fact *entails* a belief that there is a reason to respect people) or a combination of an "operative reason" and an "auxiliary reason" (the latter of which is defined residually as a reason that is not an operative one)—Raz (1990), pp. 33–35. Examples of auxiliary reasons include "identifying reasons", whose function is to "help identify the act which there is reason to perform" (ibid., 34), and "strength-affecting reasons", whose function is to "help determine the relative strengths of competing reasons" (ibid., 35). As I understand Raz, he sees directives issued by a legitimate authority as operative reasons. But I leave this claim to one side, partly because the class of legal directives I discuss is not necessarily coextensive with directives issued by a Razian legitimate authority.

in the conversation as a statement of a reason for action, we regard them as interconnected considerations that operate together—as different parts of one explanation of the action.[23] In other words, only their combination captures what we may call a complete reason for action (or, at least, comes closer to capturing it than does (a), (b), or (c) in isolation). A more formal expression of the idea of a complete reason is found in Raz's following statement:

> The fact that p is a complete reason to ϕ for a person x if, and only if, either (a) necessarily, for any person y who understands both the statement that p and the statement that x ϕ's, if y believes that p he believes that there is a reason for x to ϕ, regardless of what other beliefs y has; or (b) R(ϕ)p,x entails R(ϕ),q,y which is a complete reason.[24]

Thus, for example, Laura may believe that 'ϕ-ing in condition c would increase human happiness', and she may simultaneously believe that there is no reason to ϕ in condition c, without thereby making a *logical* mistake (though she may be making a moral mistake). But if Laura believes both (1) that 'ϕ-ing in condition c would increase human happiness', and (2) that 'human happiness is a value', she can no longer hold the belief that there is no reason to ϕ in condition c without making a logical mistake (or, at least, a mistake about the concept of reasons, assuming, as we are doing here, a value-based view of reasons).[25] Now, if we adopt the distinction between complete and incomplete reasons, and revisit Section 2's analysis in this light, it becomes apparent that our earlier observation requires some reformulation. Considered from this perspective, what has been observed is better expressed by saying that legal requirements can at most be *incomplete* reasons. Since legal requirements can only qualify as reasons for action by deriving this status from some deeper-level values or desiderata, they do not meet the criteria for being a complete reason as stated in the above quotation. We cannot say that y's belief that the law requires an action warrants a further belief in a reason for action *regardless of what other beliefs y has*, or that the mere fact that the law requires the action, in isolation from any other facts, entails a reason for action.

Whether legal requirements are best seen as capable of being reasons *tout court* or merely incomplete reasons is not a question I seek to address here. My less ambitious purpose in invoking the distinction between complete and incomplete reasons is to highlight a variant way of conceiving the issuance of a legal requirement as a

[23] The above statement refers to "explanation", but the reasons referred to in the explanation are reasons that the agent (Jenny) believes to be normative, not merely explanatory in the motivational sense.

[24] Raz (1990), p. 24. He adds the following qualification: "However, the fact that p is not a complete reason if the statement that p trivially satisfies the definition only because it entails that some person knows some fact s, and s satisfies the definition" (ibid.).

[25] I set aside here the possibility that Laura believes that the reason to ϕ has been excluded by another, second-order exclusionary reason. Note, however, that even reasons subject to Razian exclusion do not cease to exist. As Raz remarks: "Exclusionary reasons are reasons for not acting for certain valid reasons. They do not nullify or cancel those reasons …" (ibid., 184); "the reasons which are to disregard are not canceled" (Raz 1989, p. 1158).

fact whose normative significance is grounded in values external to it, but which is capable of being a genuine reason for action (even if an incomplete one).

3 Enoch on Triggering Reason-Giving

In a notable essay entitled "Reason-Giving and the Law", David Enoch has argued that when the law gives reasons for action it does so in a sense which he labels triggering reason-giving.[26] In this mode of reason-giving, law's normative significance is that it serves as a trigger for reasons; that is, it brings into operation reasons that were there in the first place, though in a dormant state. Enoch employs the following non-legal example to introduce this idea:

> [S]uppose your neighborhood grocer raised the price of milk. It is natural to say that she has thereby given you a reason to reduce your milk consumption. … But what the grocer did, it seems natural to say, is merely to manipulate the non-normative circumstances in such a way as to trigger a dormant reason that was there all along, independently of the grocer's actions. Arguably, you have a general reason (roughly) to save money. This reason doesn't depend on the grocer's raising of the price of milk. By raising the price of milk, the grocer triggered this general reason, thereby making it the case that you have a reason to reduce your milk consumption. Indeed, perhaps you even had all along the conditional reason to-buy-less-milk-if-the-price-goes-up. … But the grocer can make the conditional reason into an unconditional one, simply by manipulating the relevant non-normative circumstances. And this is what she did by raising the price of milk.[27]

As noted above, Enoch maintains that the same mode of reason-giving is at work when law succeeds in giving reasons for action, even if the dormant reasons triggered by law are substantively different to that featuring in the above example. Thus, for instance, when the law requires an action (Φ) it sometimes manages to trigger reasons "because it solves a coordination problem" or "by creating expectations that you Φ, thereby triggering the general reason you have not to frustrate people's expectations", and so on.[28]

Although there is much that I agree with in Enoch's essay, I have some doubts, or at least reservations, about the idea of triggering reason-giving as characterized by him. My doubts will be expressed by reference to the milk scenario described in the above quotation, but they apply to the legal context too. Before stating my doubts, it is worth highlighting the following aspect of the milk scenario: it involves two reasons, which correspond with two action descriptions at different levels of generality; at the more general level, there is a reason whose associated action

---

[26] Enoch (2011a), esp. 4–5, 26–33. See also Enoch (2011b). A somewhat similar notion appears in Marmor's taxonomy of norms in relation to what he terms "reason-instantiating norms" (Marmor 2018), Sect. III. But, unlike some of Enoch's remarks, Marmor's description of the mode of operation of "reason-instantiating norms" does not seem to be inharmonious with my comments in this section.

[27] Enoch (2011a), p. 4.

[28] Ibid., 28.

description is 'save money' (that is, a reason to save money) and, at the more specific level, there is a reason whose associated action description is 'buy less milk' (that is, a reason to buy less milk). With this in mind, let's consider Enoch's analysis. A first point, of lesser pertinence to my purpose, relates to the general reason, namely the reason to save money. Enoch points out that this reason was a "dormant reason". However, this does not seem to me to describe successfully the status of that reason. It is a general reason—in that the action 'save money' is general—but it was not, I think, dormant,[29] at least not under ordinary life circumstances; indeed, it was not dormant partly *because* its associated action description is general: 'save money'—which presumably you had both the need and opportunities to do, in all sorts of ways, before the grocer's action.[30] One might respond by saying that Enoch's reference to the reason to save money as dormant should only be understood to mean the following proposition: the reason to save money was not, at the time, instantiated as (part of) a reason to buy less milk. But even if this proposition is correct, I do not think it warrants describing the former reason as dormant because, once more, the action it is a reason for is the general 'save money' (rather than 'buy less milk'). Perhaps, however, Enoch would be willing to settle for another qualified proposition: namely, that the reason to save money *would be* dormant in a state of affairs where (although at some point in the future having extra money would be useful for you) you temporarily have no opportunities to save or spend money. While I am uncertain whether it is best to say, in such a state of affair, that the reason to save money is dormant or that it temporarily does not apply to you, I would in all other respects agree with the above proposition.

But more pertinent is the following point: I do not think that the second reason in the above scenario, namely the reason to buy less milk, was merely triggered. If this is what Enoch is saying—and I am not entirely sure he is—I respectfully differ. Precisely because its action description is 'buy less milk' (as distinct from 'save money'), it is a specific reason that did not exist before the grocer raised the price—it is a new reason created by the price rise, albeit a reason grounded in the desideratum to save money. Enoch mentions a similar view at the start of the above quoted passage, but he then appears to reject it. He invokes (albeit tentatively) the idea of a conditional reason to-buy-less-milk-if-the-price-goes-up that was there all along. This idea apparently harmonizes with the triggering account, but there is, I think, an air of artificiality to it.[31] It seems to me less contrived to say that the reduction of milk

[29] Possibly it was *psychologically* dormant, but Enoch, as I understand him, means something else: that it was normatively dormant.

[30] To wit, this reason was not dormant because, presumably, before the grocer's action and regardless of the milk price, you (like most people in ordinary circumstances) had at least some, and probably countless, opportunities and ways to save/spend money that would be useful in the future. As noted in the body text, however, I would agree that a reason to save money *could be* normatively inactive or temporarily inapplicable to you under some, unusual circumstances—e.g., if (and so long as) you are stranded on a desert island with no money (or remote access to money) and no need or opportunity to use money while on the island.

[31] And that doesn't seem to me to be changed by the distinction between 'wide-scope' and 'narrow-scope' conditionals about reasons (see Enoch 2011a, pp. 7–8).

consumption was simply not part of the relevant normative picture before the price rise than to say there was a conditional reason to-buy-less-milk-if-the-price-goes-up.

Now, having expressed these reservations, I should point out an alternative way of interpreting Enoch. It is possible that he intends the idea of triggering reason-giving in a weaker sense, such that it is compatible with viewing the reason to buy less milk as a newly created reason. On this understanding, it is acknowledged that the reason to buy less milk had no antecedently existing dormant counterpart awaiting to be triggered; the 'triggering' terminology, on this interpretation, is merely intended to signify that the reason is partly grounded in the desideratum to save money (which existed prior to the price rise, and which still exists, as a general, though not a dormant, reason). If this is what Enoch means by triggering reason-giving, I have no substantive disagreement with him on this matter.

In the following section, I consider an objection that could be made on behalf of more deflationary approaches than the approach I have adopted. This objection insists that, even assuming the factualist value-based conception of reasons described earlier, it is wrong to think that the fact of legality itself can be a reason for action. Later, in Sect. 5, I will attend to the opposite possibility, namely that there is a more robust, and less deflationary, sense in which law can provide practical reasons which my arguments thus far do not capture.

4 The Misattribution Objection

As clarified above, it is not suggested that the fact that law requires an action is invariably a reason for its performance, but rather that it *can* be under certain conditions, namely if and insofar as some values would be satisfied through compliance with the law (and the fact that the action is legally required is part of the explanation of why that is so). Against this background, the following objection might be raised: the reason-giving capacity that I ascribe to law is really attributable not to the fact of legality, but to certain qualities (e.g., the capacity to facilitate coordination) and circumstances (e.g., circumstances where coordination is desirable), which are sometimes present in conjunction with the law, but at other times not. Moreover, even insofar as law possesses some beneficial capabilities, they (or parallel ones with a similar function) can also be present in other, non-legal entities; for example, a charismatic citizen with a loud voice who emerges as an effective coordinator in an emergency situation, say, on board a sinking ship.[32] Such capabilities are not, therefore, uniquely legal, and this—the objector might say—casts further doubt on my argument.

---

[32] This might evoke another sinking-ship example famously used by Robert Wolff to make a different (albeit related) point (Wolff 1970, pp. 15–16). See also Hershovitz (2011), p. 17, where a similar example is mentioned.

My reply to this criticism is as follows. At least some of the beneficial aspects of law's operation are attributable not simply to qualities that coincidentally may or may not be present in conjunction with the law, but to characteristics of law and legality (even if their beneficial potential is not operative in all circumstances). And, if that is so, it appears warranted, after all, to regard the fact of legality, at least under some conditions and circumstances, as a reason for action. By way of illustration, let us revert to law's coordinating function. There are contexts or situations wherein law is comparatively well suited to facilitate coordination between people due to attributes such as its social salience, the powerful coercive apparatus at its disposal, and people's (or some people's) disposition to comply with it as a matter of their normative attitudes towards the law.[33] These are characteristic attributes of law, or, at any rate, the combination of all of them in comparatively high measures is a characteristic attribute of law. Or consider, as another example, law's function in instituting and upholding mutually beneficial schemes of social cooperation through fair sharing of burdens and adherence to restrictions (for example, as regards the use of public goods). Law is perhaps not always capable of adequately performing this function, but, to the extent that it has a comparative advantage at performing it, this is explicable in part by attributes such as its typical generality and impersonal mode of application, its relative persistence through time, and, again, the deference generally rendered to it (whether as a result of its coercive mechanism, normative attitudes towards it,[34] or both). These, once more, are characteristic attributes of law, or, at least, their conjoined presence in relatively high measures is a characteristic attribute of law. If that is true, there does not seem to be anything erroneous or strained in regarding the fact of there being a legal requirement (in circumstances of the type indicated above) as a reason for action.

The objection presented above refers also to the fact that certain bodies or individuals that do not operate on behalf of law or hold legal office may nevertheless possess attributes that allow them to perform (at least in some circumstance and to some extent) functions similar to those of law. I do not wish to deny that in certain contexts, and to some extent, functions such as conduct guidance and dispute resolution can be performed without involvement of the law. However, I should emphasize that a material part of my point refers to the *combination* of attributes associated with the law (i.e., generality, endurance through time, coercive capacity, perceived bindingness, etc.) and the *degree* to which they are present in association with law. The conjunction of these attributes, and the relatively concentrated form in which

---

[33] Attitudes whose formation and endurance may well be attributable, at least in part, to further characteristics (or perceived characteristics) of the legal system, such as its overall adherence to 'rule of law' standards and a reasonable level of fairness and justice displayed by its laws and adjudicative processes. See in this connection Sarat (1977a, b), Tyler (2006), pp. 71–178; Sunshine and Tyler (2003).

[34] There are disagreements over the empirical questions of how common normative attitudes towards legality itself are, and what part such attitudes have in the causal explanation of people's compliance with the law. The most notable study in this regard is Tyler (2006). This study has been the subject of relatively recent criticism by legal theorists such as Claus (2012), pp. 65–70 and Schauer (2015), pp. 57–67, 73–74. I have discussed this debate in Gur (2018), pp. 184–192.

they are found in legal modes of ordering, are normatively significant,[35] for they render law well suited to address certain problems of collective action that—given their large societal scale, and the type, intensity, and persistence of their cognitive and motivational precursors—other, non-legal practices or actors seem less (or not at all) capable of addressing.[36] In other words, the question of whether law can constitute reasons for action does not turn on whether there exist beneficial attributes that generally, or in the abstract, or in a necessarily qualitative sense are unique to law; rather, it turns on whether there are situations in which—due to attributes present in law, or their combination, or their concentrated level of presence—law is comparatively well placed to fulfil a valuable function.

5 Can Law-Given Reasons Acquire (System-Wide or Localized) Value-Independent Force?

So far I have argued for a qualified sense in which legal directives can be content-independent reasons. In this variant of content-independence, the reason for action constituted by a legal directive, though (relatively) independent of the merits or demerits of the directive's content, derives from—and remains invariably dependent on—other values or desiderata served through compliance with the directive, be they coordination benefits, social order, fairness, or other. The question I now wish to consider is the following. Suppose that a given legal system (S) is, overall, reasonably just and fair; and that S, overall, serves reasonably well the kind of values or desiderata that law is suited to serve. Can we say that, as a result of S's meeting the above (neither-trivial-nor-perfection-demanding) standard, its individual directives gain a more robust normative status than what has been advocated in the previous sections? Namely, can we say that S's directives thereby become reasons for action, such that their status as reasons for action crystallizes and persists independently of whether the values served by S are applicable to the directive or case at

[35] Marmor has recently argued against the thought that there is some general feature of law that renders it normatively unique (Marmor 2018, esp. 95 and Sect. VI). As I understand his argument, it focuses on law's normative modality—namely, he argues that there isn't anything unique about *the way* law gives reasons for action, for similar modes of reason-giving can be found in other normative phenomena or practices. Now, I should clarify that this argument does not stand in opposition to the claim I am making here. I am not denying that law's normative modality—the way it gives reasons—is present also in some non-legal normative phenomena or practices. I am only suggesting that there are some situations in which law (due to some of its attributes) is comparatively well placed to perform a socially beneficial function, and that, to this extent, it is capable of giving reasons for action. As far as I can see, this is not a claim Marmor denies.

[36] I should add that, even to the extent that a function performed by the law is such that it could also be performed by means other than the law, this does not seem to me necessarily to undermine the thought that the law's requirements are reasons for action—at least if those other, non-legal means are less readily available than legal means (e.g., because the latter are the method already in common use in one's society) or if there are other considerations that render the latter preferable.

hand?[37] I will offer a negative answer, following which I will touch upon two theses that involve more qualified elements of robust normativity.

I will cast my answer in terms of a value-based conception of reasons (keeping to the confines earlier set for this discussion), although a similar answer, I believe, can be arrived at on premises of a desire-based conception of reasons.[38] According to the former conception, reasons for action are ultimately grounded in some values that are served or satisfied by the performance of the action. They are not created out of thin air *simply and only* by requiring that others act in some way—they are not the mere product of someone's say-so *without more*. The utterance of a directive-issuer is no more than an artefact of the human will which cannot *alone* turn a false moral proposition into a true one or determine by way of stipulation what is wrong and what is right.[39] It can only have normative bearing, within the framework of a value-based conception, when and insofar as it appears in conjunction with some evaluative factors which make it the case that, and explain why, it is valuable or desirable to follow the directive. With this in mind, I find it difficult to grasp how the set of underlying values that is generally served by the operation of a legal system could somehow imbue the system's requirements with a type of reason-giving quality that transcends, and essentially cuts loose from, its normative origins, such that those requirements become a self-contained source of genuine reasons for action. It would take, I think, some rather mysterious form of normative alchemy for such a transition to be generated. Now, to this the following clarification is worth adding: I do not mean to deny the possibility that the law *claims* to be—or that lawmakers *intend* their directives *to be taken as*[40]—a self-contained source of genuine reasons for action in the above sense.[41] But my focus here is not on how the law presents or perceives its capacity to give reasons, but on its actual capacity to give reasons.

Having expressed doubts about robust legal normativity of the kind described above, I will now highlight two different approaches that involve more qualified variants of robust normativity. As I have discussed them elsewhere at some length, here I will only briefly comment on them. The first approach consists in Joseph

[37] The above question refers to a legal *system* (S), but a similar question can be framed by reference to a *body of laws* that forms only a part of S (say, S's body of commercial laws) and meets the above standard (i.e., the standard of being reasonably just and fair, etc.). My comments in the following paragraph of the text refer to the system-wide question, but these comments seem to me applicable, *mutatis mutandis*, to the domain-wide question too.

[38] According to which reasons for action are grounded in some ultimate desires of the agent to whom they apply.

[39] A similar argument is mentioned by Hart (1982), p. 265, though he mentions it as part of a more moderate objection to his conception of authoritative reasons.

[40] Cf. Hart's following statement (1982), p. 254: "[T]he commander intends his expressions of intention to be taken as a reason for doing them. It is therefore intended to function as a reason independently of the nature or character of the actions to be done". I am not sure whether Hart imputes to the commander an intention similar to that mentioned in the body text.

[41] Though it is worth noting that the very notion that law claims to give reasons is not free from controversy—see, e.g., relevant doubts expressed in Essert (2013).

Raz's service conception of authority.[42] Raz's service conception, it should first be emphasized, is a set of claims focused not on law in general, but on legitimate authority. As such, it applies to instances of law only where and insofar as Raz's prerequisites of legitimate authority are met. Now, Razian legitimate authorities possess a robust normative quality that finds its rational basis in Raz's distinctive view of the justification of authority. His justificatory conditions of authority make sense of the idea that the very fact that a legitimate authority requires an action is a reason for its performance (indeed, not just *a* reason, but, as will be noted below, a privileged type of reason which he labels "pre-emptive" or "protected"). The key condition, encapsulated in a thesis known as *the normal justification thesis*, is that for an ostensible authority (A) to gain legitimate authority over a subject (S), A must have the capacity to guide S to better conformity with reasons that apply to S (that is, reasons other than the directives of A)—in other words, it must be the case that S would be more likely to conform to reasons that apply to her by following A's directives than by trying to follow those reasons directly.[43] Now, if this is (at least part of) what it means for someone to qualify as a legitimate authority, it becomes easy to appreciate why Raz comes to his view about the normative force of legitimate authority: from a Razian perspective, precisely because the justification of authority lies in its ability to reach decisions that better reflect background reasons, the fact that a directive has been issued by a legitimate authority is a reason for acting as the directive prescribes, as well as a reason to refrain from trying to act directly on background reasons which the authority had power to pronounce upon.[44] This idea finds expression in another thesis of Raz, known as the pre-emption thesis, which reads thus:

> [T]he fact that an authority requires performance of an action is a reason for its performance which is not to be added to all other relevant reasons when assessing what to do, but should exclude and take the place of some of them.[45]

On this sophisticated view, the normative force of authority is thought to have the following hybrid quality: on the one hand, it is thought to retain and never break the connection with what Raz sees as the basic rationale of authority—namely, the facilitation of conformity with background reasons—and, thereby, with the deeper level of values underpinning the background reasons (the connection being that the authority is better capable of correctly tracking those background reasons than the subject is)[46]; on the other hand, there is a sense in which Razian authority-given

---

[42] Raz (1986), Chap. 3; Raz (1995), pp. 211–215; Raz (2006).

[43] Raz (1986), p. 53. In Raz's words: "[The normal justification thesis] claims that the normal and primary way to establish that a person should be acknowledged to have authority over another person involves showing that the alleged subject is likely better to comply with reasons which apply to him (other than the alleged authoritative directives) if he accepts the directives of the alleged authority as authoritatively binding and tries to follow them, rather than by trying to follow the reasons which apply to him directly" (ibid.).

[44] Ibid., 59.

[45] Ibid., 46.

[46] Thus, e.g., he notes: "No blind obedience to authority is here implied. Acceptance of authority

reasons operate independently of, and indeed supplant, relevant background reasons and their associated bedrock values, in that the subject of a legitimate authority is not supposed to act on particularistic assessments (i.e., directive-by-directive or case-by-case) of whether the authority-prescribed action comports with those background reasons and values.[47]

While the ingenuity of Raz's conception is undeniable, its claims remain contested.[48] In a critique of this conception, which I have advanced elsewhere,[49] I have highlighted what I believe to be two of its principal deficiencies. First, I have argued that the modality of pre-emptive reasons, with its exclusionary character, involves too strong a type of bindingness by authority, such that it fails to adequately accommodate situations where (notwithstanding the authority's compliance with Raz's conditions of authority) it is justified to disobey in order to avoid a directive-specific or situation-specific serious immorality.[50] The second deficiency concerns the scope of legitimate governmental authority. Raz opts for a distinctly piecemeal test for the legitimacy of authority (a choice perhaps partly driven by a wish to mitigate the relative modal stringency of pre-emptive bindingness), which, in turn, yields a rather patchy scope of legitimate governmental authority. This outcome, I have argued, is unsatisfactory since, in reality, the need to organize, and place constraints on, the operation of individuals in a political community through governmental regulation is wider and more general than the scope of authoritative power Raz's test tends to produce.[51] The analysis that led me to these conclusions cannot and need not be repeated here.

The second approach that will be touched upon is what I have put forward and defended elsewhere under the label "the dispositional model".[52] The core claim of this model can be stated, in thumbnail form, as follows: the fact of there being a reasonably just and well-functioning legal system in place is a reason to adopt a relatively settled and stable mental posture whose conative component is an (overridable) disposition to comply with the systems' requirements. Instead of reiterating my explanation and arguments in support of this model, here I will only briefly

has to be justified, and this normally means meeting the conditions set in the justification thesis. This brings into play the dependent reasons, for only if the authority's compliance with them is likely to be better than that of its subjects is its claim to legitimacy justified" (Raz 1995, p. 215).

[47] Thus, e.g., immediately after the passage in the previous footnote, Raz notes: "At the level of general justification the pre-empted reasons have an important role to play. But once that level has been passed and we are concerned with particular action, dependent reasons are replaced by authoritative directives" (ibid.).

[48] See, e.g., Moore (1989), Perry (1989), Regan (1989), pp. 1001–1033, 1086–1095; Hurd (1991), Mian (2002), Himma (2007), Martin (2014), pp. 81–89. For a relevant survey, see Ehrenberg (2011). Some of Raz's replies can be found in Raz (1989). See also Raz (2006).

[49] Gur (2018).

[50] Ibid., Chaps. 2–4.

[51] Ibid., 127–29, 168–69.

[52] Ibid., Chaps. 7–9.

highlight a couple of the model's aspects that have particular relevance to the present discussion.

It should first be noted that this model involves qualified aspects of value-independence (pertaining to the modus operandi of the foregoing disposition) alongside aspects of value-dependence (pertaining to conditions for adopting the disposition and its formation process). Starting with one of its value-dependent aspects, the dispositional model calls for adopting a law-abiding disposition on the condition that the legal system in question is a reasonably just and well-functioning system that is apt to serve valuable purposes and moral principles. And, accordingly, the model readily accepts that if a legal system descends to a pattern of repeated failures to live up to relevant moral standards (e.g., justice, fairness, and respect for persons) the result should be an erosion of its subjects' disposition to comply. On the other hand—and here I come to the qualified aspect of value-independence—once the disposition becomes a settled and relatively stable part of the agent's attitudinal profile, it operates with some degree of motivational and conative persistence.[53] It is not a mere momentary response to a particular situation or a fleeting state of mind, but rather an inclination that acquires relative embeddedness in the relevant agent and tends to endure through time. To this extent and in this sense, therefore, the motivational force it exerts gains independence of specific reasons for action as applicable to particular situations; it makes its force felt in a manner not conditional on those reasons.

At the outset of this section I rejected a type of value-independence whereby the directives of a reasonably just legal system (S) become a self-contained source of genuine reasons for action that apply independently of whether the values served by S are applicable to the directive or case at hand. Note that the dispositional model does not represent a departure from this position. For there is a difference between claiming (1) that S's directives constitute reasons for action (i.e., the action that they require), and claiming (2) that S's existence (and overall operation) is a reason for you to adopt a certain attitude or mental posture towards S, such that you become generally disposed to comply with S's directives. In claim (1), the reasons are

[53] The above-noted senses of value-dependence and value-independence are mutually reconcilable because there is a difference between, on the one hand, the factors that contribute to the formation of an attitude and a concomitant disposition, and, on the other hand, the conditions that trigger behavioural manifestations of that disposition in a particular case. The following non-legal example may help to further illustrate this point. Suppose, for example, I have acquired, through a relatively prolonged assimilation of the view that 'gambling generally tends to have destructive effects on one's life', a general and firmly embedded disposition against gambling. Having materialized, my disposition (if strong enough) may lead me to refrain from gambling even on an occasion when I am presented with arguments, which I find persuasive, as to why gambling on that particular occasion would be desirable and harmless, and why my assessment of these arguments is not prone to error in the present conditions. I have acquired the disposition through recourse to a relevant rationale, but, once the disposition is in place, it may exert its influence even when the rationale for its acquisition is absent. A similar distinction is applicable to the law-abiding disposition mentioned in the body text, thus making it possible for the disposition to be value-independent in one sense (concerning the conditions for its activation) and value-dependent in another sense (concerning the process of its formation).

ascribed to S's directives, and what they are reasons *for* are the *actions* required by those directives. In claim (2), the reason is ascribed to S's existence and general operation, and what it is a reason *for* is the acquisition of a general *attitude* towards S—an attitude that, once settled, tends to endure and exert its influence in a manner that is not contingent on reasons for action as applicable to the specific case at hand.[54] And what makes this difference all the more pronounced are situations that appear to disprove the general truth of claim (1), but which cohere with claim (2) and instantiate its practical effects—one such example being the proverbial lonely traffic light scenario, featuring a driver who comes upon a red traffic light where the road is clearly empty of other vehicles and pedestrians (the visibility is very good, the surrounding landscape is free of visual obstructions, and she can tell that there are no other vehicles or pedestrians within miles in any direction, etc.). In the latter scenario (or at least some appropriately refined version of it) the thought that there is a genuine reason for the action of stopping the car and waiting for the green light sounds counterintuitive, yet a driver who is generally disposed to comply with the law may be led by her disposition to act precisely this way.

Now compliance in the lonely traffic light scenario is also compatible with the modality of Razian pre-emptive reasons (provided that Raz's prerequisites of legitimate authority have been met), but it is worth emphasizing that, alongside this commonality, there are several significant differences between the pre-emption thesis and what I call the dispositional model. I will mention two of them. First, the dispositional model focuses on a reason to adopt a certain attitude, whereas pre-emptive reasons—and their distinctive exclusionary component: exclusionary reasons—do not have this attitudinal focus. Exclusionary reasons, as Raz has made clear, are reasons against acting for some reasons.[55] They are not reasons to adopt this or that settled and standing mental posture. Thus, whether John Doe has complied with a pre-emptive reason to φ is a question of what reasons he was acting for in performing φ (assuming he has performed it), not a question of what settled attitudinal profile he has, or what measures he has taken to change it. Second, there is a modal difference between these two conceptions. A pre-emptive reason to perform an action (φ) is a reason to φ that excludes some of the reasons that would otherwise militate against φ-ing. This means that however weighty those (excluded) contra-φ reasons might be, they should not be acted upon. Insofar as I comply with the pre-emptive reason, then, those contra-φ reasons cease to play a role in determining whether I perform φ or refrain from it. Matters are different under the dispositional model, in that the exclusionary element just noted is absent from this model. The attitude envisaged by the dispositional model implies a behavioural disposition, which is no more than a *tendency* or *inclination* to comply with legal requirements. As such, it remains overridable (or defeasible) by the weight of opposing reasons that might apply in particular cases, rather than exclusionary of

[54] As such, it is not a mere reflection of some or all of the reasons for action that apply to us in a given situation.

[55] See, e.g., Raz (1990), p. 39; Raz (1989), pp. 1156–1157.

opposing reasons. It does not exclude any reason against compliance, at least not in a sense that is not conditional on that reason's weight, which is the sense of exclusion Raz endorses.[56]

6 Conclusion

Several observations have been made here regarding law's capacity to constitute reasons. Three of these observations (if correct) seem particularly worth highlighting by way of concluding this chapter.

First, I have noted that there is a factualist value-based conception of reasons for action that seems, prima facie, intuitively plausible, and which lends credence to, or makes it relatively easy to accept, the idea that legal requirements can constitute reasons for action (or, at least, incomplete reasons for action).[57] This is because, on the above conception of reasons, saying that a given fact (F) is a reason for action (φ) is compatible with saying that F's status as a reason for action is grounded in some deeper values (V) that do not reside in F itself. F's being a reason to φ only means that F (or F in conjunction with some other facts) makes it the case that φ-ing would serve or satisfy V—and this, at least sometimes, holds true in the relation between the fact that law requires an action and the values that would be served or satisfied by performance of the action.

Second, I have discussed some relevant arguments put forward by David Enoch in his essay "Reason-Giving and the Law".[58] While there is much that I agree with in Enoch's analysis, I have expressed certain reservations about his characterization of law's normative operation in terms of triggering reason-giving. Enoch is right to note that the issuance of a legal requirement often results in specific reasons for action (e.g., a reason to drive on the left) that emerge on the back of pre-existing general reasons for action (e.g., a reason to coordinate with other drivers). But I have offered a qualification to the thought that the latter, general reasons, were dormant prior to the law's pronouncement,[59] and I have noted that, since the former, specific reasons, pertain to a distinct action description (e.g., 'drive on the left', as distinct from 'coordinate with other drivers'), there is a genuine sense in which they can be seen as newly created, rather than merely triggered, reasons.

Third, I have expressed scepticism about law's capacity to give reasons for action whose normative operation gains independence of the underlying values or desiderata served or satisfied by recourse to legal modes of regulation (e.g., coordination, social order, and fairness)—namely, reasons for action whose operation supposedly

[56] Raz (1990), p. 36, 40, 189, 190.

[57] Sects. 1 and 2.

[58] Sect. 3.

[59] Namely, I have suggested that, since these reasons are general, they were not dormant if there were other ways (even if deficient ones) to satisfy or partly satisfy them.

ceases to be contingent on whether those underlying values apply to the directive or situation at hand.[60] On the other hand, I have noted a different (qualified) form of robust normativity that pertains not to reasons for action given by specific legal directives, but to reasons for attitudes given by the overall operation of a legal system (provided it is a reasonably just and well-functioning system). This idea consists, more specifically, in reasons to adopt a (relatively settled, yet overridable) disposition to comply with the system's requirements—a disposition whose motivational and conative influence may persist and extend beyond the directive-specific or situational applicability of reasons for action, but which also remains overridable by compelling enough reasons for non-compliance when these crop up. This idea, which I have elaborated and advocated elsewhere,[61] complements my observations in this chapter to form a fuller picture of law's interaction with practical reasons.

References

Alvarez M (2010) Kinds of reasons: an essay in the philosophy of action. Oxford University Press, Oxford

Bix BH (2011) The nature of law and reasons for action. Problema 5:399–415

Bix BH (2018) Kelsen, Hart, and legal normativity. Revus 34:25–42. https://doi.org/10.4000/revus.3984

Bond EJ (1983) Reason and value. Cambridge University Press, Cambridge

Bongiovanni G (2018) Reasons (and reasons in philosophy of law). In: Bongiovanni G et al (eds) Handbook of legal reasoning and argumentation. Springer, Dordrecht, pp 3–33

Chang R (2004) Can desires provide reasons for action? In: Wallace RJ et al (eds) Reason and value: themes from the moral philosophy of Joseph Raz. Oxford University Press, Oxford, pp 56–90

Claus L (2012) Law's evolution and human understanding. Oxford University Press, Oxford

Coleman J (2001) The practice of principle. Oxford University Press, Oxford

Dancy J (2003) Practical reality. Oxford University Press, Oxford

Ehrenberg KM (2011) Critical reception of Raz's theory of authority. Philos Compass 6:777–785

Ehrenberg KM (2016) The functions of law. Oxford University Press, Oxford

Enoch D (2011a) Reason-giving and the law. In: Green L, Leiter B (eds) Oxford studies in philosophy of law, vol 1. Oxford University Press, Oxford, pp 1–38

Enoch D (2011b) Giving practical reasons. Philos Imprint 11(4):1–22

Essert C (2013) Legal obligation and reasons. Legal Theory 19:63–88

Gardner J, Macklem T (2002) Reasons. In: Coleman JL, Shapiro SJ (eds) The oxford handbook of jurisprudence and philosophy of law. Oxford University Press, Oxford, pp 440–475

Gur N (2013) Actions, attitudes, and the obligation to obey the law. J Polit Philos 25:326–346

Gur N (2018) Legal directives and practical reasons. Oxford University Press, Oxford

Hart HLA (1982) Essays on Bentham. Clarendon Press, Oxford

Hershovitz S (2011) The role of authority. Philos Imprint 11:1–19

Himma KE (2007) Just cause you're smarter than me doesn't give you a right to tell me what to do. Oxf J Leg Stud 27:121–150

Hurd HM (1991) Challenging authority. Yale Law J 100:1611–1677

[60] Sect. 4.

[61] Gur (2018), Chaps. 7–9.

Maguire B (2016) The value-based theory of reasons. Ergo 3:233–262
Marmor A (2018) Norms, reasons, and the law. In: Himma KE et al (eds) Unpacking normativity: conceptual, normative, and descriptive issues. Hart, Oxford, Chap. 6
Martin M (2014) Judging positivism. Hart, Oxford
Mian E (2002) The curious case of exclusionary reasons. Can J Law & Juris 15:99–124
Moore MS (1989) Authority, law, and Razian reasons. S Cal Law Rev 62:827–896
Parfit D (2001) Rationality and reasons. In: Egonsson D et al (eds) Exploring practical philosophy. Ashgate, Aldershot, pp 17–39
Perry SR (1989) Second-order reasons, uncertainty and legal theory. S Cal Law Rev 62:913–994
Raz J (1986) The morality of freedom. Clarendon Press, Oxford
Raz J (1989) Facing up: a reply. S Cal Law Rev 62:1153–1235
Raz J (1990) Practical reason and norms, 2nd edn. Princeton University Press, Princeton
Raz J (1995) Ethics in the public domain: essays in the morality of law and politics. Revised paperback edn. Clarendon Press, Oxford
Raz J (1999) Engaging reason: on the theory of value and action. Oxford University Press, Oxford
Raz J (2006) The problem of authority: revisiting the service conception. Minnesota Law Rev 90:1003–1044
Raz J (2011) From normativity to responsibility. Oxford University Press, Oxford
Raz J (2016) Value and the weight of practical reasons. In: Lord E, Maguire B (eds) Weighing reasons. Oxford University Press, Oxford, pp 141–156
Regan DH (1989) Authority and value: reflections on Raz's morality of freedom. S Cal Law Rev 62:995–1095
Regan DH (1990) Reasons, authority, and the meaning of "obey": further thoughts on Raz and obedience to law. Can J Law & Juris 30:3–28
Sarat A (1977a) Legal obligation: a survey study. Polity 9:384–398
Sarat A (1977b) Studying American legal culture: an assessment of survey evidence. Law Soc Rev 11:427–488
Scanlon TM (1998) What we owe to each other. Harvard University Press, Cambridge, MA
Schauer F (2015) The force of law. Harvard University Press, Cambridge, MA
Schauer F (2016) How (and if) law matters: responding to Mark Greenberg, "How to explain things with force". Harv Law Rev Forum 129:350–359
Smith M (1994) The moral problem. Blackwell, Oxford
Sunshine J, Tyler TR (2003) The role of procedural justice and legitimacy in shaping public support for policing. Law Soc Rev 37:513–547
Tyler TR (2006) Why people obey the law. With a new afterword by the author. Princeton University Press, Princeton
Wiland E (2012) Reasons. Continuum, London
Wolff RP (1970) In defense of anarchism. Harper & Row, New York

On the Alleged Problem of Legal Normativity

Frederick Schauer

Abstract Many contemporary philosophers of law believe that one of the central problems of the field is that of explaining the normativity of law. But it is not clear that this is a problem at all, or at least that it is different from the problems that have been exhaustively addressed and analyzed for generations. Once we deconstruct the alleged problem of normativity into its component parts, we can appreciate that legal normativity is either conditional, or is instead but a small variation on age-old questions about the moral obligation, if any, to obey the law simply because of its status as law. There are interesting modern versions of these positions, but in the final analysis David Enoch is correct in labeling the problem of legal normativity as a "pseudo-problem."

1 Legal Normativity: A Problem?

Explaining the so-called normativity of law has preoccupied positivist philosophers of law for at least several decades. How can the very fact (or existence) of law, which for the positivist is a contingent social fact whose facticity need not depend on moral considerations, create obligations?[1] That, to put it too starkly, and too briefly, is what is understood as the problem of legal normativity, the problem of explaining the normative force of a phenomenon which exists as a matter of human creation and whose existence, for the legal positivist, need not rest on moral criteria. For the legal positivist, the existence of law is conceptually independent of the

[1] This framing of the question tracks Shapiro (2011), pp. 25–50. See also Coleman (2001a), pp. 89–90, Coleman (1996, 2001b), Perry (2001). Couching the problems of law's authority and law's reason-giving capacity as problems of normativity can be traced largely to Hart (1982). It is worth noting that the (alleged) problem of normativity that I address in this paper is almost completely unrelated to the questions labeled as questions of normativity arising within Kelsenian and related legal theories. See Bjarup (2005).

F. Schauer (✉)
University of Virginia, School of Law, Charlottesville, VA, USA
e-mail: fschauer@law.virginia.edu

N. Bersier Ladavac et al. (eds.), *The Normative Force of the Factual*, Law and Philosophy Library 130, https://doi.org/10.1007/978-3-030-18929-7_12

moral worth of a particular law or of an entire legal system, and thus, to put it more precisely, morality is not a necessary condition of law properly so called, and is not a necessary condition of legality in all possible legal systems in all possible worlds.

Those who are puzzled by law's normativity purport to be puzzled by the tension between the fact that morality is not necessarily a criterion of legality, on the one hand, and the way in which law creates obligations, on the other. Thus, the problem is sometimes understood (Stelmach 2011) as one of attempting to understand how an "ought"—the obligations that law is thought to create—can be derived from an "is"—the facticity of law's existence. My goal in this paper, however, is not to solve the problem, or puzzle, of legal normativity. Rather, I want to question why normativity is seen as a problem or puzzle at all. In one sense, I propose to argue against legal normativity, but that way of expressing the goal of this paper is too quick. Rather, the central theme of this paper is the proposition that the so-called problem of legal normativity is, contra many contemporary positivist legal philosophers, not a distinct puzzle at all, but merely the non-puzzling instantiation of a several different traditional perspectives, none of which is especially puzzling in its own right, and all of which, although still debated, suggest that contemporary inquiries into the normativity of law are less novel and less important than most legal philosophers now tend to believe.

2 An Obligation to Follow the Law?

As widely understood, the problem of normativity is the problem of explaining how the fact of law—a content-independent understanding of legal directives[2]—can provide reasons for action. Sometimes this is put in terms of the possibility of law's creating obligations, but this is simply another way of stating the possibility that the fact of law may itself provide a reason, such that to ignore the reason is to ignore an obligation. But more specifically, those who believe that normativity is a problem insist that the reasons that law provides are not moral reasons, but rather are reasons of some other variety. There is, they maintain, some idea of a legal ought that is to be distinguished from the more familiar and far less controversial moral ought (Hage 2011; Marmor 2011).

The nature of the reasons that law might provide is thought to be crucial in distinguishing the alleged problem of normativity from the longstanding debates about the moral obligation, if any, to obey the law just because it is law.[3] At least as far

[2]Understanding authority as content-independent is central to understanding the very idea of authority. When we treat a directive as providing a reason for action because of its source and not its content, we have treated that source as an authority, and the directive emanating from that source as authoritative solely because of its source. Hart (1982), Schauer (2008), Shapiro (2002). On content-independent reasons more generally, see Sciaraffa (2009).

[3]An excellent analytical overview of the literature on the moral obligation to obey the law is (Edmundson 2004).

back as Socrates in the *Crito* and the *Apology* (Plato 2003), theorists have argued that there is a content-independent moral obligation—non-absolute, to be sure[4]—to obey the law just because it is the law. For Socrates, for John Rawls (Rawls 1964) more recently, and for many others (Nozick 1974, pp. 90–95), the obligation has something to do with reciprocity, or gratitude, or fair play. For John Locke, among others, the obligation stems from ideas of consent generally and the social contract more specifically.[5] And even more recently, for Gerald Postema (1982) and others (Green 1983; Reynolds 1989) the obligation is a consequence of the moral obligations to participate in cooperative arrangements from which all benefit, and which provide a (partial) solution to Prisoners' Dilemma and other problems of collective action.

Against such arguments, so-called philosophical anarchists—theorists such as Robert Paul Wolff (1970), Smith (1973), and John Simmons (1979)—have argued that there is simply no such obligation at all. There is, of course, the anarchists acknowledge, a moral obligation to do the right thing as a matter of first-order substance, but the existence (or non-existence) of a legal (or political) directive adds nothing to the moral calculus. The fact of legal authority, sanctions, aside, is, for the anarchist, morally inert.

The debates between those who believe in a moral obligation to obey the law or other form of political authority and those who are described as philosophical anarchists is by now a familiar one. And it should be clear that *if* there is a moral obligation to obey the law, then law can be considered to be normative by virtue of the fact that the existence of a legal directive provides a moral reason that would not have existed but for law. And so although there may be debates about the existence or not of such a moral obligation, there seems nothing especially puzzling about these debates. Socrates, Locke, Rawls, and many others on one side and the anarchists on the other disagree about a great deal, but they do not appear to be disagreeing about what they disagree about, and in this sense these hoary debates can hardly considered to be puzzling.

3 Instrumental Purposes

To some extent the nature of law's normativity is a function of the nature of reasons, moral and otherwise. To be more specific, there are some accounts of legal obligation that locate that obligation in the obligation to participate in a collective enterprise in the pursuit of a collective goal. Scott Shapiro's planning theory of law (Shapiro 2011) is one such account, Gerald Postema's focus on coordination and

[4] Some would say "prima facie," and others would say "pro tanto," but the basic idea is the same—the existence of an applicable duty or obligation that is less than absolute may fall in the face of conflicting duties or obligations, but such overridable duties or obligations nevertheless provide reasons for action that would otherwise not exist (Loewer and Belzer 1991).

[5] See Plamenatz (1968), Plamenatz (1963), pp. 220–241.

convention (Postema 1982) is another, and there are still others. But what all of the variations on this theme share is the basic idea that law serves certain instrumental purposes, that these purposes are socially desirable, and that as a result law's normativity is a function of the valuable instrumental purposes that law does or might serve.

If these instrumental purposes are understood to be moral, then this variation on the theme of normativity is no different from that discussed above—the normativity that derives from a prima facie moral obligation to obey the law just because it is the law. But if these purposes are not understood as moral ones, then the nature of normativity might be different. That is, if the reasons for participating in a collective or cooperative social enterprise are not forms of moral reasons, then such reasons might ground law's normativity in a non-moral way. But insofar as most of the proponents of a moral obligation to obey the law believe that such pro-social reasons are themselves moral reasons, the debate now appears to be at least in part a terminological one, depending entirely on the extent to which the domain of the moral does or does not encompass the full domain of the rational.[6] And thus the basic idea is the same. If law is understood to have some value, even if that value is not understood in moral terms, then the normativity of law is still derived from the value that law is perceived to serve. And thus the normativity of law might be understood as a variant on the normativity of cooperation, or on the normativity of participation in a collective enterprise. This form of normativity might well be important, but it seems sufficiently close to the traditional understanding of the moral obligation to obey the law that it is difficult to understand why the normativity of cooperation represents a different and in some way less tractable issue than the traditional one of the normativity embodied in questions about the moral obligation to obey the law.

4 The Voice of the "Ought"

It is of course true that the voice of law is the voice of prescription—the voice of the "ought." Although law in its constitutive aspect tells us what we may do and how we may do it (Hart 2012; Schauer 2015; Pound 1945), law in its regulatory mode tells us not what we may do, but what we must (or must not) do—what we ought (or ought not) to do.[7] And it is often thought that explaining how law in this regulatory mode can create non-moral obligations to act or refrain from acting, and to do so in and because of this characteristic voice, is at the heart of the problem of normativity.

[6] On the question whether the moral is a subset of the rational, or the rational is a subset of the moral, or whether the two are congruent, or whether there is no overlap at all, see Audi (2001), pp. 162–164. And see also Portmore (2003).

[7] The terminology of "constitutive" and "regulatory" comes from Searle (1969), pp. 33–42.

One response to this is to distinguish, following Joseph Raz (1979, 1986, 1990),[8] between what the law claims to its addressees (or subjects) and what those addressees or subjects in fact have an obligation to do. Law does indeed claim that its subjects have countless obligations, including of course the obligation to obey the law, but law's claiming it does not make it so. In other words, although law claims that its addressees have an obligation to obey, its addressees might still not have an obligation to obey, and certainly do not have an obligation to obey just on account of law's claiming that they do. And thus for the actual existence (if any) of an obligation to obey the law, we must look elsewhere, and beyond the claims of the law, and thus once again to the question whether there is in fact a moral obligation to obey the law. And so although the law itself has what might be labeled as the legal point of view,[9] whether law's addressees have the legal point of view is a function of something other than the fact of law's claiming it, or even of the language that law happens to use in claiming it.

5 Conditional Normativity

There is a stronger sense in which we might understand the characteristic voice of the law, a sense in which not only the law but also its addressees genuinely internalize the language of ought. The subjects of the law appear also to say that they or others ought to do this or that because the law says so. And when a subject of the law says this, that subject is speaking from a legal point of view, or, to put it in different terms, is presupposing the existence of an obligation that arises solely from the fact of law. As a result, such statements of ought and ought not, where the "ought" or the "ought not" arises from the fact of law and where the obligation thus arises because of the law,[10] might be thought to support the idea that the law is indeed normative.

From this perspective we might understand law's normativity not as absolute or universal or unqualified, but as conditional. More specifically, and following Andrei Marmor (2011), pp. 26, 71–73; Enoch (2011a), and others (Schaubroeck 2011; Silk 2019), we can understand the normativity of law as conditional upon participation in a particular enterprise. It is true, for example, that chess players use the language of ought in saying that you ought not (or should not or must not) move your rook

[8]An especially valuable commentary on Raz and on the ability of law to claim is offered by John Gardner (2012).

[9]Raz (1990), pp. 170–171 at times puts it exactly this way. The particular locution appears to be an adaptation from Baier (1958).

[10]It is crucial to distinguish genuine compliance from mere consistency. In many instances, agents engage in acts—refraining from murder, for example—that are consistent with law's commands but are not motivated by the existence of law. If we are attempting to focus on law's normative power, therefore, we must look not at the ubiquitous cases of behavior that happens to be consistent with the law, but instead at the smaller class of acts that are undertaken *because* of the law, as I explain in (Schauer 2015, pp. 48–56).

(castle) diagonally. And thus the normativity of the language of chess, and thus the normative force of that language, derives from and hinges upon the fact of being a participant in an enterprise with its own rules that those within the enterprise are expected to follow. But, importantly, the obligation is conditional on playing chess. If you are not playing chess, you are under no obligation to move little pieces of wood in one way or another, and the obligation to move them in a particular way, or not in a particular way, is conditional upon participation in the enterprise. If you are playing chess, then this is what you should or must do, but if you are not playing chess then there is no obligation at all. Of course there might be an obligation to play chess that comes from outside the institution of chess and outside the rules of chess. I might, for example, have promised my mother that I would become a chess player, and in that sense the "chessal" obligation—the otherwise conditional internal obligation of those who are inside the institution and the rules of chess—would itself be parasitic on the (arguably non-conditional) moral obligation to keep promises to one's mother, but here the initial obligation to play chess at all would not come from the rules and obligations that chess imposes, conditionally, upon those who choose to play it.

And so too with law. Legal obligation, insofar as it exists as a distinct form of obligation, might be conditional upon "playing" law, or entering into a legal system, and in that sense legal obligation might be very much like "chessal" obligation—not independently moral and perhaps not even instrumental, but conditional upon being within the system. But if the addressee of law's directives were to ask why she should consider herself part of the system, the most plausible answers would track the answers to the question whether and why there is a moral obligation to obey the law. Perhaps it is a (social) contract, perhaps a duty of gratitude, perhaps a duty of fair play, perhaps a moral duty to participate in a collectively beneficial collective enterprise, or perhaps, as the philosophical anarchists would claim, nothing at all. But the basic point is that "you ought to do this because the law says so" is conceptually no different from "you ought to move bishops diagonally because the rules of chess say so." Insofar as one is part of the enterprise, then the obligations are real, but the obligations are conditional upon being part of the enterprise. And insofar as there is an obligation to become part of the enterprise, that obligation comes not from the enterprise and its rules, but from some obligation outside of the enterprise itself. Just as the Wittgensteinian insists that rules cannot determine their own application, so too can the rules of law, or law itself, not determine their or its own obligatoriness.

6 A "Pseudo-Problem"?

For those who insist that that there is a real problem of legal normativity, the argument from conditionality is insufficient. Legal obligation is unconditional, they say, and thus is different from and stronger than chessal obligation. As a result, they maintain, the problem of legal normativity is a real problem in a way that the problem of chessal normativity is not.

But now it is far from clear that there is a problem in need of a solution. Or, as Enoch (2011b) puts it, what we have is not a real problem but a "peudo-problem." If legal obligation is unconditional, that obligation might, as discussed above, simply be a function of the fact that the law *claims* that its demands are unconditional. But Raz and others have demonstrated that the mere fact of law's claiming it does not make it so, and thus that law's claims about the unconditionality of its obligations do not establish that law in fact does impose unconditional obligations. But if it does, then we must find the actual fact of law's normativity in the moral obligation to do what the law says just because the law says it. This is a real problem, but it is not a new problem, nor is it a distinct one. It is simply the language of the traditional question whether there is a moral obligation to obey the law just because it is the law.

7 Moral Impact

One final possibility needs to be considered, and that is the possibility that law's normativity might consist not in creating reasons, but in some way operating on the reasons that we already have. Donald Regan (1987, 1989a, b), for example, importantly distinguishes between *intrinsic* and *indicative* reasons. An intrinsic reason is the kind of reason we have been discussing, but an indicative reason is something different. It is epistemic, in that it indicates the existence of some other reason. I might, for example, have a reason to drive safely, and this reason exists independently of the law. But when the law says that I must drive no faster than 120 kph, it indicates to me what a safe speed would be. When I follow the speed limit, therefore, I am following the speed limit's indication, but my reason for driving safely is antecedent to the law's prescription. The law tells me what safe driving would be, but does not itself give me a reason for driving safely. That reason existed all along.

In many respects Regan's (sound) distinction between indicative and intrinsic reasons foreshadows David Enoch's distinction (Enoch 2011a, b) between *triggering* and *robust* reasons or reason-giving.[11] There are interesting differences, to be sure, but the basic idea is again that some reasons are self-standing, and others merely operate on other pre-existing reasons, reasons that may derive from notions of authority,[12] or from antecedent moral obligations. But Enoch's robust reasons, like Regan's intrinsic reasons, rest on a firmer foundation. The question, then, is whether the fact of law can provide such intrinsic or robust reasons. If it can, however, there appears to be no sound argument for it doing so that does not go through, depend on, or largely duplicate the traditional debates about the existence (or not) of a prima facie moral obligation to obey the law.

[11] A valuable response is Rodriguez-Blanco (2013).

[12] Which might include conceptions of democratic or procedural authority. See (Stone 2016, 2017).

Much the same might be said about Mark Greenberg's notion (Greenberg 2016) of law's changing our "moral profile."[13] Greenberg is plainly on to something, and there are again interesting and important differences among the accounts of Regan, Enoch, and Greenberg. But Regan's indicator reasons, Enoch's triggering reasons, and Greenberg's changing of a moral profile all presuppose an existing and not law-created obligation, or an existing and not law-created reason for action. Once such reasons and obligations exist, it is true that the presence of law may instantiate, indicate, shift, or otherwise operate on these pre-existing reasons. But law does not create these reasons, and all of the ways in which law may operate on those reasons require that we accept that law will have some "moral impact," to use another of Greenberg's terms. But for law to have a moral impact, it must have a moral status, and thus the question cannot be as divorced from the traditional questions about whether law in fact has such status as the proponents of law's normativity as a distinct issue seem at times to believe.[14]

8 Conclusion: Against Normativity

In some sense this paper might be understood as being an argument against the normativity of law, but to be "against" normativity is not to be against the idea that law can or does have normative force just because it is law. But this normative force is either non-existent, as the philosophical anarchists have argued, or in some sense moral, as Socrates and his successors have argued, or conditional, making it very much like the obligation to follow the rules of an enterprise that one has, conditionally, entered.

Those who argue that there is a distinct problem of legal normativity thus have two tasks and not just one. First, they must explain why legal normativity even presents a problem not covered by any of the just described alternatives. And, second, they must then offer a solution that does not simply dissolve into conditionality or rest on the existence of a moral obligation to obey the law. And thus far neither of those tasks appears to have been accomplished with any degree of success.

Acknowledgments This paper was presented first at the workshop on "Law and Normativity: Cross-Disciplinary Dialogues in a Troubled Relation," held at Queen Mary University of London on 19 May 2017 and organized by Noam Gur, and then at the special workshop on normativity organized by Christoph Bezemek and Nicoletta Ladavac at the IVR Congress in Lisbon on 18 July 2017. A previous version of this paper has been published in "Lo Stato" (2017) 8.

[13] For my response, see (Schauer 2016).

[14] For a compatible conclusion, see (Bix 2013).

References

Audi R (2001) The architecture of reason: the structure and substance of rationality. Oxford University Press, Oxford

Baier K (1958) The moral point of view: a rational basis of ethics. Cornell University Press, Ithaca

Bix B (2013) Law and reasons: comments on Rodriguez-Blamco. Problema Anuario de Filosofia del Derecho 7:27–39

Bjarup J (2005) Continental perspectives on natutral law theory and legal positvism. In: Golding MP, Edmundson WA (eds) The Blackwell guide to the philosophy of law and legal theory. Blackwell Publishing, Oxford, pp 287–299

Coleman J (1996) Authority and reason. In: George RP (ed) The autonomy of law: essays on legal positivism. Clarendon Press, Oxford, pp 287–320

Coleman J (2001a) The practice of principle. In: Defence of a pragmatist approach to legal theory. Oxford University Press, Oxford

Coleman J (2001b) Incorporationism, conventionality, and the practical difference thesis. In: Coleman J (ed) Hart's postscript: essays on the postscript to the concept of law. Oxford University Press, Oxford, pp 99–147

Edmundson WA (2004) State of the art: the duty to obey the law. Legal Theory 10:215–259

Enoch D (2011a) Reason-giving and the law. Oxford Stud Philos Law 1:1–38

Enoch D (2011b) Giving practical reasons. Philos Imprint 11:1–22

Gardner J (2012) How law claims, what law claims. In: Matthias K (ed) Institutionalized reason: the jurisprudence of Robert Alexy. Oxford University Press, Oxford, pp 29–44

Green L (1983) Law, co-ordination, and the common good. Oxf J Leg Stud 3:299–324

Greenberg M (2016) How to explain things with force. Harv Law Rev 129:1932–1979

Hart HLA (1982) Commands and authoritative legal reasons. In: Hart HLA (ed) Essays on Bentham: jurisprudence and political theory. Oxford University Press, Oxford, pp 243–268

Hage J (2011) Legal transactions and the legal ought. In: Stelmach J, Brozek B (eds) The normativity of law. Copernicus Center Press, Wasaw

Hart HLA (2012 [1961]) In: Bulloch PA, Raz J, Green L (eds) The concept of law. Oxford University Press, Oxford

Loewer B, Belzer M (1991) In: Lepore E, Van Gulick R (eds) Prima Facie obligation: its deconstruction and reconstruction. Basil Blackwell, Oxford, pp 359–370

Marmor A (2011) Philosophy of law. Princeton University Press, Princeton

Nozick R (1974) Anarchy, State, and Utopia. Basic Books, New York

Perry SR (2001) Hart's methodological positivism. In: Coleman J (ed) Hart's postscript: essays on the postscript to the concept of law. Oxford University Press, Oxford, pp 312–354

Plamenatz JP (1963) Man and society. Longmans, Green, London

Plamenatz JP (1968) Consent, freedom, and political obligation. Oxford University Press, Oxford

Plato (2003) The last days of Socrates – Euthyphro – apology – Crito – Phaedo (trans: Tredenick H, Tarrants H) Rev edn. Penguin Books, London

Portmore DW (2003) Position-relative consequentialism, agent-centered options, and supererogation. Ethics 113:303–332

Postema G (1982) Coordination and convention at the foundations of law. J Leg Stud 11:165–203

Pound R (1945) Book review. Tex Law Rev 23:411–418

Rawls J (1964) Legal obligation and the duty of fair play. In: Hook S (ed) Law and philosophy. New York University Press, New York, pp 3–35

Raz J (1979) The authority of law: essays on law and morality. Clarendon Press, Oxford

Raz J (1986) The morality of freedom. Clarendon Press, Oxford

Raz J (1990 [1975]) Practical reasons and norms. Princeton University Press, Princeton

Regan DH (1987) Law's Halo. In: Coleman J, Paul EF (eds) Philosophy and law. Basil Blackwell, Oxford, pp 15–30

Regan DH (1989a) Authority and value: reflections on Raz's morality of freedom. South Calif Law Rev 62:995–105

Regan DH (1989b) Reasons, authority, and the meaning of "obey": further thoughts on Raz and obedience to law. Can J Law Jurisprud 3:2–28

Reynolds N (1989) Law as convention. Ratio Juris 2:105–120

Rodriguez-Blanco V (2013) Reasons in action and triggering reasons: a reply to Enoch on reason-giving and legal normativity. Problema Anuario de Filosofia del Derecho 7:3–25

Schaubroeck K (2011) Legal normativity and the instrumental principle. In: Bertea S, Pavlakos G (eds) New essays on the normativity of law. Hart, Oxford

Schauer F (2008) Authority and authorities. Va Law Rev 95:1931–1961

Schauer F (2015) The force of law. Harvard University Press, Cambridge

Schauer F (2016) How (and if) law matters. Harv Law Rev Forum 129:F350–F359

Sciaraffa S (2009) On content-independent reasons: it's not in the name. Law Philos 28:233–260

Searle J (1969) Speech acts: an essay in the philosophy of language. Cambridge University Press, Cambridge

Shapiro SJ (2002) Authority. In: Coleman J, Shapiro S, Himma KE (eds) The Oxford handbook of jurisprudence and philosophy of law. Oxford University Press, Oxford, pp 382–439

Shapiro SJ (2011) Legality. Harvard University Press, Cambridge

Silk A (2019) Normativity in language and in law. In: Plunkett D, Shapiro S, Toh K (eds) Legal norms, ethical norms: new essays on meta-ethics and jurisprudence. Oxford University Press, Oxford

Simmons AJ (1979) Moral principles and political obligations. Princeton University Press, Princeton

Smith MBE (1973) Is there a prima facie obligation to obey the law? Yale Law J 82:950–976

Stelmach J (2011) And if there is no ought? In: Stelmach J, Brozek B (eds) Studies in the philosophy of law: the normativity of law. Copernicus Center Press, Krakow, pp 15–20

Stone R (2016) Legal design for the "Good Man". Va Law Rev 102:1767–1830

Stone R (2017) Law's motivational landscape. Jurisprudence, 9. https://doi.org/10.1080/20403313.2017.1333261

Wolff RP (1970) Defense of anarchism. Harper & Row, New York

CPSIA information can be obtained
at www.ICGtesting.com
Printed in the USA
BVHW042127020919
557411BV00006B/19/P

9 783030 189280